The Capitalist Alternative

By the same author:

Subjectivist Economics

The Capitalist Alternative:

An Introduction
to Neo-Austrian Economics

Alexander H. Shand

SENIOR LECTURER IN ECONOMICS
MANCHESTER POLYTECHNIC

FOREWORD BY G.L.S. SHACKLE

Wheatsheaf
Books

DISTRIBUTED BY HARVESTER PRESS

First published in Great Britain in 1984 by
WHEATSHEAF BOOKS LTD
A MEMBER OF THE HARVESTER PRESS PUBLISHING GROUP
Publisher: John Spiers
Director of Publications: Edward Elgar

©Alexander H. Shand, 1984

British Library Cataloguing in Publication Data

Shand, Alexander H.
  The Capitalist alternative.
  1. Austrian school of economists
  I. Title
  330.15'7   HB98

  ISBN 0-7108-0231-5
  ISBN 0-7108-0262-5 Pbk

Typeset in 10 point Times by Photobooks (Bristol) Ltd.
Printed and bound in Great Britain by
Butler & Tanner Ltd, Frome, Somerset

THE HARVESTER PRESS PUBLISHING GROUP
The Harvester Press Publishing Group comprises Harvester Press
Limited (chiefly publishing literature, fiction, philosophy,
psychology, and science and trade books), Harvester Press
Microform Publications Limited (publishing in microform
unpublished archives, scarce printed sources, and indexes to
these collections) and Wheatsheaf Books Limited (a wholly
independent company chiefly publishing in economics,
international politics, sociology and related social sciences), whose
books are distributed by The Harvester Press Limited and its
agencies throughout the world.

To my wife, my loving Tim

*   *   *

Capitalism created the proletariat, but not by making anyone any the worse off; rather by enabling many to survive who would not otherwise have done so.

F.A. Hayek, *Encounter*, May 1983

Contents

Foreword *by G.L.S. Shackle*   xi
Preface   xiii

1   Methodology   1
    1. Introduction   1
    2. The methodology of neoclassical economics   2
    3. Praxeology and apriorism   2
    4. Subjectivism and social science   3
    5. Methodological individualism   4
    6. Scientism   6
    7. Knowledge, uncertainty and unintended consequences   7

2   Mathematics, Statistics and Econometrics   15
    1. Definitions   15
    2. Historical background   16
    3. Neoclassical dissent   18
    4. Austrian views   22

3   Equilibrium   32
    1. Introduction   32
    2. Historical perspective   33
    3. Definition and proof   34
    4. Criticisms from within the neoclassical school   35
    5. The Austrian view   37

4   Value   43
    1. The long debate: a brief history   43
    2. Subjective value: a general statement   44
    3. Demand   46
    4. Costs and supply   53
    5. The labour theory of value   57

5 The Market   63
   1. Terminology: alternative names   63
   2. The nature of markets   65
   3. The Austrian view of the market   66
   4. Economy and catallaxy   71

6 Profit and the Entrepreneur   77
   1. Introduction   77
   2. Modern theories of enterprise and profit   79
   3. Is there an Austrian theory of profit and
      entrepreneurship?   82
   4. Are entrepreneurs capitalists?   86
   5. Other criticisms of neoclassical theory   90
   6. The 'supply' of entrepreneurs   92

7 Market Failure I   98
   1. Introduction   98
   2. Collective consumption goods   98
   3. Neighbourhood or over-spill effects   103
   4. Consumer preferences   106
   5. Prisoner's dilemma situations   107
   6. Welfare economics   108

8 Market Failure II   114
   1. Self-interest   114
   2. Consumer manipulation   116
   3. The alleged immorality of the profit motive   119

9 Monopoly   125
   1. The 'mainstream' picture of monopoly   125
   2. The Austrian critique of orthodox monopoly
      theory   126
   3. The Austrian definition of monopoly   126
   4. Origins of monopoly   127
   5. Oligopoly   128
   6. Monopolistic competition   129
   7. Are monopolies harmful?   130
   8. Monopoly and the state   130
   9. Trade unions   131

10 Macroeconomics   136
   1. Introduction   136
   2. Keynesian analysis: a general view   137
   3. The Austrian critique of macroeconomics   137

11 The Business Cycle   147
   1. Definition   147
   2. Historical background   147
   3. Keynes and the Austrians in the 1930s 148
   4. The dissolution of the Keynesian consensus 154

12 Money and Inflation   158
   1. What is money?   158
   2. Origins of money   159
   3. The demand for money   160
   4. The meaning of inflation   161
   5. Effects of inflation   162
   6. A general view of Austrian monetary theory 162
   7. Austrian policy recommendations   164

13 The State   174
   1. Theories of the state   174
   2. Austrians on the state   178

14 Planning   186
   1. The planning urge   186
   2. The failures of planning   188
   3. The Austrian critics of planning   189
   4. The tendency for government intervention to
      accelerate   192
   5. The socialist calculation debate   193

15 Liberty and the Market   199
   1. Introduction   199
   2. What is freedom?   200
   3. Arguments for positive freedom   201
   4. Arguments for negative freedom   203
   5. The Austrian concept of liberty   205

16 Equality and Social Justice   210
   1. Equality as an ideal   210
   2. Austrian view of social justice   212

17 Conclusion   220

Biographical Notes on the Leading Representatives of the
  Austrian School   224
Selected Bibliography   228
Index   237

Foreword

Subjectivism is the belief that human affairs – the takings-place in all their subtle complexity that we experience, see and hear of – begin as individuals' thoughts, who use the suggestive impressions of the world on their minds to imagine, each for himself, alternative feasible uses of the means he has at hand, and for each such use, plural rival possible results. It is amongst such alternatives, creations of his own thought, that he must choose. There is no other source from which rival, choosable actions can present themselves. The chosen actions of the many individuals depend upon and affect each other, and thus produce results unknowable in advance by any person. There is, however, a means by which some of these results, when they have occurred, can, in effect, be known by everyone. This means is the market, the spontaneously evolved facility for all-encompassing exchanges of goods. Many choices of action will look for their effects far in time-to-come, and not even the market can show these until that time does come.

The scene described by subjectivism has essential characteristics. First, *non-determinism.* Subjectivism credits the individual with the power of the alchemist who can throw into his crucible whatever his fancy has invented but knows not what will emerge. At the extreme (I may be allowed to cite myself) the subjectivist may believe that the content of time-to-come is non-existent until the decisions have been taken whose effects (much of them undesigned) will create it.

Secondly, therefore, subjectivism asserts that history-to-come is *unpredictable.* Human affairs could not be made ultimately predictable by any centralised coercion, but the proliferant germination of ideas in millions of brains could instead be killed by it. That fertility of invention could not conceivably be approached, let alone matched or surpassed, by a centralised total control. *Freedom,* despite the range of its meanings, implications and problems, is not only the indispensable condition of individualist efficiency but is surely in itself the supreme good.

Mr Shand has surveyed the vast field of subjectivist themes, implications, problems and presentations; has given us concise illuminating contacts with dozens of writers from Plato (no democrat) to the great figure of Hayek, still splendidly at work. Mr Shand's style of exposition is easy and readable but behind the march of words, most especially in the chapters on liberty, we can sense a drum-beat of conviction. His book can provide endless suggestions for thought, reading and original work, and shows economics as an enterprise of mind going to the heart of human concerns.

GLS Shackle
1 August 1983

Preface

The main aim of this book is to introduce the ideas of the neo-Austrian school of economics and to compare these ideas with the more familiar methods of conventional or orthodox economics. Many well-known introductory textbooks meant for the use of prospective accountants or business studies graduates, whose main interest is not in economics, typically make great use of graphical diagrams of equilibrium situations. These often appear to students to have little usefulness or connection with reality, and unfortunately many people are put off economics as a result. Sometimes attempts are made to water down or force into rather unconvincing 'case studies' the apparatus of modern economic analysis, but this does not always work well. As a consequence, much that is both interesting and relevant tends to be missed out.

There are today several varieties of identifiable dissenting movements which reject the methodology of mainstream economics as it appears in most textbooks. The two most sharply opposed are Marxian economics (which is sometimes found under the label, Political Economy) and the neo-Austrian school. But criticism is commonly heard from many other directions. Nicholas Kaldor's view, as expressed in a lecture given in 1973, was that economic theory, as it appears in most regular university textbooks, is thoroughly misleading and useless. More recently Lord Balogh (1982) has attacked economists for their pretensions as scientists and their ceaseless construction of mathematical models that ignore so much of human nature, history and the uncertainty of expectations.

It is the claim of the neo-Austrian school that they offer some promising ways forward from the present 'crisis'. Whether the neo-Austrian school should be regarded as an entirely new and different perspective – an *extraordinary* science, to use Kuhn's term – or merely as an attempt to 'save late capitalism' is debatable.

Certainly there are some quite fundamental and apparently irreconcilable differences between the neo-Austrian school and conventional economics, but there are several Austrian ideas which have begun to influence mainstream economics, for example, the renewed interest in the micro-foundations of macroeconomics and the role of expectations in the theory of inflation.

The main title of this book reflects the Austrian conviction that capitalism offers the best guarantee of personal freedom and economic and social well-being. This belief is, of course, shared with many other economists, such as Milton Friedman, but there remain some quite significant differences on questions of methodology.

The topics of this book may be divided roughly as follows: Chapters 1 to 3 deal with methodology; Chapters 4 to 9, micro-economics; Chapters 10 to 12, and 14 are on macroeconomics; and Chapters 13, 15 and 16 cover some topics which are not usually given much space in books on economics. The justification for this is that the Austrian school regard questions of liberty and justice as inseparably bound up with their analysis of the processes of free markets, the defence of capitalism and the principle of the private ownership of property; this is particularly evident in the work of F.A. Hayek. Needless to say, in two such short chapters, only a very approximate outline is possible of subjects which touch upon questions which involve many areas of specialist study and controversy. However, an important corollary of the Austrian view of economics is that on such concepts as liberty, equality and social justice their philosophy leads to some truly radical conclusions which are sharply distinguishable from the 'conventional wisdom'.

ACKNOWLEDGEMENTS

My thanks go to my academic friends and colleagues, and especially to Jim Lord and John Phillips for many invariably stimulating discussions and to George Zis for his helpful encouragement; to my son John for his guidance in some philosophical matters, (but who should be absolved of blame for any solecisms which remain); to the staff of the Manchester Polytechnic Library, especially those of the Aytoun Site; to Mrs Olive Donohue for her cheerful and efficient attention to the typing of the manuscript; and above all to my wife and sons for their indispensable help, unfailing devotion and patience I owe the greatest debt.

1 Methodology

1. INTRODUCTION

For the purposes of this chapter, the term methodology is to be understood as being mainly descriptive of those methods of study favoured by the Austrian school. The broader use of the term, in which not only the methods but also the underlying philosophy is analysed must necessarily receive only summary consideration.[1]

The following exposition will treat Austrian methodology under the separate heads of praxeology, subjectivism, methodological individualism, scientism, knowledge, uncertainty and unintended consequences. To some extent there is a certain arbitrariness in this division since there are strong interconnections between these topics. Its justification is that it may bring out more clearly the main principles which lie behind Austrian views on economics and enable these to be related to specific questions, such as why Austrians favour free markets and are so critical of some of the assumptions and methods of neoclassical mainstream economics. There are, of course, some important differences as between individual Austrians on questions of methodology, but in the present context it seems unnecessary to devote any detailed discussion to such comparative aspects. In what follows, therefore, the aim is to identify a few of the principles with which most Austrians are in agreement and which are the most relevant to an explanation of the Austrian attitude to economic and social theory and policy. There is, however, one area in which Austrians' differences of opinion demand some specific discussion: this is what might be called the 'later Hayek' attitude to the empirical testing of hypotheses. This will be done in the section on scientism.

2. THE METHODOLOGY OF NEOCLASSICAL ECONOMICS

The mainstream methodology, with which that of the Austrian school is being compared, is positive economics. Very briefly, this consists of subjecting economic phenomena to study by similar methods to those of a natural science such as physics. It is believed by its advocates that it is possible to produce testable propositions about the world which may objectively be falsified.[2] It involves a considerable use of mathematics and statistics since many economic variables are thought to be quantifiable. Great stress is laid on the value of theories which yield testable predictions and which may be useful for policy-making.

3. PRAXEOLOGY AND APRIORISM[3]

Praxeology literally means the study of human action and was first applied to Austrian methods by Mises, who set out to construct, purely by deduction mainly from a basic simple axiom, a whole body of economic theory in his treatise *Human Action.* The fundamental axiom is that individuals act purposefully to achieve chosen ends. This, at first sight, seems a remarkably trivial and obvious idea from which to begin.

Mises taught that this fundamental postulate is a true axiom and that, therefore, any propositions deduced from it, if arrived at by sound logic, must also be true. The fact that people act purposefully to achieve certain ends implies an act of choosing between alternatives and a set of valuations. Thus already some of the basic ideas of consumer theory are implied by the original axiom. There is no implication however that the individuals' ends or goals may be judged as to their rationality by an external observer. 'The ultimate end of action is always the satisfaction of some desire of the acting man' (Mises, 1949 p. 19); there is no way of objectively deciding that an individual's actions are irrational. Also, there is no possibility of testing these logical implications of the basic axiom and neither is there any necessity to do so. One question which obviously arises is: what is the justification for regarding the original axiom as true? Mises took the view that the concept of action is prior to all experience and requires no empirical 'proof'. It might, however, be argued that the fact that human beings act is itself a matter for observation by anyone and has therefore a strong empirical basis.[4] Furthermore, if someone attempts to refute the axiom of human action, they must themselves act and choose means in order to reach their aim of refuting the axiom.[5]

4. SUBJECTIVISM AND SOCIAL SCIENCE

Subjectivism is the name given to a theory which takes the private experience of an individual to be the sole foundation of factual knowledge. Austrians do not deny the existence of objective measurable facts in the natural sciences, but it is fundamental to their attitude to the social sciences that in these the situation is quite different. The social sciences, unlike the natural sciences, deal not with 'the relations between things, but with the relations between men and things or the relations between man and man' (Hayek, 1952, p. 41). Most of the objects of human action are not 'objective facts' as this term is understood in the natural sciences, but they are what people *think* they are. This has important implications for economic theory, the most obvious being that it suggests that there is no such thing as an objective standard of value. Such terms as 'price' and 'cost' cannot be defined in concrete terms, but only in terms of what people think. The Austrian view of subjectivism in the social sciences should not be confused with the contention of some philosophers that objectivity is impossible either in the natural or the social sciences – for example, the idea that the laboratory experimenter has (subjectively) to *select* what to look for in the first place.[6] The Austrian adherence to subjectivism does not rest on this basis, but on the proposition that what people think – their evaluations for example – are the proper object of study for economists.

It is on this issue of subjectivism that one of the greatest differences between the Austrian and neoclassical methods exists. In general, the latter proceeds on the assumption that there are objective economic facts with reference to which theories may be tested; it is this which makes economics a 'positive' science.[7] Professor Shackle has sought to push back the origins of subjectivism to an earlier phase than how the individual reacts to stimuli. This he has described as 'imaginative–critical' origination, the sorting-out of 'the imagined, deemed possible'.[8] Shackle's thesis is that individual economic decisions are not only subjective but are based on the selection of a particular course of action from conceivable sequels to each of a list of possible actions. Thus any economic theory which assumes the existence of a mechanism of rational decision-making is misguided.

The Austrian belief that the social sciences are significantly different from the natural sciences is supported by the doctrine of certain German nineteenth-century philosophers of *Verstehen* (understanding from within) by means of empathy. The term was used by the sociologist Max Weber and implies that in studying society human beings have the advantage of knowing intuitively how other human beings might react to given circumstances, whereas in the natural sciences this route to understanding is inherently impossible. The Austrian contention that *Verstehen* presupposes that the actor and the observer of his actions have something in common has led to the misunderstanding that this means that, for example, 'only a war historian can tackle a Genghis Khan or a Hitler' (Barry, 1979, p. 26). The nature of this confusion lies in thinking that we need to have a similar character to those whose actions we wish to understand. But all that is necessary is that we be made of the same 'ingredients', however different the mixture may be. For example, it is easy for almost anyone to understand an outburst of anger in another person without being oneself constantly or even frequently angry (Hayek, 1967, p. 59).

5. METHODOLOGICAL INDIVIDUALISM

This is the name given to that aspect of Austrian methodology which, in its extreme form, asserts that all statements about groups are reducible to statements about the behaviour of the individuals composing those groups and their interactions. It is to be contrasted with methodological *holism*[9] which postulates the existence of social wholes which have purposes or needs, or which cause events to occur. Individualists regard the holist use of terms such as 'committee', 'crowd', 'the economy', 'the state', as at best incomplete and at worst misleading for social and economic understanding.[10] The Austrian school's rejection of holism tends to explain much of their criticism of those parts of neoclassical economics such as macroeconomics which deal in interacting aggregates. Examples of holistic thinking abound on all sides. For example, politicians, economists and newspaper leader writers constantly refer to 'the economy' as an entity which, by implication, has an existence and which may be analysed without much reference to the individuals of which it is composed.[11] The habit of thinking in holistic terms is widespread and deep-rooted. Individualists maintain that this approach is not only methodologically fallacious but also politically and socially dangerous. According to Sir Karl Popper, holists not only plan to study society by an 'impossible' method, but also to control and reconstruct society 'as a whole'. He describes this as 'the totalitarian intuition'.[12]

The Austrian defence of the individualist method is explained in Hayek (1952), chapter 4. He stresses the importance of distinguishing between what he calls the 'speculative or explanatory views which people hold about the wholes' on the one hand, and 'the motivating or constitutive opinions' of individuals which will exist irrespectively of the wholes. In other words, a 'society' or an 'economy' could continue unchanged in respect of the interactions of all the individuals within it, even if somehow there was no outside observer to see it as a whole.

Methodological individualism has frequently been criticised, often in the form of refuting examples, as too restrictive of enquiry. It has been pointed out that to deny the existence of social wholes, such as 'crowd hostility', or a 'symphony orchestra' in the sense that they are not observable, is like denying that we can ever observe a forest, on the grounds that when we do so the only things we really see are individual trees.[13] This view, however, only supports the contention that collective terms need not be redefined in individual terms, but it does not refute the Austrian point that society is composed of purposefully acting individuals the consequences of whose actions are unpredictable: trees cannot be analogous to individual human beings. According to Nagel,[14] Mises and Hayek use microeconomic theory based on methodological individualism to explain the operations of a whole economy, rather in the same way as physicists explain the temperature of a gas in terms of the movement of individual molecules; this involves making a special assumption about a statistical property of all the molecules considered as a whole. However, Hayek seems to argue that there is no causal connection between macro totals and micro decisions (1978a, p. 14).

One writer[15] contends that the debate between individualists and holists has become too much associated with political divisions between the former and collectivists, describing it as a 'sterile polarity' and maintaining that a separation should be preserved between the relative usefulness of the two methods on the one hand, and their ideological implications on the other hand.[16] Another line of attack on the individualist approach is to observe how difficult it may be in practice to describe particular types of individual without implicit reference to their membership of social wholes, e.g. 'working-class deferential Conservative' (Lukes, 1973, p. 122).

Whatever may be said in criticism of the Austrian school with regard to their rigid insistence on individualism, their continued critique of holism has served to alert people to the dangers of treating all kinds of social wholes as if they were impersonal forces,[17] and that the social scientist will be wary of attributing non-observable properties to equally non-observable group entities,[18] even though he still wishes to cling to the idea that not all holist concepts are either useless or dangerous.[19] One of the most important implications of methodological individualism is that there exist no social tendencies which are beyond the power of individuals to alter provided they have the will and the necessary information.

6. SCIENTISM

Scientism is defined as the slavish imitation of the methods of science in fields for which they are not appropriate, such as the study of society. To be 'scientistic' is to fall short of being truly scientific which is to be engaged in critical disinterested enquiry. Scientism is not scientific because it involves the uncritical use of the mechanical methods of science. Developing this theme and showing the consequences of scientism has been largely the work of Hayek, especially in his famous study *The Counter-Revolution of Science* (1952), the sub-title of which is 'Studies on the Abuse of Reason'.

Before the nineteenth century the study of economic and social affairs was carried on by various methods and without much worry over whether or not what was being done was 'scientific'. Political economy, for example, before the nineteenth century, could be regarded as either a branch of science or of moral or social philosophy. During the first half of the nineteenth century attitudes changed. The term science came to be regarded as confined to the study of the natural world and, in disciplines such as physics, soon became associated with prestige, rigour and certainty of prediction. This led increasingly to attempts to apply these dazzling techniques to the study of human society, especially in its economic aspect. The term science became not only a description but also an encomium. Hayek regards the attempts by social scientists to show their equal status as contributing scarcely anything to our understanding of social phenomena. In Part I of *Counter-Revolution* he sets out this theme, and in Part II traces the historical roots of scientism to the work of L'Ecole Polytechnique 'the source of the Scientistic Hubris' in Paris at the end of the eighteenth century, a new institution which embodied the growing pride in the achievements of science. Both the two great intellectual forces which have since transformed social thought – modern socialism and scientism – sprang from the members of this institution, especially Henri de Saint-Simon and his disciple Auguste Comte.

Hayek uses two main arguments against scientism: first, that most of the 'facts' of the social sciences are subjective and therefore not susceptible to the objective methods of the natural sciences; and secondly, that social facts and systems are too complex, having too many variables and attended by much difficulty in establishing their magnitudes.[20] In the study of such a complex phenomenon as the market, for example, all the circumstances which will determine the result of a process will hardly ever be known or accurately measurable and much of the data may not lend themselves to measurement. One unfortunate consequence of this is a tendency to treat only what is measurable as important, which is sometimes carried to the point where theories are constructed so as to include only measurable variables. Even worse, because some facts cannot be quantified, they are simply ignored. This could result in the extreme case in some elegant mathematical models which comprise all the facts except the important ones.[21]

Hayek's views on scientism later underwent a slight change, when he accepted Popper's view of what scientists actually do as distinct from what Comte and his followers claimed they do. In his Preface to *Studies* (1967) Hayek acknowledged that, as a result of what he had learned from Popper, the gap between the natural and social sciences had been greatly narrowed, but that he continued the argument 'only because so many social scientists are still trying to imitate what they wrongly believe to be the methods of the natural sciences'.[22] This misunderstanding over the actual methodology of science has, it has been suggested, led to damage to social and economic enquiry by confusing historicism with the proper use of historical method.[23] What has been described as 'fundamental dilemmas' for modern Austrians lies in the 'later' Hayek's attempt to combine two different philosophies of social science: the Austrian praxeological school with its axiomatic rejection of empirical testing, and the hypothetico-deductive approach of Popperian falsifiability. This was not a problem for Mises since he rejected the Popperian approach (1962, p. 70), but it is a dilemma for later Austrians who evidently must choose between two incompatible philosophies.[24]

7. KNOWLEDGE, UNCERTAINTY AND UNINTENDED CONSEQUENCES

The players listen very carefully and respectfully to all that the clever men have to say about what is to happen in the next generation. The players then wait until all the clever men are dead, and bury them nicely. They then go and do something else.[25]

A basic element in Austrian methodology is the belief that there is an inherent unpredictability and indeterminacy in human knowledge. This implies, not merely that the future is difficult to predict, but that it is inherently unpredictable. Of course this does not rule out the common sense of individuals, or groups of individuals, or even the government arranging their affairs with awareness of possible outcomes. What the Austrian school have always emphasised, however, is the dangers of over-confidence whether it be among economists drawing up forecasts,[26] or of politicians acting on the basis of such forecasts. Because of uncertainty all human purposive action has unintended consequences which may turn out to be beneficial, of course, but equally may be very unpleasant and unwanted. A modern example of the second kind which has now become obvious to everyone is the disaster which resulted from the wholly well-meaning and enormous schemes of slum clearance and subsequent rehousing of people into high-rise flats in Britain in the 1960s and 1970s. A less dramatic and less obvious example is the adverse effect on employment opportunities for young people consequent upon such developments as the demand for educational certificates, trade union restrictions and employment protection laws (Bauer, 1981, pp. 33–4).

Carl Menger argues in *Problems* that many social institutions have developed spontaneously. Although unplanned, their results have often been of great benefit. Such social phenomena as law, language, markets and the state are given as examples (Menger, 1963, p. 130),[27] and are seen by Menger as the 'unintended results of historical development'. He also emphasises the fact that much human action resulted in mistakes because of ignorance. It was Hayek who combined this insight with the largely British classical tradition of individual liberty as derived from Locke, Mandeville and Hume, to develop his theory of knowledge.[28] It is this theory which, together with Shackle's wholly original ideas, has become one of the most influential methodological foundations of modern Austrian economics. Hayek added to this in *The Sensory Order* (1952) a theoretical psychological justification to support the contention that there are inherent limits to the human mind's capacity to comprehend complex systems. By analogy with Gödel's theorem (i.e. that it is impossible to prove the consistency of a formal system within the system itself),

Hayek argues that for all rational processes there must always be some rules which cannot be stated or even be conscious. In other words, we know more than we can speak of, therefore not all knowledge is objectifiable. Austrians see competitive markets as processes for the discovery and articulation of such inarticulate knowledge.

The starting-point for the development of Hayek's speculations on the theory of knowledge began with his essay on 'Economics and Knowledge' in which he set out to explain what he had come to regard as the main task of economic theory: 'how an overall order of economic activity was achieved which utilised a large amount of knowledge which was not concentrated in any one mind but existed only as the separate knowledge of thousands or millions of different individuals' (1967, pp. 91–2). A view of the world, derived from Ancient Greece, was that it could be divided into what was natural and what was man-made, and this dominated European thought for centuries. Since, according to this dichotomy, everything was either natural (i.e. independent of human will and action), or artificial (i.e. the intended result of human action), it left no place for any phenomena which were the result of human action but not of human design. Dr Bernard Mandeville is credited by Hayek with showing the way of escape from this dilemma in his *Fable of the Bees* (1728). He influenced David Hume, Adam Smith and Edmund Burke and through the latter the German 'historical' schools and men such as Savigny who, in turn, influenced Menger. Thus it would appear that the third possible view of institutions – that there were some which were the product of human action but not of design – reached Hayek essentially from the same root, but by two complementary paths.

Alongside the mainly British tradition and almost entirely opposed to it were the French Encyclopaedists such as Rousseau, Condorcet and Voltaire, who became dominant in continental Europe. These men were strongly influenced by the teaching of Descartes who contended that all useful human institutions were and ought to be deliberately created by conscious reason. This led to the belief that only institutions which are the products of human design can be beneficial, giving rise to a contempt for tradition, custom and history in general. Man's reason alone should enable him to construct society anew. This 'Cartesian rationalism' is traceable to Plato, and Hayek sees it as continued by Hegel and Marx. Hayek's preferred term to describe this view is now *constructivism*; he had originally used the term 'engineering type of mind'. It is seen by modern Austrians as naive, arrogant and dangerous, being the source of socialism and totalitarianism. The Austrian alternative to constructivist rationalism has also been described as *critical rationalism*, a term which Hayek credits to Popper.

The implications of critical rationalism may be summarised as follows. Reason is not omnipotent and separable from the processes of society, it grows out of them. Most institutions are not the result of human intention, and individuals must be willing to abide by rules which are not the products of human design. No group of people such as a government, can possibly ever know all they would need to know for 'social' planning. Of all the human institutions which are the result of unintended action, such as money, the market and the rule of law, the last is seen as vital in making possible that unintended spontaneous order which is an essential condition of liberty. It should be noticed that Hayek's view of law is inseparable from his theory of knowledge. He sees the system of common law as a product of countless decisions, made over centuries, by kings or any other human authority, who could only 'declare or find existing law . . . and not create law' (1960, p. 163). Only gradually did rulers change from law-finders to law-creators. The idea which has now become almost universally accepted, that it is the government's function to lay down detailed rules, is seen by Hayek as a threat to liberty, even when the government is democratically elected. Most laws should be a product of spontaneous order not what the government decides, since in this situation a democratically elected government can easily tyrannise minorities.

Hayek's view of human action has been criticised as an example of 'self-referential inconsistency'. He sees human action as governed by general rules that people have not chosen; they are just adopted. Nowhere in his analysis is there apparently any room for free will; human behaviour is mostly outside human control. 'Human actions spring from a sort of evolutionary force.'[29] But Hayek's own activities as a theoretician deny his own theory about human action.

Finally, it is interesting to note that Popper sees unintended consequences arising from the very processes of scientific study itself, 'the moment we have produced these theories, they create new, unintended and unexpected problems to be discovered' (1979, p. 161).

In this chapter, the foundations of Austrian methodology have been discussed in the form of separate, fairly brief expositions of its various aspects; it is, however, clear that there exist strong linkages between all these concepts, and subjectivism is the key to almost all the other elements of Austrian methodology.

If the private experience of an individual is regarded as the foundation of factual knowledge in the social sciences, then the rest of the structure follows without much difficulty. Hayek's criticism of scientism was precisely that it was fallacious to treat the social sciences as if, like the natural sciences, they could deal in observable facts. The doctrine of subjectivism involves the belief that there are no directly observable facts in the social sciences, that only the evaluations and attitudes of the human agents are accessible to the observer. The validity of this proposition has been criticised on various grounds. For example, it might be argued that although no one can deny that the 'value' of a work of art is subjectively determined by the 'eye of the beholder', there may be many circumstances in which objective facts cannot and should not be ignored by the social scientist – facts which may themselves constitute unquestionably legitimate fields of enquiry. Inflationary expectations, for example may be revised downwards in the light of people's experience of the actual course of prices as observed in the economy. A subjectivist might, however, reply that these very prices are themselves the product of thousands of individuals' subjective valuations. (For discussion of this and other objections to subjectivism see Nagel, 1961).

Other elements of Austrian philosophy are likewise linked directly or indirectly to subjectivism. For example: if only individually and subjectively known attitudes and evaluations matter, then the object of study must be the individual – hence the advocacy of methodological individualism. This in turn explains among other things, the Austrian objection to aggregation in economics and has, as we shall see later, important policy implications, such as the Hayekian opposition to Keynesianism.

There is a clear connection between Mises' axiom that human beings act purposefully, and the interest of Austrians in the unintended consequences of such human action. The term *action* is to be contrasted with a happening or an event; things 'just happen' to inanimate objects such as stones or machines but, by contrast, human action *purposefully* affects inanimate objects as well as possibly human beings. If A shoots B thus killing him, many unintended consequences are conceivable: B will not live to draw his pension, he will not have children (or at least he will not have any *more* children), the children he might have had, but for A's *purposeful* action will not themselves get married, etc. If A had not shot B, he would still be alive and all the infinitely extending chain of consequences would be different. It is difficult at this point to resist the feeling that this is nothing but an uninteresting and boring story. It seems to be quite unremarkable and a statement of the obvious, for example, to point out that if a man had not crossed a road he could have avoided being struck by a car, and then to imagine to the point of tedium all the different events which, as a consequence, would have been unchanged. Amartya Sen has pointed out the importance of distinguishing between the results of an action which are the *opposite* of what was intended and results which even though unintended are not the opposite of what was intended.[30] Adam Smith's 'invisible hand' case, although seen as working through self-interested actions which benefit others is not one in which the self-interested agents *intended harm* to others, even though they were behaving selfishly. Why then do the Austrians think the unintended consequences concept is so significant? There are two possible answers, to the importance of which the Sen view perhaps attaches insufficient weight. One answer rests upon the Mises/Hayek stress on the Darwinian type of evolutionary character of some of the most beneficial of human institutions, such as markets, money and the rule of law. The second part of the Austrian defence is based on the contention that the obviously beneficial nature and supreme importance of such institutions is clear proof of the superiority of unplanned evolution through the actions of countless individuals, as compared with the conscious deliberate creation of Utopian systems, the belief in what Hayek calls 'constructivism'.

In the following chapters it will be seen how the Austrians' methodology helps to explain their attitude to specific aspects of economics and political economy. We begin by examining two subjects which are of general importance throughout economic theory – mathematics and equilibrium – and in regard to which there arise some of the sharpest divergences of opinion between the Austrian School and orthodox mainstream economics.

NOTES

1. See Hutchison (1981), chapters 6 and 7, for an account of Austrian philosophical foundations.
2. Whether mainstream economists actually live up to their own pretensions has been questioned. See e.g. Blaug (1980), chapter 15. Some suggested explanations are offered by Lawrence A.

Boland (1982), *Foundations of Economic Method*, London: Allen & Unwin.

3. See Rothbard, in Dolan (1976), pp. 19–39; and Mises (1949), pp. 11–29.
4. See Rothbard (ibid.), p. 24.
5. ibid., p. 28.
6. See Katouzian (1980), pp. 137–41.
7. As Barry (1979, p. 23) points out, this is the area of greatest disagreement between the two most famous free-market proponents, Hayek and Friedman.
8. See Shackle (1979), chapter 6.
9. The terms 'individualist' and 'holist' will be used as abbreviations in what follows.
10. For a full discussion of holism versus individualism, see Brodbeck (1968), chapters 14, 15, and 16.
11. Austrians would not deny that there is a meaningful sense in which terms such as 'the economy' may be used, but merely that it encourages fallacious ideas, for example, that there exists a 'national cake' and that it is somebody's responsibility to divide it up. Another common holistic phrase, 'the needs of society', is the source of much confused thinking.
12. See Popper (1957), pp. 76–93 for a classic critique of holism.
13. See, e.g. Nagel (1961), pp. 539–46.
14. ibid., p. 543.
15. Patrick Burman, 'Variations on a dialectical theme', *Journal of the Philosophy of Social Science*, 9 (1979), 357–75.
16. Blaug makes a similar point in respect of Popper's 'illegitimate' linking of criticisms of holism to the defence of 'political individualism' (1980, p. 50).
17. 'The fight against inflation' is a typical example, suggesting that inflation is due to some non-human agency like an earthquake or a drought.
18. See Brodbeck (op. cit.).
19. Further sources on this topic are: Watkins, J.W.N., 'The alleged inadequacy of methodological individualism', *Journal of Philosophy*, 55 (1958), 390–5; Dray, William H., 'Holism and individualism in history and science', in Paul Edwards (ed.), *Encyclopedia of Philosophy*, vol. 4. New York, pp. 53–8.
20. See 'The pretence of knowledge', in Hayek (1978c).
21. It has often been remarked that Keynes' followers tended to sweep under the carpet his emphasis on the importance of expectations as a determinant of the business cycle.

22. See the comment by Popper in 'A pluralist approach to the philosophy of history', in Streissler (1969), p. 190 in which he acknowledges this point, and reminds us of his own long opposition to scientism.
23. See Katouzian (1980), pp. 40–1.
24. See Barry (1979), p. 40, and Hutchison (1981), pp. 219–20.
25. From G.K. Chesterton, 'Introductory remarks on the art of prophecy', in *The Napoleon of Notting Hill* (1904).
26. As we have previously noted many economists still continue to follow what they wrongly believe to be the methods of the natural sciences. The models used by economists are seen by one modern physicist as based on an 'outmoded paradigm' (Professor M. Berry in a talk given on BBC, Radio 3, 11 May 1983: 'The Electron at the End of the Universe'). This included some graphic illustrations to show how modern physics has to take account of uncertainty. In recent years there has been among economists, a considerable increase in interest in the subject. See, e.g. John D. Hey, *Uncertainty in Microeconomics* (1979), Oxford: Martin Robertson.
27. Popper contends that a large part of the 'world of actual and potential theories and books and arguments arises as an unintended by-product of the actually produced books and arguments. We may also say that it is a by-product of human language' (Popper, 1979).
28. See Hayek's essays, 'Dr Bernard Mandeville', and 'The place of Menger's *Grundsätze* in economic thought', in *New Studies* (1978); also chapters 1 to 4 and 6 in *Studies* (1967).
29. See Tibor Machan, 'Reason, morality and the free society', in Cunningham (1979), pp. 268–93.
30. See n. 3, p. 123.

2 Mathematics, Statistics and Econometrics

1. DEFINITIONS

Mathematical economics is the application of the techniques of mathematical analysis to economic variables, the relationships between such variables being described as functions, for example, 'quantity demanded is a function of price'. Functions may be represented graphically as curves and herein lies some of the fascination which these techniques have held for generations of economists and teachers since their first application. The resulting smooth curves, being susceptible to precise manipulation through the techniques of calculus, have formed the basis for almost endless clever mathematical exposition and development, and have undoubtedly, in their time, served to disperse much verbal fog which has pervaded economic theory. Indeed, many of the controversies which engaged economists before the possibilities of the usefulness of mathematics was realised are now regarded as rather futile, and sometimes the product of those having a knowledge of mathematics confronted by simple ignorance of its power to clarify thinking.

The use of statistics in economics ('political economy') appeared quite naturally and much earlier than did the application of mathematics. Originally it meant simply the collection and arrangement of quantitative facts. Such activity preoccupied the economists of the seventeenth and eighteenth centuries, and was known in England as 'Political Arithmetick'. The advances initiated by Sir William Petty, by which the mere collection of data began to progress into 'statistical method', the forerunner of modern econometrics, received a set-back from the unsympathetic reaction of Adam Smith: 'the suggestive program . . . wilted in the wooden hands of the Scottish professor and was practically lost to most economists for 250 years' (Schumpeter, 1954, p. 212).

Econometrics is that branch of economics in which hypotheses are mathematically expressed and then tested empirically by collecting data and subjecting these to statistical tests. One of the main preoccupations of modern neoclassical economics is the construction of econometric models of the economy at either macro or micro levels or a combination of both. The extraction of predictions from models has, of course, been greatly advanced by the use of computers. Econometric models are, to some extent, comparable to those employed by meteorologists in weather forecasting. In principle, if enough simultaneous equations showing functional relationships between variables can be assembled, and if the correct values are assignable to the variables, then a computer may be programmed to generate predictions. The validity of the comparison between economics and a branch of applied natural science such as meteorology has been questioned by critics of the methodology of modern economics, and especially by the Austrians.

2. HISTORICAL BACKGROUND

The differential calculus was invented almost simultaneously by two men in the seventeenth century (Newton in England, and Leibniz in Germany) and was probably the most important single tool in the beginnings of mathematical economics, being admirably suited to lend an air of precision to the marginalists after 1870. It was seized enthusiastically, especially by Jevons.[1] Although there were a number of men who started to employ mathematical techniques before the 'marginal revolution', such as H. Lloyd, Bernoulli, Dupuit, von Thünen and others, it would not be appropriate here to go into their work in any detail,[2] which often apparently went unread because of the lack of comprehension of their methods; but mention must be made of the outstanding work of Augustin Cournot (1801–77) in which many of the elements of later developments in mathematical economics were foreshadowed.

The remarkable Stanley Jevons had begun to think of the possibility of using mathematical functions in economics as early as 1860, and wrote a paper on the subject which was read at the 1862 meeting of the British Association. It attracted no attention, and remained unpublished until 1866. This contained all the basic ingredients of his later work but again went unremarked.[3] By the time his *Theory of Political Economy* was published in 1871, Jevons' work no longer appeared as original as it would have done in 1862, since 'several economists, notably Walras and Marshall . . . were scribbling equations with x's and y's big Deltas and little d's' (Keynes, 1972, p. 131). Nevertheless, Jevons' *Theory* was the first rounded exposition of economic principles using the now familiar techniques of algebra and diagrams. Keynes found Jevons' approach superior to that of Marshall: 'chiselled in stone, where Marshall knits in wool' (ibid.) Jevons, unlike Marshall, had few doubts about the validity of mathematical methods.

It seems perfectly clear that Economy, if it is to be a science at all, must be a mathematical science. Most persons appear to hold that the physical sciences form the proper sphere of mathematical method, and that the moral sciences demand some other method, I know not what. (Jevons, 1971. p. 3)

Jevons attempted to forestall one commonly held objection to the use of mathematics: that unlike the 'exact' sciences economics does not consist of precise data. He pointed out that even in astronomy, a more exact science than most, many of the measurements are approximations: for instance, that the earth is a perfect sphere. In mechanics a perfectly inflexible lever or a perfectly hard fulcrum never exists (ibid., p. 7). Jevons' confident devotion to the introduction of mathematics, and especially to differential calculus, was given a grudging reception. Cairnes, who represented the 'establishment' economists, the school of J.S. Mill, said that he could not understand Jevons through his ignorance of mathematics but this did not prevent him from disagreeing with it:

unless it can be shown that either mental feelings admit of being expressed in precise quantitative forms, or, on the other hand, that economic phenomena do not depend on mental feelings, I am unable to see how this conclusion [that mathematics cannot be applied to economics] can be avoided.[4]

It may well be that Cairnes' objections were based on ignorance but that his instinct would later appear as sound. Marshall, who in 1871 was of the younger generation, thought Jevons' *Theory* would have been improved if the mathematics had been omitted but the diagrams retained. But his lack of sympathy for Jevons' methods may, it would appear, have had deeper causes than his disapproval of the way in which he used mathematics: Marshall could not accept Jevons' criticisms of Ricardo. He did, however, stress the difficulty in getting a 'clear full view' of the principles of marginalism without the use of either mathematical symbols or diagrams, but for the most part he preferred diagrams as their use 'requires no special knowledge, and they often express the conditions of economic life more accurately . . . than do mathematical symbols' (Marshall, 1916, p. xvi).[5]

The application of mathematics to economics flourished greatly after Jevons with the publications of Walras (*Elements*, 1874), Edgeworth (*Mathematical Psychics*, 1881), Fisher (*Mathematical Investigations*, 1892) and Pareto (a number of published works in the first decade of the twentieth century). On these foundations was subsequently built the familiar apparatus of modern neoclassical exposition, such as indifference curves and tangency solutions. Although the subject improved its analytical precision as a result of all these endeavours it was also the start of a period in which ever more finely-spun mathematical theoretical structures moved the focus somewhat away from humanity and history. The founding of the Econometric Society in 1933, with its journal *Econometrica*, was evidence of a will to apply the developed mathematical armoury to the creation of models which could yield predictions to be statistically tested in 'real world' circumstances.

Since the end of the second world war, economics has become more and more dominated by mathematical formulation. For the young, aspiring economist the inducement to rush into print with an article or two, well-embellished with mathematical symbolism, has been the almost certain prospect of obscurity ahead which faced him should he fail to show his fitness to join the 'college' of the mathematical economists. (This has given rise to complaints that economics undergraduates have become more brightly numerate but in some other respects rather duller and narrower.)

3. NEOCLASSICAL DISSENT

Almost from the beginning of the process by which economics became increasingly mathematical there were to be heard the voices of those who were not happy with the way the subject was going. The opposition to mathematics was, and continues to be, directed from those who, in their formative years, experienced nothing but the literary style of presentation and whose hostility roused the suspicion that it rested not on a clear-headed appraisal of the usefulness and limits of mathematics so much as an unwillingness or inability to master the necessary essentials; sometimes this appeared merely anti-intellectual or obscurantist. At the other end of the spectrum there have been many doubts expressed by economists whose mathematical competence is beyond question, yet who, in a full understanding of the issues, did not accept the flood of mathematisation which has now come to dominate the learned journals, and for which a high degree of mathematical skill is essential for comprehension.[6] A few among the great number of such criticisms will now be mentioned merely to illustrate something of the nature and extent of the disquiet even amongst quite orthodox and respected economists.

It should be mentioned that no clear ideological lines divide the mathematical economists from their critics and there is a measure of irony in that Marxist economists are apparently just as keen as neoclassicists to prove their credentials by employing increasingly sophisticated quantitative methods in order to convince, even though they also often deplore the 'box of tricks' approach of the typical modern economics textbook, with its apparent lack of awareness of the historical and sociological aspects of the subject.

As has previously been noted, reservations were felt from the beginning about the wisdom of over-reliance on mathematics, as shown by the attitude of Marshall. As well as preferring graphical methods to algebraic symbolism, he showed himself alert to the dangers involved in allowing mathematicians the freedom to produce whatever complexities they were capable of, working with data which they had been provided with by economists, without regard for the possibility that the data too may be imperfect; not that the mathematicians would be to blame – it was the duty of the economist to warn them: 'He [the mathematician] takes no technical responsibility for the material, and is often unaware how inadequate the material is to bear the strains of his powerful machinery' (*Principles*, Appendix D).

This cautious attitude to the new 'machinery' was found amongst others of the literary school such as Cairnes who had been taken aback by Jevons' calculus, and even Keynes writing in the 1930s, though himself an outstanding statistician and a mathematician of note, deplored the fact that much of 'recent "Mathematical" economics' consisted of 'mere concoctions, as imprecise as the initial assumptions they rest on, which allow the author to lose sight of the complexities and interdependencies of the real world in a maze of pretentious and unhelpful symbols' (Keynes, 1973, p. 298). Often, however, between the two world wars, and into the 1950s, the tendency was for mathematical economists to increase both in numbers and influence, being observed with a mixture of admiration and apprehension by their not so numerate colleagues.

By the 1950s and 1960s impressive amounts of paper had been

covered in the pursuit of quantification and yet there began to be heard critical voices – and from the most respectable quarters.[7] Kenneth Boulding, the author of a very widely recommended and strictly orthodox textbook, in the course of a memorial lecture to the prestigious American Economics Association in 1966, spoke of economists as having become obsessed with 'piddling refinements of mathematical models'. Five years later he criticised contemporary economics education for its 'anti-historical' method which leads into what he called ' "*Ptolemaic*[8] economics" . . . finding out more and more numbers which mean less and less.'[9] Further denunciatory presidential addresses and lectures by the eminent appeared fairly soon afterwards. In 1970 Leontief used his presidential address to the AEA to charge economists with caring more for formal mathematical reasoning than they did for observable reality; and in 1971, Professor Phelps-Brown, in his address to the Royal Economic Society, criticised the inappropriate use made of statistical aggregates, calling for less mathematical rigour and more attention to history; he also declared the contemporary degree of mathematisation to be premature, because economics lacks sufficient empirical data on which to build securely the mathematical structures.[10]

About the same time, G.D.N Worswick, in his presidential address to the Economics Section of the British Association,[11] whilst acknowledging that the econometricians had been 'a powerful force in bringing economic theory back into touch with reality'[12] with their insistence on the collection of data and the testing of hypotheses, declared it to be his impression 'that the predictive power of econometrics is rather low, certainly very much lower than what one expects in natural sciences.' He illustrated this contention by reference to the case of the Phillips curve in which 'a quite unjustified stability and precision were imputed to relationships of this type'. Also, 'Too much of what goes on in economic and econometric theory is of little or no relevance to serious economic science.' Similar complaints came in 1970 from Professor Ragnar Frisch, himself a much respected econometrician, who condemned the production of 'queer assumptions' leading to attractive intellectual games ('playometrics'). These assumptions he declared were frequently made more 'for the convenience of *mathematical manipulation* than for reasons of similarity to concrete reality' (my emphasis). This divorce from reality was seen by Professor H.G. Johnson, then at the London School of Economics, as having caused the best work in econometrics to have been on the theory of econometrics and not on the solution of economic problems.[13]

In the face of questioning from within the ranks of their profession one response from the mathematically-inclined economists has been to suggest that the criticisms are invalidated by reason of the critics' ignorance of modern mathematics and especially of the possibilities of the computer. No such reply is adequate however in respect of most of the critics referred to above, and a most damaging critique has come from one of the outstanding academic mathematicians of the post-war period, Norbert Wiener, Professor of Mathematics at the Massachusetts Institute of Technology and creator of cybernetics. Here are two short extracts from his observations which seem worth quoting:

> Just as primitive peoples adopt the western modes of denationalised clothing and of parliamentarism out of a vague feeling that these magic rites and vestments will at once put them abreast of modern culture and technique, so the economists have developed the habit of dressing up their rather imprecise ideas in the language of the infinitesimal calculus.

> Very few econometricians are aware that if they are to imitate the procedure of modern physics and not its mere appearance a mathematical economics must begin with a critical account of these quantitative notions and the means adopted for collecting and measuring them.[14]

A similar note on the dangers of assuming the universal applicability of mathematical instruments had been struck by Nobel Laureate Koopmans in 1957: 'the success of a mathematical tool or theory in one field (such as physics) creates no presumption either for or against its usefulness in another field.'[15]

So far as the use of statistics is concerned, the limits to the applicability of frequency-ratio probability had been set out in Keynes' *Treatise on Probability* (1920) and were analysed and refined by Shackle in, *Expectation in Economics* (1949). In a later work, Shackle observes that although frequency probability has become dominant in scholarship of every kind: 'The central question is whether probability . . . is any more rational than the ordinary man's contemned "pre-scientific" procedures. For it can offer itself as a guide of life only in the *absence* of knowledge, only when science is not there to be appealed to' (Shackle, 1972, p. 395). Nevertheless frequency-ratio probability continues to be used in analysing economic situations for which it is not appropriate. The effect of such misuse has led to unwarranted assumptions of the equiprobability of whatever is not known.[16] In view of the rising chorus of criticisms even from the highest ranks of the economic establishment it is a matter for some wonder to observe that successive editions of learned journals and new textbooks continue to dazzle us with their apparently undeterred devotion to many of the principles which have been under fire.[17]

4. AUSTRIAN VIEWS

A first reaction from the reader at this point might well be to ask, in view of what has been noted of the scale of the criticisms from among the orthodoxy, what could possibly remain to attack. Certainly with many of the strictures mentioned the Austrians would be in agreement. But two preliminary and general points should be noted. First, the Austrian school were saying some of the things which we have recounted as coming from the orthodox, but were saying them much earlier, and indeed received some derision for their 'unfashionable' ideas; secondly, the Austrians do not agree with the possibility that, through continued patient efforts to refine and sharpen their techniques, the mathematical economists and econometricians will eventually 'win through'. They tend rather to view the whole approach, for various reasons, as quite fundamentally misguided.

Menger's book containing the marginal principle was first published in the same year as Jevons' *Theory of Political Economy* (1871), but the methods of presentation of the two could scarcely have been more different. Jevons' was not only presented mathematically but positively asserted that economics 'must be a mathematical science' (ibid., p. 3) simply because it deals with measurable quantities.[18] Menger's approach was entirely non-mathematical, nor did he use a single diagram, although he used simple numerical illustrative examples. Despite his avoidance of algebraic symbols his work has been considered by some to be more thorough and careful than that of Jevons. However, even though allowances must be made for the difficulties imposed by translation from German the relatively tortuous wordy version of marginal utility given by Menger as compared with the crisp lucidity of Jevons' differential calculus makes it easy to see why the mathematical method eventually came to dominate in economic theory; though this may have turned out ultimately to have been for the wrong reasons. Schumpeter thought that the founders of the Austrian school were gravely handicapped by their lack of ability to 'understand a set of simultaneous equations', but found Menger's achievement all the more impressive given his lack of the 'appropriate mathematical tools'.

The fact that the older Austrians avoided (either voluntarily, or involuntarily, as a consequence of their alleged lack of familiarity with the necessary skills) the use of mathematics, it has been suggested, is rooted in their basic education which included the philosophy of Aristotle[19] – Menger and his disciples, especially Böhm-Bawerk, Wieser and Mises had been required to read Aristotle's *Metaphysics* in the original Greek in Austrian secondary schools. This, so it has been claimed, influenced among other things, their attitude towards the role of mathematics in economics. According to this view economic laws as expressed in equations are 'only arbitrary statements'. Economics is not about the quantities of phenomena, 'but the underlying *essences* of such real entities as value, profit, and other economic categories'. This apparently somewhat mystical approach is bound to strike the modern positivist as quite simply wrong or even obscurantist, but it does fit consistently with Austrian subjectivism, which maintains that all the interconnections between economic magnitudes such as value, cost, supply and demand are best explained, not by functional equations or diagrams but by the fact that the wants of the consumer directly or indirectly determine all the other economic variables. It is not very obvious why, in principle, we cannot have functional relationships between consumer wants and other variables without lapsing into the objectivism to which the Austrians are opposed. It should be noted that Hayek seems to accept as perfectly reasonable the use of functional relationships depicted graphically, even though being himself firmly subjectivist.[20]

Although the founders of the Austrian school avoided, for various reasons, the use of mathematics, they did not go out of their way to denounce its use to the extent which followed in the writings, for example, of Mises. The confident – some would say sweepingly general and dogmatic – style of his critique is seen in reference to mathematical method in economics in terms such as 'barren', 'vicious', 'false assumptions leading to fallacious inferences'. The syllogisms of mathematics he regarded as sterile and serving to distort the true nature of the relations between phenomena (Mises, 1949, p. 350). Mises' main criticisms are centred on his belief that mathematics simply distracts attention away from market processes. All investigations of prices and costs involve money, but the equations and curves of the mathematical economists in no way describe reality. 'They strongly impress the gullible layman. In fact they only confuse and muddle things which are satisfactorily dealt with in text books of commercial arithmetic and accountancy' (ibid., p. 353). Whilst in a subject like mechanics or physics equations can be useful in the sense that they can enlarge our knowledge, this is not so in respect of economics. One reason for this is that although constants in the natural sciences exist and have reality, no such constants exist in economics.[21] Mises distinguishes between what he calls the 'logical' and the 'mathematical economists' in their analysis of equilibrium. Although both agree that human action tends towards equilibrium states, the logical economist is not content only to analyse such states:

He shows how the activities of enterprising men, the promoters and speculators, eager to profit from discrepancies in the price structure tend toward eradicating such discrepancies and thereby also toward blotting out the sources of entrepreneurial profit and loss. . . . The mathematical description of various states of equilibrium is mere play. The problem is the analysis of the market process. (ibid., p. 356)

Mises had noticed that there were critics who wanted to see economics use mathematics to analyse dynamic change rather than static equilibrium situations, and this has, of course, since become a fruitful field of activity for mathematical economists. Instead of welcoming what might have been judged to be attempts at a more realistic approach, Mises condemned such efforts as misguided. It was not enough to introduce time into economic models because time alone as a variable adds nothing to our understanding of market process:

The differential equations of mechanics are supposed to describe precisely the motions concerned at any instant of the time travelled through. The economic equations have no reference whatever to conditions as they really are in each instant of the time interval between the state of nonequilibrium and that of equilibrium. Only those entirely blinded by the prepossession that economics must be a pale replica of mechanics will underrate the weight of this objection. (ibid., pp. 356–7)

Not only does he see no merit in such analysis but goes out of his way to block off any suggestion that mathematics should be tried out. Thus: 'the problems of process analysis, i.e. the only economic problems that matter, defy any mathematical approach' (ibid., p. 356). Whilst accepting that Mises' criticism is justified in respect of some 'pretentiously optimistic quantifiers'[22] his case suffers somewhat by reason of his own dogmatic stance. Furthermore, his implicit message that all enquiry by mathematical methods should be given up must be contrasted with the fact that he does not clearly tell us how 'market process' should be analysed. Perhaps it should not be enquired into and the important thing is simply to know that it exists, is complex in its operation, and should be respected. This does not satisfy those who cling to the idea that economics is, or is capable of becoming (cf. Popper), a fully-fledged science.

Mises' attitude to statistics and econometrics is almost equally uncompromising: 'there is no such thing as quantitative economics. All economic quantities we know about are economic history.' The point he is making is that whereas a laboratory experimenter can observe what is now happening, all the statistics of prices, etc. which the econometrician works with are data about 'yesterday', and current change is unobservable. Also the problem is made more difficult because of the subjective basis of the quantities observed: 'external phenomena affect different people in different ways' (ibid., p. 351).[23] As an example of what he regards as the pretensions surrounding certain kinds of econometric studies, Mises cites the case of some research which determined the price elasticity of demand for various commodities, published in 1938. For example, a value was calculated for the elasticity of demand for potatoes in the USA between 1875 and 1929. It was praised by an eminent professor of economics and compared in its significance for economic science with the determination of atomic weights for the development of chemistry. Mises had picked an easy target; he simply pointed out the obvious difference, namely, that the elasticity of demand for potatoes in the USA during those particular years is not comparable to a value such as the atomic weight of hydrogen (the latter is thought to be true for all times and places). Mises concluded that such researches are 'rather questionable and unsatisfactory contributions to economic history' (ibid., p. 352).[24]

Thus, Mises' opposition to econometrics is compounded of two main elements based on his subjectivism, first, the habit of treating the facts of economic behaviour – historical facts – as if they were the kind of observations available to the chemist in his laboratory; secondly, to make matters worse, some of these observations having been quantified, are treated as if they were constants. Given the ever-changing conditions of human behaviour such constants appeared to Mises to be impossible.[25]

Although Hayek has, of course, been greatly influenced by Mises, his reservations on mathematics appear mild in comparison and his emphasis is mainly concerned with the false assumption of knowledge involved in objectivity if applied to the social sciences. In 1945, for instance, he wrote of the way in which 'much of mathematical economics with its simultaneous equations' starting 'from the assumption that people's *knowledge* corresponds with the objective *facts* of the situation, systematically leaves out what is our main task to explain' (Hayek, 1945, p. 91). Like Mises, Hayek has constantly warned of the inappropriateness of the kind of mathematical methods common to natural science when they are applied to the social sciences. For example:

the blind transfer of the striving for quantitative measurements to a field in which the specific conditions are not present, which gives the desire for quantitative data its basic importance in the natural sciences, is the result of an entirely unfounded prejudice. It is probably responsible for the worst abberrations and absurdities produced by scientism in the social sciences. (ibid., p. 89)

In a footnote Hayek does concede that mathematics is probably 'absolutely indispensable' to the description of certain complex structural relationships in economics even though he again, like Mises, is highly sceptical as to the validity of the numerical values which appear in formulae ('misleadingly called "constants"' (ibid.)). Hayek was still largely of the same opinion twenty-nine years later when, in his Nobel Memorial Lecture,[26] having first again recognised that 'we could scarcely have achieved that comprehensive picture of the mutual interdependencies of the different events in a market without this algebraic technique', and is anxious to avoid giving the impression of rejecting mathematical method, nevertheless declares it to be illusory to think that by such means we can calculate the prices and quantities of all goods traded. Pareto, one of the founders of mathematical economics, is quoted in support as saying that it would be absurd to assume that we could ascertain all the data. The coming of the computer, it might be supposed, would do something to meet these criticisms but Hayek remains unimpressed. However great is a computer's power of digesting facts it is of little help in ascertaining such facts (Hayek, 1982, I, p. 148, n. 14).

A common feature of mathematical economics is the use of continuous functional relationships yielding smooth curves which are amenable to differentiation and this practice has been criticised by Austrians as tending to suggest a false view of economic activity. Most economists evidently consider the assumption of continuity a harmless enough device and would defend it on the grounds of its immense usefulness in clearing the way for mathematical analysis. It is significant that in an introduction which takes up some of the criticisms made of mathematical economics very lucidly, the authors of an elementary book[27] on the subject do not appear to consider the question of continuous smooth functions worth mentioning. But Rothbard, for example, points out the obvious difference between assuming continuity in physics[28] and assuming it in economics: 'There are no infinitely small steps in human action . . . they will always be finite and discrete' (Rothbard, 1962, p. 265). He even regards the very idea of a function as inappropriate in a study of human action: 'no causal, constant, external determinants of action can exist. The term "function" is appropriate only to the unmotivated, repeatable motion of inorganic matter.'[29] As for the econometricians' pretensions to produce accurate predictions, these are dismissed: 'when the forecaster attempts to make quantitative predictions he is going beyond the knowledge provided by economic science' (Rothbard, 1962, p. 256).

Even in physics – a subject whose methods have been to some extent the model for econometricians – there are many signs that prediction is not so certain as was once imagined. As one modern physicist put it recently:

Suppose we have a gas in which we wish to predict the behaviour of molecules: a single electron at the 'end of the Universe' will upset our predictions within a time of micro-seconds. (See n. 26, p. 14)

Although, as we have noted, Hayek sees a useful place for functional relationships in economics, it has been contended that acceptance of Austrian methodology necessarily involves rejection of econometrics as a tool of economic study. This follows from the presumption that true axioms concerning human behaviour can be discovered; hence that the theories based on the axioms must also be true (given the accuracy of the logical steps involved) and that, therefore, there is no requirement for the predictions of such theories to be subject to Popperian falsification.[30] It has been pointed out by Barry and Hutchison that such apriorism puts Hayek, who latterly became influenced by Popper, in a somewhat ambiguous methodological position.

Statistical aggregation and the use made of the 'law of large numbers' has come in for criticism by Austrians. This principle, which is dependent on the notion that if there are a large number of elements in the set being measured, random changes will be mutually compensated for, cannot be used to account for the stability of aggregates in economics, because the number of elements is, in practice, too small and the constant adjustments which go on in markets are often unquantifiable (Hayek, 1945, p. 83). In particular, statistics gathered by a central authority tend to aggregate data by ignoring those minor differences between individual elements which are crucial ones, e.g. the location and quality of goods and services. (See also Hayek, 1952, pp. 107–9, for further discussion on the limitations of statistical aggregates.) The current tendency to compile statistical aggregates, it has been suggested, is a symptom of the desire to promote central 'control'. Bureaucracy requires the classification of economic facts into a relatively few broad bands of manageable 'homogeneity' and, whilst there is no harm in using such aggregates as a rough measure of *past* social and economic events, it is a fallacy to assume them as causally operative upon one another.[31]

Hayek's contention that statistics can lead to a false picture of society is given support by a quotation from Roger Williams:

People who study statistics, even such very important subjects as demography, do not study society. Society is a structure, not a mass phenomenon, . . . we do not have a sufficient number of specimens to treat the behaviour of the wholes statistically. . . . The problems have nothing to do with the law of large numbers. (Williams, *You are Extraordinary* (1967), New York, pp. 26–7; See Hayek, (1982), III, p. 201).

In conclusion, the reader is recommended to consider some of the arguments for mathematics and statistics as stated, for example, in a concise and persuasive manner in the book by Archibald and Lipsey (See note 27). He might then ask himself to what extent the Austrian critique has been refuted.

In many respects the Mises critique of the misuse of mathematics and statistics is unduly harsh, distorting the actual state of affairs, and it is noteworthy that Hayek has a more temperate view. Mises presents us with a picture of econometric forecasters which leaves them looking incredibly naive. Of course, the degree of accuracy attained by the various institutes and research centres is often disappointing and the Austrians serve a useful purpose in pointing to the dangers which this involves, such as the consequent over-confident and faulty 'management of the economy' by politicians. Nevertheless, the suggestion that all econometric models are constructed with complete unawareness of some of the inherent difficulties involved in forecasting is undoubtedly exaggerated. Some quite elaborate models have been developed as explanatory systems, but attempts to draw inferences from them about the future have often been approached with a good deal of caution. The most notable triumphs of econometrics have been those which have turned a searching light on historical data and which have made necessary radical reappraisals of cherished theories.

Derision for mathematical models can degenerate into crude anti-mathematical obscurantism which is just as deplorable as a devotion to measurement which ignores the unmeasurable. However, the tendency to spurious objectivism and the attempt to treat the human science of economics too much like physics would not have been possible without the application of mathematics. The use made of the concept of equilibrium, considered by Austrians to be an important example of such tendencies, forms the subject of the next chapter.

NOTES

1. It is perhaps surprising that it took so long for economists to see the possibilities of the calculus, but economics was for long regarded as a 'moral' science, unsuited for treatment by mathematical techniques. It is even more surprising to observe the lateness of the application of calculus in natural science, and even in technologies, such as mechanical engineering.

2. For details on early developments see Schumpeter (1954), Lekachman (1959) or Routh (1975).

3. This account of Jevons' early work relies chiefly on Keynes (1972), pp. 128–30.

4. See Rothbard (1962), pp. 450–1, n.3.

5. Marshall provided a mathematical Appendix to his *Principles*, in which 'A few specimens of those applications of mathematical language which have proved most useful for my own purposes have . . . been added.' (p. xvi).

6. Professor Alan Prest remarks that 'it is a commonplace that each generation of new entrants to economics has more mathematical experience than the last. A few years ago an immigrant from engineering could cut a dash in economic theory. Now it requires an immigrant from pure mathematics.' (See 'Letter to a young economist', *Journal of Economic Affairs*, vol 3, no. 2, January 1983, 130–4) which is also to be recommended for its witty satire on some contemporary practices.)

7. An early post-war critical note was by George J. Stigler, *Five Lectures in Economics* (1949), London School of Economics.

8. 'Ptolemaic' refers to Ptolemy, the Ancient Greek astronomer, whose theory was that the heavenly bodies revolved about the earth in eccentric circles and epicycles.

9. See Hutchison (1977), p. 95, for the quotation from which the extract in the text is taken.
10. See 'The underdevelopment of economics', *Economic Journal*, vol. 82, no. 325, March 1972, 1–10.
11. See G.D.N. Worswick, 'Is progress in economic science possible?', *Economic Journal* vol. 82, no. 325, March 1972, 73–6).
12. Worswick's criticism of contemporary economic theory was that much of it has 'no links with concrete facts' and is 'almost indistinguishable from pure mathematics' (ibid.).
13. For further more detailed versions of these and other criticisms see Hutchison (op. cit.), pp. 69–73.
14. See Bauer (1981), chapter 15, for this reference and other relevant discussion, which is taken from Norbert Wiener, *God and Golem Inc.* (1964), Cambridge, Mass.: MIT Press.
15. Tjalling Koopmans, *Three Essays on the State of Economic Science*, (1957), New York: McGraw Hill, p. 182.
16. See also J. Marschak, 'Probability in the social sciences', in P.F. Lazarsfield (ed.), *Mathematical Thinking in the Social Sciences* (1954), Glencoe, Ill.: Free Press.
17. Wassily Leontief, 'Theoretical assumptions and non-observed facts', *American Economic Review*, March 1971, p. 3.
18. So far as knowledge of mathematics is concerned, however, Schumpeter declares that Jevons 'knew very little – much less than would have been good for him to know' (Schumpeter, 1954, p. 956, n. 5).
19. See Murray N. Rothbard, 'New light on the prehistory of the Austrian school', in Dolan (ed.) (1976), pp. 69–70, from which the following account is taken. Rothbard draws upon Emil Kauder, 'Intellectual roots of the older Austrian school', *Zeitschrift für Nationalökonomie*, 17, December 1957, 411–25.
20. See, for example, Hayek (1982), II, p. 118.
21. See Mises (1949), p. 55.
22. See Hutchison (op. cit.), p. 6, for the rest of the sentence from which this phrase is taken. It should be noted that in this sentence the author speaks also of 'non-mathematical apriorists'.
23. Hayek recognised Mises' subjectivism as the governing factor of the latter's attitude to the measurement of economic phenomena. (See Hayek, 1952, pp. 52–3, n.7.)
24. Perhaps the famous Phillips curve is a similar case.
25. See Rothbard, 'Praxeology: the methodology of Austrian economics', in Dolan (ed.), (1976), p. 33.

26. Delivered at Stockholm, 11 December 1974, and reprinted as 'The pretence of knowledge', in Hayek (1978c), pp. 23–34.
27. G.C. Archibald and Richard G. Lipsey, *Introduction to a Mathematical Treatment of Economics* (1967), London: Weidenfeld & Nicolson.
28. Even in physics there may be problems: substituting a continuous smooth function for a function consisting of a finite number of ordered pairs obtained from data may be reasonable if the intervals between the pairs is relatively small and unusual behaviour is improbable, but if the pairs are few and far between, the assumption that there will be no unusual behaviour between may not be justified, e.g. a smooth curve representing the density of water against temperature and based on readings taken at 0°, 30°, 60° and 90°C would not reveal the important point at 4°C where water is at its most dense. (I am grateful to Douglas Francis for this illustration).
29. Rothbard's implication that functional relationships are only appropriate with respect to inorganic matter would remove all biological phenomena from mathematical analysis. This seems plainly at variance with all the evidence.
30. Dolan (ed.) (1976), p. 7.
31. See Louis M. Spadaro, 'Averages and aggregates in economics', in Sennholz (ed.) (1956), pp. 159–60, on this point and a discussion of the possibilities of error or distortion arising from the use of averages.

3 Equilibrium

1. INTRODUCTION

In this chapter we are concerned with that all-pervasive concept 'equilibrium' as a general method, and with particular emphasis on what is known as Walrasian 'general equilibrium', that is, the possibility of the existence of an equilibrium arising from the interaction of thousands of separate but interacting markets and the usefulness of such a concept. There are other models of general equilibrium which originated with the work of J.M. Keynes and unfortunately for the cause of clarity these are also referred to in some textbooks simply as general equilibrium theories but they perhaps are better described as *aggregative* general equilibrium theories in order to emphasise the way in which their methodology differs from the Walrasian type. (Keynesian macroeconomic equilibrium, conventionally, is usually considered as a separate topic and this is the procedure to be followed here, although there are recent signs that the integration of Keynesian and Walrasian equilibrium may soon enter introductory text books as a usual feature[1].)

In essence, equilibrium means a balance of opposing forces and its use in economics is probably in imitation of its use in physics. In *partial* equilibrium analysis of markets the equilibrium price is that price at which the supply of, and demand for, a commodity are equal, to put the matter as briefly as possible. In *general* equilibrium analysis the problem is to determine whether each of the thousands of markets acting independently, but affecting each other, can reach a simultaneous equilibrium. These sketchy definitions will serve as a starting-point; some of their finer points will be brought out later.

2. HISTORICAL PERSPECTIVE

According to Schumpeter the 'scholastic doctors' of the Middle Ages developed the rudiments of the concept of equilibrium (e.g. Duns Scotus in the thirteenth century) and one eighteenth-century economist, Count Pietro Verri, appears to have grasped the idea at least as well as his illustrious successor, Adam Smith. Although the latter did not use the term, he was quite close to the idea of equilibrium as when he spoke of prices converging to 'this centre of repose and continuance'.[2] The convergence was, however, between the 'natural' price (as determined by costs of production) and the actual price on the market, and the idea, although apparently serving as a starting-point, needed much refinement. It would seem to be the case that the desire to import into economic method the mathematical instruments which had shown their power in the natural sciences was originally the motive for the introduction of the equilibrium concept into economics, along with other mathematical techniques. In the Preface to his *Theory of Political Economy* (1871), Jevons proposed that the understanding of economics could be greatly advanced by the introduction of elementary calculus and compared equilibrium in economics to equilibrium in natural science: 'The Theory of Economy thus treated presents a close analogy to the science of Statical Mechanics, and the Laws of Exchange are found to resemble the Laws of Equilibrium of a Lever' (1871, p. viii).[3] Alfred Marshall also compares economic forces to those of mechanics and biology: 'A business firm grows and attains great strength, and afterwards perhaps stagnates and decays; and at the turning point there is a balancing or equilibrium of the forces of life and decay' (Marshall, 1890, p. 323) and: 'to prepare the way for this advanced study [of markets] we want first to look at a simpler balancing of forces which corresponds rather to the mechanical equilibrium of a stone hanging by an elastic string' (ibid.) From then on, the concept of partial static equilibrium was a dominant influence in the methodology of the neoclassical school.

From the beginning the Austrian school, as represented by Menger, although awake to the idea of equilibrium, never explained their theories with the extensive use of mathematics found in Jevons and Marshall. In his explanation of exchange Menger uses the equilibrium concept albeit in an entirely verbal way. As with his follower Mises, Menger's work is devoid of mathematics or even diagrams. This might be explained as due simply to the lack of mathematical competence of the older Austrians (Schumpeter's opinion) or as a consequence of their mistrust of quantification.

It was Léon Walras who, in 1874, pioneered[4] the idea of general equilibrium (GE), and provided a mathematical proof. Marshall, although he was an outstanding mathematician, and apparently an admirer of Walras' work, preferred the static equilibrium method as being more applicable to concrete, everyday problems;[5] but he had every hope that the study of economics would eventually move from partial to general equilibrium analysis.

Vilfredo Pareto, who succeeded Walras at Lausanne, extended and refined Walras' general theory, but used it chiefly as the basis for the solution of welfare propositions. Modern refinement of GE theory began with Gustav Cassel, a member of the Swedish school, of which Wicksell was the first and probably the most original member. Cassel set out a clear, simplified account of the Walrasian system in the early 1930s. In this decade the preoccupation of most economists with Keynes' *General Theory*, which appeared at the time to have little in common with Walrasian general equilibrium, resulted in only slight interest in the latter. But by the end of the 1930s there existed, according to Weintraub (1979, p. 222), rigorous and detailed models of the Walrasian system. Modern developments began seriously in 1954 with the work of Arrow, Debreu and McKenzie. Debreu, through his *Theory of Value* (1959) has probably become the best-known and influential of these modern theorists. Today, the tendency is for neoclassical theorists to concentrate on the entirely logical idea that macroeconomics can be reconciled with its micro-foundations; to work on the basis that the long-lived dichotomy always was fallacious. But as to what are the 'right' foundations in micro-economics for macroeconomics neoclassical economists have not, as yet, provided a definitive answer, but the modern Austrian school would not dissent from the view that the roots of macroeconomic aggregates must be sought in the microeconomy. From their point of view the Keynesian revolution is seen as something of an aberration.

3. DEFINITION AND PROOF

The problems to which neoclassical economists address themselves in equilibrium will now be briefly outlined,[6] followed first by some possible criticisms which have come mainly from neoclassical economists themselves.

A general equilibrium is defined as a state in which all markets and all economic agents (i.e. firms and households) are in simultaneous equilibrium. GE emerges from the solution of a system of a large number of simultaneous equations, a solution which is possible if there are the same number of unknowns as there are equations. Three problems arise: (i) the existence problem, (ii) the uniqueness problem and (iii) the stability problem. Existence of equilibrium requires that quantities supplied and demanded in all markets are, in principle, capable of being brought into equality; uniqueness requires that there be only one set of equilibrium prices and quantities; and stability depends on the relationship between the slopes of the supply and demand curves. (For example, if a demand curve was of positive slope and a supply curve of negative slope – the reverse of the usual assumptions – the equilibrium would be unstable, having no tendency to persist.) Mathematical theorems have been worked out which, given some quite restrictive assumptions (e.g. perfect competition in all markets, constant returns to scale and no externalities) support the idea that the three problems of GE theory are soluble.[7]

4. Criticisms from within the neoclassical school

GE theory has been assailed almost as much by the practitioners of positive economics as by anyone – for its unreality and uselessness, among other things. Sometimes it sounds rather as if some of the critics should re-examine their basic methodology. If following similar methods to those of physics yields unacceptable conclusions in economics, perhaps the positivist approach is simply inappropriate for the study of economic behaviour.

Janos Kornai (1971) has argued that the main defect of GE is its extremely limited power to describe the real economy. Weintraub (1979), although acknowledging that GE theory has flaws, rejects much of Kornai's criticism as being based on faulty methodology (ibid., pp. 36–7).

Hutchison has, by means of some conclusive quotations, shown how one eminent neoclassical economist has grown from being an admirer of the concept of equilibrium to a severe critic. In 1934 Lord Kaldor evidently regarded equilibrium as one of the main achievements of the previous fifty years, but by 1972 in his article 'The irrelevance of equilibrium economics'[8] he had come to regard it as a major obstacle to proper understanding (Hutchison, 1977, pp. 74–5).

Frank Hahn, who has himself contributed many important essays to the development of GE theory, has some strong reservations. In defending neoclassical theory from the attacks of Sraffa and his followers, and whilst arguing that neoclassical theory has 'nothing to fear' from this quarter, he admits that as an explanation of how equilibrium comes about, it is 'highly unsatisfactory'.[9] Hahn's criticisms and his suggestions for modification are summarised concisely in Bell and Kristol (1981), pp. 123–38.[10] Amongst these criticisms are: that Arrow–Debreu economics takes no heed of time and expectations and that in this regard rational expectations theory cannot help much. Nevertheless, after all his reservations, Hahn concludes optimistically that GE theory has been a major intellectual achievement, a useful starting-point and is the basis for the way forward even though it will eventually be superseded (op. cit., p. 137). But Hutchison criticises Hahn's defences of GE at some length (op. cit., pp. 81–7) as not refuting the charge that it is entirely without real world interest or significance. Hutchison sees GE theory as a prime example of what he calls 'the crisis of abstraction' in economic theory, this is, the danger inherent in extreme abstraction from reality and the adoption of unreal assumptions. In particular, argues Hutchison, so much concentration on equilibrium situations leads to 'deluded utopianism', in which unjust criticisms fly between the advocates of rival economic systems (ibid., p. 90).

Blaug is also in profound disagreement with Hahn with regard to the fundamental merit of GE theory as a fruitful starting-point from which to explore the economic system:

Its leading characteristic has been the endless formalization of purely logical problems without the slightest regard for the production of falsifiable theorems about actual economic behaviour, which, we insist, remains the fundamental task of economics. (Blaug, 1980, p. 192)

GE, as its creators have envisaged it over the years since Walras, was to be a shining example of the power of mathematics to dispel the dark cobwebs of ignorant subjectivism associated with political economy. The disillusion now being felt by some of its former devotees may not be the fault of the method *per se* but more of its appropriateness to its subject matter. That this is now more widely realised is shown by the increasing amount of recent research which concentrates not upon equilibrium but on disequilibrium, the product of uncertainty. This, however, involves an even more varied set of mathematical tools of analysis than does equilibrium theory. With regard to the basic Walrasian GE model however, even after the incorporation of disequilibrium, it seems that there remain many problems. As one writer, though critical of equilibrium theory remains in his methodology firmly within the neoclassical fold, puts it: 'one is perpetually plagued by the suspicion that a complete restructuring of the basic framework [of the Walrasian general equilibrium model] is required before substantial and significant progress can be made' (Hey, 1979, p. 221). And: 'Despite the amount of attention devoted in economics to the study of equilibria, the process by which an equilibrium is reached is not well understood. It has been called the fundamental problem in economic theory' (S. Kawasaki *et al.*, 'Disequilibrium dynamics: an empirical study', *AER*, vol. 72, no. 5, December 1982, 992–1004).

4. THE AUSTRIAN VIEW

A succession of Austrian economists have expressed their dissatisfaction with Walras' GE theory from its beginning. Mises rejected the notion of general equilibrium as 'a superficial analogy spun out too long'. He not only criticised GE theory, but argued for its replacement by the concept of 'market process'. A clear exposition of Mises' objections to GE theory is to be found in Lachmann (1977), pp. 181–93). On the subject of 'market process' he concedes that 'conceptualization and unification are painfully slow', for even though it might be widely agreed that GE theory is entirely useless, there is clearly some difficult work ahead for Austrians in specifying exactly what is involved in 'market process'.

Although Mises introduced the concept of the 'evenly rotating economy' (ERE) he stresses that it is a purely imaginary concept, 'a limiting notion'. Mises' ERE is seen as a state of affairs in which all changes of data and time are eliminated. It is not to be confused with the imaginary construction of a 'stationary economy'. The latter appears to be, in Mises' view, what mainstream economists mean by general equilibrium. The purpose of the hypothetical ERE, is simply to enable the problems of changes in the data and time to be analysed. But, according to Mises, the 'mathematical economists' ignore the fact that the data are always changing. He appears to claim that although by his praxeological method one can make sensible use of such an entirely imaginary concept as the ERE, the mathematical economists devote too much attention to describing various equilibrium states as if they were real and not a limiting notion, 'a mere tool' (Mises, 1949, pp. 244–50).

Mises' critique as set out in *Human Action* is not notable for its clarity and, of course, it is not true today that any economists regard equilibrium models as anything but hypothetical constructions.

Given the methodology of positive economics the construction of 'unreal' models is unobjectionable so long as falsification of their predictions is possible. Nevertheless much economic theory, and particularly GE theory, has been built on the imaginary model of perfect competition, coherent plans of economic agents and apparently instantaneous adjustments to change – all this embodied in a system of simultaneous equations.

Although Mises and his followers are able to accept the idea of equilibrium in a very simple market as being a reasonable proposition, the broader its application the more it is seen as remote from reality. Thus, although equilibrium for an individual or a firm is an acceptable idea, the equilibrium of an industry is less so; and equilibrium of the 'economic system' even less so. As for 'equilibrium growth' – an economic system in motion – this 'borders on absurdity' (Lachmann, 1969, p. 89). From the Austrian point of view, although individuals or firms may realistically be conceived of as being in equilibrium, there is no justification for extending the principle to multitudes of individuals. In the case of 'the economy' this would seem to be implying the necessity of a single 'super-mind'. From the point of view of methodological individualism this idea is untenable.

Another relevant basic assumption of the Austrian school concerns the role of knowledge; that is, that human preferences, expectations and knowledge are unpredictable. The use by economists of the term equilibrium is regarded by Hayek as unfortunate because it presupposes an unwarranted degree of knowledge. In various of his articles and books Hayek has stressed that the equilibrium condition implies that all the facts are known and all discovery of new ones has ceased. Furthermore, two distinct kinds of facts are discernible. First, there are real objective facts as an observer might know them, and secondly, subjective facts which are known only to the people whose behaviour we are trying to explain. The difficulties which this distinction raises for general equilibrium were thoroughly analysed by Hayek in the 1930s (Hayek, 1937). His main conclusion was that equilibrium conditions would constantly be disrupted by the changing of plans consequent upon the continual acquisition of new knowledge,[11] much of it of a subjective nature, by economic agents. It also follows from Hayek's subjectivism that there can be no way of determining when an equilibrium exists as is implied in neoclassical economics.[12] But Hayek, like Mises, does not entirely reject the concept of equilibrium: 'I have long felt that the concept of equilibrium . . . has a clear meaning only when confined to the analysis of the action of a single person' (Hayek, 1937).

The Austrian theory of money, as advanced by Mises, would, incidentally, reveal a significant problem for the original version of Walrasian GE theory. In a world of perfect knowledge every individual's cash balances would be zero, since there would be perfect foreknowledge of future sales and purchases. According to Rothbard if the demand for cash falls to zero, all prices rise to infinity, and the entire general equilibrium of the market 'falls apart' (Rothbard, 1976, p. 172). Mises does not go quite so far as this, but simply rests his case on the proposition that 'there is no room left for money in a "static" system. But the very notion of a market economy without money is self-contradictory' (Mises, op. cit., p. 249).

The lack of applicability in neoclassical GE theory has been the basis of another major criticism by Austrians which allegedly fails even by the standards of Popperian falsifiability – a principle by which many economists now claim to be guided. For example, Loasby concluded that the GE research programme has generally combined 'Fierce rigour in the theory and unheeding slackness in its application' (as quoted approvingly by Blaug, 1981, p. 192). It should be noted, however, that Blaug rejects the 'anti-Popperianism' which follows from some interpretations of Austrian methodology (ibid., p. 185). He has in mind, for example, the alleged implications of Shackle's approach.

It has sometimes been argued that the Austrian school's attitude to the grand structures of neoclassical equilibrium tends to be negatively critical and does not offer much suggestion as to what might be considered as a replacement. There is something in this; the writings of the Austrians are dominated by hostile criticism of the neoclassical system. But an important point should be noticed with regard to this matter. One of the consequences of the use of equilibrium in conventional economic theory is that we almost subconsciously look for modifications of that theory, expressed in its *own terms* and propounded via algebra and graphs; not being able to find many examples, we tend to conclude that Austrians have not real alternative to offer. One has also heard the Austrian school criticised as yielding 'no policy prescriptions'. But the answer to this is: why must it? We move into deep waters here. And the question is inevitably raised: what is economics for?

Austrians have suggested that one way by which economic theory might be substantially modified – or at least our approach to it – is to reverse the roles of equilibrating and disequilibrating forces (Lachmann, 1977, p. 39). In neoclassical theory equilibrium is central, and processes which move either towards or away from it are regarded as of subsidiary importance. For Austrians, on the other hand, it is the reverse: the disequilibrating forces are accorded the position of central importance and the market is seen as a continuous process with temporary equilibria which appear and dissolve rather like a speeded-up film of clouds. The economy is, however, even less capable of being observed than a sky full of clouds.[13]

The ever-shifting nature of knowledge and expectations has led Shackle to a similar view of equilibrium to that of Hayek and Mises and there are other similarities.[14] In GE theory some constancy of data over time is usually assumed. This demands knowledge of the future on the part of the economic agents, but strictly speaking this is impossible in a kaleidic world of ever-changing knowledge; thus GE theory becomes impossibly difficult – so difficult, that it has been said of Shackle's view that it 'leads to total despair'. Shackle's work certainly cautions a high degree of humility towards the complexity of human affairs but not 'total despair'.[15] What it certainly does is to argue that economic theory should avoid over-confident prediction.

What damages equilibrium theory as much as anything in Shackle's view is its inability to cope with the passage of time: 'the theoretical ideal applies to mutually *isolated* days or moments, each to be treated as perfectly self-contained and looking to no yesterday and no tomorrow' (Shackle, 1972, p. 150). But in the real world circumstances are constantly changing, rendering each successive equilibrium obsolete. In GE theory time was banished. The theoretician 'did so because *time* and *complete knowledge* are utterly incompatible' (ibid., p. 151). Shackle has suggested the concept of kaleidic method as an alternative approach. This method of enquiry into economic affairs would involve not seeking to predict what will happen, but what is the range of (short-run) possible outcomes of various situations:

The notion of kaleidic equilibrium is an explicit recognition of . . . the overwhelming fact that the *economic* affairs of society are not self-contained and independent. They may be compared to a sailing-boat in tempestuous and tide-swept waters'. (ibid., p. 438)

To sum up: criticisms of GE theory do not fall easily into two neat categories – neoclassical versus Austrian. To some mainstream economists GE theory is seen as unsatisfactory because of its failure to generate falsifiable hypotheses and as having no real-world significance. GE is nevertheless seen, by Hahn for example, as a valid basis for further progress; but he appears to agree with the Austrians and with Professor Shackle that GE theory ignores the importance of time and expectations. Austrian criticism is based on the following propositions: not enough attention is given to the *process* through which equilibrium is reached; it is implied that all the relevant facts can be known which, because of constantly changing plans is impossible; and Austrian suspicions that the scientistic basis of GE could tend to favour centralised control on the grounds of improvements in economic efficiency. Although the Austrian criticisms are undoubtedly usefully corrective in their insistence upon the greater importance of market *process* rather than general equilibrium, they do not offer any clearly stated *comparable* alternative to GE in the form of a mathematical model, but, of course, they would regard such an enterprise as largely a waste of time. This does, however, open the Austrians to the charge that their methodology lacks the clarity necessary for the creation of a coherent, precise account of how a complex of interacting markets works; possibly they would be quite happy to accept the validity of this criticism in the belief that such precision is incompatible with subjectivism.

NOTES

1. The macroeconomic equilibrium of the Keynesian model of national income determination differs in its methodology from the Walrasian system, but many theorists today see Keynesian concepts as having had their micro-theoretic foundations strengthened by the work of those who have built on the Walrasian foundations, such as Arrow and Debreu. In principle there would seem to be strong reasons for thinking that the two general equilibrium 'research programs' may be integrable.
2. As quoted by William J. Barber, *A History of Economic Thought* (1967) Harmondsworth: Penguin, p. 33.
3. Jevons employs the equilibrium concept, for example, in his analysis of exchange (1871, p. 97).
4. See Lekachman, *A History of Economic Ideas* (1959), New York: Harper & Row, pp. 270–1. Credit must be given to Augustin Cournot in 1838 for an insight into the possibility of a general equilibrium but which remained undeveloped until 1874 by Walras. (See Weintraub, 1979, p. 19.)
5. Keynes said of Marshall, 'He had an inclination to undervalue

those intellectual parts of the subject which were not *directly* connected with human well-being or the condition of the working classes or the like' (Keynes, *Essays in Biography* (1972), London: Macmillan, p. 200).

6. Any good second- or third-year textbook published recently will provide greater detail than is here appropriate on general equilibrium theory, e.g. Koutsoyannis (1979).
7. For an introduction and bibliography, see Gravelle and Rees (1981), chapter 16.
8. *Economic Journal*, December 1972, 1237–55.
9. Frank Hahn, 'The Neo-Ricardians', *Cambridge Journal of Economics*, vol. 6., no. 4. December 1982, 353–74.
10. Also in 'The winter of our discontent', *Economica*, August 1973, 322ff.
11. The possibilities of 'learning' by economic agents so that the expectations of different individuals converge to the 'correct' values have now become the subject of attention by neo-classical economists (see Arrow, 1974). Whether such convergence would overcome the problem of the subjectivism of individual knowledge seems uncertain.
12. For a concise, non-mathematical, but logical exposition of several reasons why perfect competition is incompatible with subjectivism, see W. Duncan Reekie, *Industry, Prices and Markets* (1979), Oxford: Philip Allan, pp. 153–4.
13. In the air mass known as polar maritime, cumulus clouds are constantly being born, growing to a maximum depth (their 'equilibrium' which may last only for a few moments) decaying, and finally vanishing.
14. See Lachmann, 'From Mises to Shackle: an essay on Austrian economics and the kaleidic society', *Journal of Economic Literature*, Spring 1976, 54–62.
15. Kenneth Boulding, in a review of Shackle's *Epistemics and Economics*.

4   Value

The question which agitated the minds of economists perhaps more than any other in the nineteenth century was: what causes the prices of goods and services to be what they are, and what makes them change? The great division in the history of ideas – subjectivism or objectivism – is seen clearly in value theory. Although mainstream economics today seems to have settled the matter to the satisfaction of its practitioners, Austrians contend that the neoclassical approach contains important anomalies.

The picture presented in most histories of economic thought is often roughly as follows. If we begin with the medieval period the contemporary orthodoxy on price is an obsession, derived mainly from religion, with the concept of the 'just price'; this is dismissed as pre-scientific nonsense in most modern accounts.[2] After this, Adam Smith and David Ricardo are presented as the first to adopt anything approaching scientific method, followed by Karl Marx who adapted Ricardian objectivity. Then, in the late nineteenth century, the 'marginal revolution' ushered in by Menger, Jevons and Walras was eventually merged with the classical theories of costs by Alfred Marshall to become the fount from which has flowed the orthodox stream of modern neoclassical value theory. Since the time of Marshall what has really been happening in economic theory is a matter for some disagreement. Many economists seem to have been striving to exorcise subjectivism, but others regard these efforts as doomed to fail and hold that only via subjectivism have any really significant advances in economic theory been made (Hayek, 1952, p. 31).

A substantially different account, however, of the changes in value theory stresses the continuity of the Austrian view of value – that it was not so much a 'revolution' as a revival of a much older line of thought which had been temporarily eclipsed by the classical school. The notion that value depended upon utility was prevalent, for instance, among the Spanish scholastics of the sixteenth century;[3] and Thomas Aquinas had held the view that goods are only valued relative to human wants. Such utility theories of value had much influence in Europe as seen, for instance, in the work of Abbé Ferdinando Galiani (1728–87). In Schumpeter's view (1954) the English classical economists, Smith and Ricardo, are therefore seen as directing economic science on the wrong track and that it was due to the Austrians that a sound basis for value theory was restored in the 1870s.

One interesting suggestion has been put forward to account for the fact that subjectivism became more dominant in Europe than in Britain; Kauder suggests a connection with religion. The pre-nineteenth century subjectivists were French, Italian or Spanish Catholics. British economists, such as Locke and Smith, on the other hand, were influenced by Calvinism with its emphasis on the divine nature of labour, and would presumably be predisposed to search for a theory of value based on labour. Kauder also notes that Marshall (who tended to favour cost-of-production theories) had a strong Evangelical and Calvinist background.[4]

2. SUBJECTIVE VALUE: A GENERAL STATEMENT

In propounding the Austrian approach to value in parallel with neoclassical theory there is an initial problem of methodology. Neoclassical theory divides the theory of price conveniently into two components: demand and supply. Although modern demand theory may claim some success in having dispensed with subjectivism this has not been so marked as the apparently quite objective treatment of costs of production – the supply side. It has become the accepted procedure in textbooks to treat demand and supply separately. The Austrian view, however, is that there exists a common factor which links demand and supply: that *both* are wholly subjectively determined by human evaluation. Therefore to treat them as though they are quite separate is to present a false picture. Of course, the neoclassical theory of factor pricing does rest partly on the theory of marginal productivity, which in turn must depend on the subjective valuations of producers, but the conventional textbook theory of costs of production often gives an appearance of objectivity. Therefore, in treating value theory as we propose to – in terms of demand and supply – there is a certain artificiality. This must be accepted, however, for the sake of taking a parallel path to the neoclassical approach.

Before looking at the two aspects of price determination in this way, a word on the Austrian approach to value in general. From the economic point of view no objects or services can be defined solely by physical descriptions. For example: 'Economic theory has nothing to say about the little round discs of metal as which an objective or materialist view might try to define money' (Hayek, 1952, p. 53). On this basis, Austrians reject any attempt to discover 'physical laws of production' as did Ricardo and Marx: 'in economics . . . [they] . . . are not physical laws in the sense of the physical sciences but people's beliefs about what they can do' (Hayek, ibid., p. 52). Hayek's insistence on the wholly subjective nature of value is typical of the Austrian school and many examples can be found, e.g. 'Market prices are entirely determined by the value judgements of men as they really act' (Mises, 1949, p. 332); and since the prices of factors of production are ultimately determined by the prices of goods, the prices of factors are also subjectively determined. But Mises does, following Menger and Böhm-Bawerk, make one distinction between producers' and consumers' goods. This distinction is between the direct valuation of factors which takes into account the anticipated value of the product and the value of all the complementary factors being employed on the one hand, and, on the other, the prices of each factor on the market which is determined by the actions of competing bidders (Mises, ibid., 333–8). According to Buchanan, in their search for a general theory of value, the subjectivists did little to develop any analysis of *expected* value, a concept which classical theory, based as it was on costs of production, could provide (Buchanan, 1969, p. 8). The classical theory's predictions might be tested and rejected, whereas subjectivism is not amenable to such tests.

In concluding this section mention must be made of the important distinction made by Austrians between the use of the term 'value' in the sense of subjective *valuation* or preference, and the objective concept of purchasing power or price on the market. When a good is being subjectively valued it is being ranked by an individual in relation to other goods on his value scale, but when an individual is estimating how much a good could be sold for he is 'appraising' its purchasing power. It is the *appraised* value of goods, including factors of production which is the foundation of all economic activity (Rothbard, 1962, pp. 271–2; Mises, 1949, p. 332). (The apparent contradiction between subjectivity in valuation and 'objectivism' of appraisement is presumably reconciled by insisting that the appraised purchasing power of a good observable by an individual is merely the net outcome of hundreds of other individuals' *subjective* valuations.)

3. DEMAND

(i) Development of marginal utility
Well before the 1870s there were a number of forerunners of marginal utility: H.H. Gossen, J. Dupuit, A.A. Walras (father of Léon), W.F. Lloyd and M. Longfield. The last two mentioned were followers of the classical school yet came near to proposing a theory of subjective value.[5] Longfield (1802–84) suggested that utility lay behind demand and spoke of the 'intensity of demand'. 'He had assembled all the building blocks for a satisfactory theory but did not take the final decisive steps' (O'Brien, 1975, p. 103). W.F. Lloyd, in a lecture given in 1833, 'distinguished total and marginal utility more clearly than any writer before Jevons' (O'Brien, ibid., p. 105). According to Schumpeter the reason that Lloyd's idea failed to exert more influence was because the economists who read it (the classical economists) were 'blind to the analytic possibilities enshrined in it' (Schumpeter, 1954, p. 464). But Schumpeter does not think Lloyd was the first thinker in any country to explain the dependence of value on marginal utility as proposed by Seligman (*op. cit.*, p. 1055, n. 3). 'Even the "paradox of value" – that comparatively "useless" diamonds are more highly valued than is "useful" water – had been explicitly posited and resolved by many writers, for example, John Law, in the 17th century' (ibid., p. 1054).

The founders of modern utility theory were Menger (*Principles*, 1871), Jevons (*Theory of Political Economy*, 1871) and Walras (*Elements of Pure Economics*, 1871). In England the new theory was popularised by William Smart, who translated Wieser and Böhm-Bawerk, and P.H. Wicksteed, a follower of Jevons. The Ricardians had rejected marginal utility theory on the ground that from observation there seemed to be the widest discrepancy between the usefulness of commodities and their prices; Ricardo gave gold and iron as an example. Marginal utility theory focused attention firmly on demand which the classical economists had taken for granted.

The similarities between Menger's, Jevons' and Walras' books are apparently not to be explained by any collusion on their part, and although, as we have seen, the idea of utility was not itself all that new, the refinement of *marginal* utility was.

The advent of marginal utility theory provided the solution, among other things, to the old so-called paradox of diamonds and water. It was now clear that the relevant comparison is not between the utility of *all* water and *all* diamonds, but between the utility of an *additional* pint of water and an *additional* single diamond. But the spread of marginal utility theory was relatively slow and 'real cost' theories remained influential until the turn of the century.

(ii) The bourgeois counter-attack?

As it seems difficult to account for the simultaneous appearance of marginal utility theory by any general changes in philosophy and scientific method it has been suggested that we should look to the influence of economic and social forces. The new subjectivist theories had first appeared only three years after Marx had published *Das Kapital* in 1867. It was contended by their Marxist opponents that the marginalists were nothing more than propagandists for the consumption habits of the bourgeoisie and a weapon against communism. Nikolai Bukharin, in *The Economic Theory of the Leisure Class* (1927), regarded the Austrian economists as 'advertising agents of the bourgeois class'. But if the Austrians had been motivated by ideology it is plausible to think that they would have tried to conceal rather than advertise the true interests of the ruling class. Furthermore, the marginal utility theory applied to all classes. Another view is that the Austrians used their theories as an attack on Marxism. This appears more convincing; there is Böhm-Bawerk's famous attack on Marxism (Böhm-Bawerk, 1949) first published in 1898.

However, the timing will not support the 'bourgeois counter-attack' idea. Walras, Jevons and Menger had produced their solution to the value problem between 1860 and 1870 at the same time that Marx was writing *Das Kapital.* Also it is difficult to sustain a picture of Menger as a mere agent of the bourgeoisie in view of what is known about him. He was, in many ways, no traditionalist 'reactionary'. He was opposed to militarism and was very critical of the clergy, army and nobility. Although he regarded economic freedom as desirable, he did not regard it as a panacea for all social evils. 'Carl Menger was no defender of the leisure-class; he has an outspoken resemblance to the welfare economists of today' (Kauder, 1965).

An alternative explanation for the appearance of marginalism in the late nineteenth century is that it was associated with the perceived decline in the ability of the economy to increase resources at the rates previously achieved (the 'Great Depression'). This led to greater emphasis on more efficient allocation of given resources. Thus, 'Bukharin was wrong in characterising the theory of marginal utility as the ideology of a new *rentier* class, but right in associating it with a particular stage in the development of capitalism[6].' Although contemporary events must, of course, influence the selection of subjects for attention by economic theorists to some extent,[7] there is no strong evidence to support the view that environment plays the decisive role and if economics is to be regarded as a science it is important that this should continue to be so.[8] 'The leading theoretical chemists are not working on detergents or headache remedies and the leading economic theorists need not be concerned with urban renewal or oil embargoes' (Stigler, 1960, p. 38). But, on the other hand, a preoccupation with high theory gets social scientists a bad name with a wider public.[9] In order to 'explain' the contributions of the marginalists to economic theory without reference to current events, we do not require anything very profound; the idea was an essentially simple one and the wonder is that it took so long to be enunciated clearly, 'Menger, Jevons and Walras took the most pedestrian, even vulgar "fact" of diminishing marginal utility . . . and with it reconstructed a large part of the theory of value' (Stigler, ibid., p. 40).

(iii) Marginal utility in neoclassical theory

Although much of the Austrian theory pointed the way to a wholly subjectivist explanation of value there were two forces pulling in the opposite direction. First, Marshall's synthesis of marginalism with classical ideas still depended on Ricardianism in its theory of costs; and secondly, there was an effort to place demand theory on a non-subjectivist basis. The idea of entirely subjective choice was discarded in the 1930s, which Austrians regard as a mistake. The direction taken by the neoclassical school of orthodox economic theory departed more and more from the demand theory of Menger and strove always for measurement and testable hypotheses; it was in fact built more on the mathematical foundations of Walras than on those of the Austrian school.[10] The tendency was to assume that Austrian marginal utility was now simply absorbed into mainstream economics.

It is chiefly to Alfred Marshall (1842–1924) that we owe the familiar supply and demand curves which are to be found in any modern textbook. His theoretical approach to demand theory was, in general, the same as that of Jevons, Menger and especially Walras, although there is some uncertainty surrounding how much Marshall owed to them and to what extent he was an originator (Schumpeter, 1954). Walras' brilliant formulation of a general theoretic system of general equilibrium, with its use of mathematics, was a very different road from that of the Austrians, but became in many ways a methodological ideal to be emulated by twentieth-century economists with their desire to identify equilibrium states.

Although indifference curves had been introduced by Edgeworth in 1881, it was not until 1934 that this analytical tool was used by Allen and Hicks to produce an ordinal theory of demand. (The marginal utility theory was 'cardinal' rather than 'ordinal', appearing to assume that utility could be measured. In ordinal theories the aim is to get away from this 'unreal' notion.) This was followed in the late 1930s by Samuelson's revealed preference theory which appeared finally to dispel subjectivism.

(iv) The modern Austrian view of demand theory
The main element in Austrian thinking today is to push demand back to pure subjectivism and to abandon attempts at elaborate theoretical constructions which often appear merely as underpinnings for the 'simple' proposition that demand curves are normally negatively sloping. Hayek, although firmly attached to subjectivism as a guiding principle – that 'observation' implies a *Verstehen* [understanding] and that 'there is still much that could be said in defence of the original position of Menger . . . on this issue' – appears to think that indifference analysis and especially revealed preference have gone some way to make possible hypotheses about behaviour independently of 'psychological' assumptions (Hayek, 1978c, p. 277).

One way of basing demand theory firmly on subjectivism is simply to deduce preferences from what has been chosen.[11] The clearest formulation of this method is in Mises' work. The American economist Fisher expressed this as: 'Each individual acts as he desires', but Sweezy (1934) regarded this as a meaningless tautology which was reducible to 'Each individual acts as he acts'. The riposte to this, using the apriori praxeology of Mises, is as follows: Sweezy's criticism is rooted in a fundamental error about the nature of knowledge of human behaviour and is the result of applying the methods of physics ('scientific empiricism'). Whereas in physics hypotheses can be tested but never absolutely established, in economics the reverse is the case. The necessary axioms for a study of economics are 'implicit in the very existence of human action' (Rothbard, 1956, p. 226). If these axioms are absolutely valid then the truth about the real world is deducible through logic. The concept that preferences are deducible from what is chosen has been designated 'demonstrated preference'. The objection to demonstrated preference is that it is not capable of being falsified empirically and is therefore tautologous; the statement that 'each man acts as he desires' is circular reasoning because desires are only discoverable through the action itself. But it is the distinguishing property of human action that it is motivated by desires and hence there is nothing inconsistent in 'deducing the specific desires of real actions' (ibid., p. 228). The term 'revealed preference' could well have been used instead of demonstrated preference but for the fact that it had been pre-empted by Samuelson. The difference between the two is that Samuelson assumes constancy over time for which there is no justification, since preferences are determined at the moment when the consumer is confronted with choices and these will be in a constant state of flux.

The Hicks–Allen abandonment of marginal utility in the 1930s is seen as too hasty. They assumed that the term 'marginal' is equivalent to the sort of incremental change in differential calculus and hence that total utility was the sum of the marginal utilities. However, if we regard the word 'marginal' as meaning, not an increment of utility (and hence being measurable) but as simply the utility attached to an increment of a commodity then this objection to marginal utility theory disappears (ibid., p. 235). If the demonstrated preference approach is adopted, then indifference theory becomes superfluous. Indifference cannot be shown by action, since action signifies a choice; action is the contrary of indifference. It is questionable, however, whether, if we dispense with indifference, there is any way in which we can distinguish between a commodity as such and a unit of that commodity. Particular goods X and Y will be the same good only if all choosers are indifferent between them. Without the concept of indifference, how can we have the idea of a good or of a unit of a good? And if we cannot have the idea of a unit of a good we have no way of stating the law of diminishing marginal utility (Nozick, 1974, p. 371). A more sustainable objection to indifference analysis from the Austrian point of view is that it is open to the same general criticism as many other pieces of economic theory: i.e. that in drawing smooth, differentiable functions to which tangents may be drawn it makes unwarrantable assumptions about real economic behaviour which is concerned with discrete variations, not those of infinitely small magnitude.[12]

Attempts to introduce measurability into consumer theory using the Neumann and Morgenstern theory of games is equally unacceptable from the Austrian point of view for several reasons, the most important of which is that it uses probability theory where it is inappropriate. Human actions are unique, they are not a class of homogeneous members (Shackle, 1949, pp. 109–23).

It has been proposed that Austrian-type objections to trying to measure subjective states are invalid on the grounds that, for example, a feeling of warmth may be converted to a temperature. But a thermometer simply shows a measurable expansion of mercury in response to its environment. The fact is that people do not always agree on whether the weather is cold or mild. (We cannot escape from this by discovering, say, that 90 per cent of a population agree that when the temperature is below 3°C, that it is describable as cold weather: Siberians and equatorial inhabitants would not agree.)

A fundamental objection to indifference theory is that it conceives of consumers as having a comprehensive list of alternative plans before them covering all possibilities. 'Spontaneous action has been turned into a response to stimulus' (Lachmann, 1977, p. 157).

(v) Footnote on demand: Some criticisms of Austrian theory

Austrian methodology as applied to value theory has vulnerable points, some of which have been noted in passing in the preceding sections. A rather serious criticism concerns the foundations of the subjectivist view of consumer preference. An Austrian axiom, as we have seen, is that if an individual does action A, then this in itself is sufficient evidence that he preferred A to any other action that was available to him at that time. But simply because someone does A it only follows that he was willing to do A but not that, at the same time, he was unwilling to do B – he might have been willing to do B also, in other words be indifferent between A and B (Nozick, 1974, p. 370).

Another assumption which is implied by the Mises–Rothbard view is that the idea of preference makes no sense apart from the actual choice made (and observed). Nozick regards this as wrong, and illustrates why through the following analogy:

A substance is *soluble* in water if it *would dissolve* if placed in water. Substances which are never placed in water may yet be water-soluble, even though they never actually dissolve. 'Prefers A to B' is like 'soluble'; 'chooses A over B' is like 'dissolve'. The claim that it makes no sense to say a person prefers A to B unless he's actually chosen A over B, is like the claim that it makes no sense to say something is soluble unless it already has actually dissolved. Both claims are mistaken. (ibid., p. 374)

The economist however has no other way of discovering an

individual's preferences unless they show in his actions, so how is it possible to describe a substance as soluble unless there is some evidence that it has (at some time in the past) actually been observed in solution? Does Nozick mean, perhaps, that by knowledge of the chemical structure of a substance plus knowledge of the criteria of solubility we are able to infer its solubility without ever actually carrying out the experiment?

As we have seen, Rothbard defends his concept of demonstrated preference on the grounds that it is inappropriate to adopt the methods of physics in the social sciences. To the criticism that the statement 'each individual acts as he desires' is a meaningless tautology, he replies that it is 'rooted in a fundamental epistemological error that pervades modern thought' (Rothbard, 1956, p. 226). Rothbard identifies such criticism as 'positivism'. It is therefore rather puzzling to note that one critic of mainstream economics sees its practitioners as forbidden to ask questions designed to unearth the basis of an individual's preferences; they may only note what individuals choose. This is described as 'a position central to positivism' (Nell, 1981, p. 176). But it looks very like the method advocated by Rothbard who is against positivism in economics.

This point of Edward J. Nell's is only one of a number of criticisms from a Marxian viewpoint in the same article. These are not specifically directed against Austrian economic methodology but in so far as the latter has entered mainstream economics they are relevant to any account of criticisms of Austrian demand theory. For the present only one of these will be mentioned.[13]

This is the objection to the way in which neoclassical economics (and by implication, also Austrian) does not seek to explain why a consumer prefers one bundle of goods to another; 'this is obviously wildly at variance with everyday life. . . . When we choose a bundle of goods we can always explain why, and we frequently have to, to our wives, children, employers, and tax collectors' (ibid., p. 177). Whatever relevance there may be in this criticism it would seem to be the case that although, of course, we 'can' always explain our choices, we are not compelled to and certainly not by 'our economists', who mostly are interested only in underpinning the negatively-sloped demand curve. Nell's point however is only part of his general criticism that economic theorists almost ignore the institutional, historical and social context in which individuals act (but see note 13).

Finally, there are those who want to know what all the fuss is about, and think that there would be no great loss if the whole apparatus of consumer theory were forgotten, and the 'law of demand' simply taken on trust:

after all the display of technical virtuosity associated with such theorems, there is nothing the practising economist can take away with him to help him come to grips with the complexity of the real world. (Mishan, 1961)

This economist also sees in some aspects of consumer theory debate 'a prepossession with mathematical problems rather than with economic ones'. Scepticism about the elaborations of consumer theory and of the use made of mathematics is welcomed by the Austrian school, especially when it comes from such a source.

4. COSTS AND SUPPLY

(i) Origins of Austrian cost theory
Until the 1870s the dominant concept of 'supply', derived from the work of Ricardo, was that costs could be determined by the quantities of factors of production involved in a given output, and especially by the quantity of labour, either direct or indirect. As we have seen, the Austrians of the 1870s not only brought demand into the dominant position in value theory, but, following the logical implications of their subjectivist assumptions, began to show that on the supply side costs might also ultimately be shown to be equally subjectively determined. Marshall, in the 1890s, carried out something like a synthesis of classical (i.e. Ricardian) cost theory with the new marginalism on the demand 'side', establishing what proved to be such a pervasive and useful idea: the famous Marshallian 'cross' – the supply and demand curves which have become as unconsciously accepted as breathing to generations of economists. This was expressed in the analogy of the 'scissors'. In answer to the question, what determines value (price)?, the answer was that this is like asking which blade of a pair of scissors does the cutting; both blades are equally important in cutting as are demand and supply in determining value. Marshall thought that although the real cost theory of the classical economists required correction, it was fundamentally sound and that the criticisms of it by the Austrians and Jevons were too severe; his scissors analogy was to illustrate this point.[14]
    The Austrians were not, however, questioning the reasonableness of the scissors metaphor, what they were saying was that both blades were made of the same material: 'They stood in no need of being told about the two blades of Marshall's pair of scissors' (Schumpeter,

1954, p. 922). The Austrians wanted to show that not only demand depended upon utility but so did supply. Furthermore, an important implication of the utility concept followed; one which was not fully worked out until much later, though the idea was well understood by Jevons. This was that expenditures on the production of goods, once they have been incurred, have no influence on the future value of the goods. 'In commerce bygones are forever bygones and we are always starting clear at each moment, judging values of things with a view to future utility' (Jevons, 1871, p. 164). One view of the influence of Marshall is that he 'blocked and reversed' the 'enormous advance' of the Austrian school (Rothbard, 1962, p. 304) and that it led to the unfortunate idea that anything worthwhile of the Austrian school had been incorporated satisfactorily in Marshall's *Principles*, the rest of Austrian economics being best forgotten, or at least confined to histories of economic thought. It is this attitude which the modern Austrians wish to refute.

(ii) The Austrian influence at the LSE

The view that Austrian ideas were not as dead and buried as the foregoing suggests is supported by the continuing influence of them seen at the London School of Economics.[15] Buchanan, although crediting Austrian sources with a vital part in the 'London tradition', insists that 'uniquely characteristic features were added and that the whole construction reached operational validity only in London' and that Wicksteed was at least as important an influence as were the Austrians. But there is no question about the influence of Hayek, who, following Mises, attempted to rid neoclassical theory of objectivity (Hayek, 1937). For Hayek and Mises there is no possibility of the objective measurement of costs, and one puzzle is why their work was of such comparatively slight influence on the body of neoclassical theory. The explanation probably lies in the reluctance of the neoclassical school to accept such a denial of the very validity of their methods. The very possibility of objectively measuring costs for instance, provides a necessary foundation for the orthodox theory of the firm.

Others who showed the influence in their work of Austrian subjectivism were R.H. Coase and G.F. Thirlby, who has in turn several times expressed his debt to G.L.S. Shackle. Although the London tradition was heavily influenced by the Austrians it is distinguished from it by Buchanan as 'the commonsense approach' (ibid., p. 35). But neither the Austrian subjectivist approach nor its London version, although they flourished side by side in the 1930s and 1940s, were able to exert much influence, ultimately, on mainstream economics. In the neoclassical theory of the firm it is of little consequence how a producer determines his costs. For the purpose, for example, of stating the profit-maximisation condition that marginal cost should be equal to marginal revenue there is no need to know how the firm arrived at the value of marginal cost; but there arises a problem when, as in welfare economics it becomes necessary to measure costs objectively – cost must then be capable of being observed and measured by anyone, not just the decision-maker himself. An excellent example of the results of the London–Austrian subjectivist merger is found in the work of G.F. Thirlby.[16] Although the idea of opportunity cost was quite familiar to economists, the full consequences were not explicit in mainstream economics. In the London–Austrian approach such implications were fully explored.

As well as the basic concept that opportunity cost is the consequence of preferring one course of action to another, the following important additions were made to the idea. The cost involved is not the things (e.g. money) which will flow along certain channels as a result of a chooser's decision, it is the loss, prospective or realised, of the foregone possibility of using those things alternatively. This cost cannot be discovered by another person who observes these channels because cost exists only in the mind of the decision-maker before the flow began. Cost is ephemeral. The cost involved in a particular decision loses its significance with the making of a decision because the decision displaces the alternative course of action. There can never be an objective way of measuring cost because the relevant alternative (the real measure of the cost) can never be realised and therefore there can be no actual revenue to measure. It would follow from this that it is hard to see how any precise meaning can be attached to the concept of 'social cost', since this rests on the possibility of objectivity. It also seems to undermine the possibility of central planning of production in an 'efficient' way, using objectively measured costs.[17] If all costs are ultimately subjectively determined, what costs are accountants measuring in a firm's budget? The budget measures projected expenditures which will arise if particular choices are made. But it cannot say anything about the value of those choices which have been rejected by the firm, as these cannot be known other than at the moment they would have been realised.

As previously noted, the London-Austrian cost concepts were strongly influenced by the work of G.L.S. Shackle, but some lingering doubt is evident as to whether even he had rid his ideas of objectivism as applied to cost theory (Buchanan, 1969, p. 36), and that he does not fully endorse the concept of opportunity cost (White, 1978). There is not, however, an inevitable clash between opportunity-cost and Shackle's view.[18]

(iii) Austrian cost theory today

Mises (1949) and Kirzner (1963) incorporate the Austrian view of costs in their general treatment of markets and these ideas have been further developed by Rothbard (1962).

From a strictly subjectivist viewpoint one surprising conclusion is that, once a good has been produced, its actual sale is costless. The fact that if an entrepreneur had known in advance the present price he would not have made the cost outlays does not affect the present situation: 'At present, there is no alternative to the sale of the good at the market price, and therefore the sale is costless' (Rothbard, 1962, p. 291). If costs have no direct bearing on price, what exactly is their role? The modern Austrian view is that prices are initially determined by the evaluations made of goods by consumers according to their assessment of the goods' utility. The goods have been produced by decisions of firms who have compared expected revenue with the subjective costs which would have been incurred. Throughout the process of price formation, therefore, only the subjectively deter-mined utilities of individuals count. There are no other 'objective' costs which can be observed. This lack of objectivity worries mainstream economists and especially those who like the idea of 'social engineering'. Subjective economics produces a sceptical approach to the very possibility of central decision-making.[19]

Finally, the Austrian view throws a different light on 'fixed costs'. In orthodox economics these are defined as those costs which do not vary with output (they are often referred to as overhead costs or unavoidable costs). Two modifications to this usual depiction of fixed costs are derived from the subjectivist version. First, so-called fixed costs are entirely incurred without there being any output, and so cannot influence decisions on the level of output and are therefore best considered not as 'fixed' but as not being costs at all. (One presumes that although 'fixed' costs would be one determinant of a decision whether or not to try to produce something rather than nothing, they would then be like variable costs in their effect on output.) The second point is that there may be a number of degrees of 'fixity' in costs, corresponding to the many points during the production process at which a producer may be forced to make decisions (and at which the expenditures previously irrevocably incurred are no longer weighed as cost factors in arriving at decisions) (Kirzner, 1963, p. 192).

5. THE LABOUR THEORY OF VALUE

The earliest Austrian response to Marx's theoretical system was Böhm-Bawerk's, *Karl Marx and the Close of His System* (1896).[20] This became the classic critique of Marx, in which Böhm-Bawerk argued that Marx's 'error' lay in his use of the labour theory of value instead of the 'more scientific' subjectivist theory. In spite of his attack on the Marxian system, he ends with a generous tribute to Marx himself as a philosophical genius who built up 'a most ingeniously conceived structure', but 'a house of cards'. Rudolf Hilferding replied to Böhm-Bawerk's critique in 1904, recognising the fundamental difference in outlook of the subjectivist and Marxist schools ('mutually exclusive outlooks upon the whole of social life'). The crucial question for Hilferding was whether economics should begin with the individual or society. If it is the individual then, like Böhm-Bawerk, we consider the individual with relation to objects instead of the 'social relationships of human beings one with another'. Schumpeter saw Böhm-Bawerk and Marx as similar in many ways: they both attempted to be scientific in their approach and each had borrowed their basic idea from others. Menger was for Böhm-Bawerk what Ricardo was for Marx.

In assessing the labour theory of value today, the non-Marxian is bound to experience some bewilderment. The theory is one form of the productive resources theory of value. Such theories hold that the value of a commodity is equal to the sum total of resources embodied in it. The labour theory of value holds that labour is the only productive resource. Thus commodities exchange according to the ratio of the values of the labour embodied in them. However, this leaves the obvious problem of where profit comes from. The neat answer given by Marx is that it is the difference between the quantity of labour embodied in the product and the quantity of labour necessary to produce and maintain the labour force. This, in brief, is the theory of surplus value and exploitation and it rests on the labour theory of value. Now it requires no great effort to show that the theory in this, its simplest form, is full of holes. For example, labour is not all equally skilled, so how can the value of different amounts of labour time be compared? Other difficulties are exemplified by very rare goods that cannot be reproduced, such as 'Old Masters', antiques, and such things as old wine, for which the value increases as a function of *time* not the labour embodied in them.

Marx, however, was careful to attempt to avoid these difficulties by introducing the concept of socially necessary labour time, whereby the value of a good is proportional to the socially necessary labour hours which were needed to produce it. What is socially necessary labour time? If, for example, the quantity produced of a good is too large for the market to clear at a particular price, then less of the good should have been made; not all the labour embodied in it was socially necessary. Whether or not some labour is socially necessary is ultimately determined by what happens in the market in the process of exchange, including what customers think something is worth.[21] An extract from Marx on this point:

the use-value of the social mass of products depends on the extent to which it satisfies in quantity a definite social need for every particular kind of product in an adequate [sic] manner, so that labour is proportionately distributed among the different spheres in keeping with these social needs, which are definite in quantity.[22]

But is not one of the virtues of the Marxian theory, according to its proponents, that it rids us of subjectivism, the preoccupation with the relationship between men and things, commodity fetishism or whatever?

Having had fun at the expense of the labour theory of value the innocent enquirer may now be satisfied that subjective value theory must surely command universal assent. However, the modern proponents of productive resources theories of value have many more cards which they can play. For example, Professor Steedman maintains that if the labour theory of value is interpreted as the proposition that the relative prices of commodities will tend to equal the relative quantities of labour time embodied in them 'no labour theory of value would merit ten seconds' consideration and . . . no serious economist has ever entertained such a theory.'[23] Steedman's view is that the labour theory of value should be stated as the proposition that 'the rate of profit and normal prices under capitalist conditions can be *explained in terms of* labour quantities.' Another writer, though sympathetic to Marxian ideology, appears to come close to rejecting any objectivist method of valuation: 'there can never be any invariable measure of value, be it "labour", "money" or the currently fashionable Sraffian "standard commodity".'[24] Karl Kühne, admitting that there are 'difficulties' associated with the labour theory of value, favours the thesis supported by Mandel 'that Marxian "prices" are not prices at all, but rather, values in the proper sense of the word, i.e. "socially necessary" labour hours valued in money terms.' He acknowledges that, even so, 'socially necessary' labour time 'remains somewhat nebulous', because of the fact that technical advances often lead to 'a reduction in labour time for a given produce'.[25]

The foregoing are, of course, but small selections from some of the modern attitudes of productive resources theorists to the labour theory of value and cannot possibly do them full justice nor convey a proper idea of the richness of their variety. Nevertheless, there is a sufficient basis to occasion some degree of incomprehension in the mind of the unbiased enquirer after truth. There may be a tendency among modern students of Marx to want to steer the discussion away from the technical aspects of value and its causes and more towards Marx's stress on alienation,[26] in the sense that a worker puts something of himself into an object and later this very thing, if it is a piece of capital such as a machine, 'confronts him as something hostile and alien'. Things become dominant over men. The attraction of Marx is that he 'gives us an agonizingly real picture of the steel worker, stripped to the waist and dripping sweat' (Sherman, op. cit., p. 361) unlike other economists who only see 'statistics and graphs' (ibid., p. 360.) This seems to imply that although Marx did not make his theory of value clear he had more important humane points to make of a moral kind. Why a desire to place value theory on a firm and usable basis should automatically debar anyone from human feelings of sympathy is not obvious.

A final point of criticism of the labour theory of value from the Austrian point of view is that it is part of the general Ricardian–Marxist search for a physical cause of value which assumes that prices are determined by what has occurred in the past, rather than as a signal telling them what they must do in order to be able to sell their products (Hayek, 1982, III, p. 170).

The apparently simple question with which we began this chapter is now seen to have generated much discussion and divergence of views. The differences between the Austrians and the neo-Ricardian productive resources theorists are obviously fundamental. Although modern mainstream economic theory has absorbed the part-Austrian introduction of marginal utility and the subjectivist nature of consumer's preference, there remain important differences. The most important of these are: the differing attitudes to costs which Austrians see as just as subjectively determined as final prices; and the regrettable (as the Austrians see it) and unsuccessful attempts to banish subjectivism from consumer demand theory.

NOTES

1. For amply detailed accounts of developments in the history of value theory see, for example, Schumpeter (1954) and Blaug (1968).
2. In spite of this, many people including, regrettably, a few economists, still apparently believe in the possibility of 'just' prices. How otherwise is the search for prices and incomes policies to be explained?
3. Murray N. Rothbard, 'New light on the prehistory of the Austrian school', in Dolan (ed.) (1976) pp. 52–74.
4. Emil Kauder, 'The retarded acceptance of marginal utility theory', *Quarterly Journal of Economics*, 67, November 1953, 564–75.
5. This tends to undermine Kauder's view (see note 4 and text).
6. Ronald Meek, 'The marginal revolution and its aftermath', in E.K. Hunt and Jesse G. Schwarz (eds), *A Critique of Economic Theory*, (1972) Harmondsworth: Penguin, p. 89.
7. The example of Keynes in the 1930s is the classic case, of course.
8. See Karl Popper's devastating critique of 'sociologism', the thesis that all ideas are determined by our total ideology (1966, vol. 2, pp. 208–23).
9. One of the chief criticisms of neoclassical theory by Austrians is that it has become somewhat divorced from reality because of the inappropriate use of abstraction.
10. A glance through any modern text on demand theory is sufficient to show the degree to which neoclassical mainstream economics regards the proper method of enquiry as being a search for objectivity through the use of mathematics. (For a good exposition using this approach see, for example, Green (1971).)
11. Much of the following section relies on Rothbard (1956).
12. For a detailed Austrian critique of indifference analysis see Rothbard (1962), pp. 264–8.
13. For further discussion on Marxian value theory see pp. 57–60.
14. Marshall distinguished between the 'short run' and the 'long run' in assessing the relative importance of demand and supply.

He took the view that although demand may be the dominant influence in the short period, the longer is the period under consideration, the greater is the importance of costs of production.

15. The brief account given here of the 'London' tradition is mainly taken from Buchanan (1969a).

16. G.F. Thirlby, 'The subjective theory of value and accounting cost', *Economica*, XII, February 1946, 32–49. See Buchanan (1969a), pp. 30–1, for reference to this and other articles by Thirlby.

17. See 'The socialist calculation debate', in Chapter 14, Planning.

18. Shackle does not reject the opportunity cost concept, but although recognising its basis in foregone alternatives he insists that the act of choice is a more subtle and complex affair than would be evident in the orthodox view of opportunity cost. See Shackle (1973), pp. 65–6; (1972), pp. 131–2.

19. 'Suspicion lurks that a not unwelcome implied conclusion is that one should minimise the number of policy-makers.' (A. Sutherland, review of Buchanan, *L.S.E. Essays on Cost* (1969), in *Economic Journal*, March 1974, p. 240.) This comment implies that any economics which does not help policy-makers is in some way erroneous. The idea that a study of economics leads to the conclusion that 'policy-makers' should be 'helped' cannot be accepted as inherently obvious. It depends, among other things, on who are the policy-makers referred to, and the proper role for economists in a society is not a subject on which there is unanimous agreement.

20. The translation of the German *abschluss*, as 'close' would perhaps be more accurately rendered as 'conclusion', or 'winding up'.

21. See Nozick (1974), who quotes Marx himself and Ernest Mandel, an eminent Marxist theoretician, in support of this view (pp. 253–62 and p. 349, n. 15).

22. Part of an extract from *Capital*, vol. 3., reprinted by Howard J. Sherman in Hunt and Schwarz (1972), p. 354. Sherman later asks what it is that makes people keep reading Marx while other economists gather dust on the shelves (ibid., p. 360).

23. Ian Steedman (ed.), *The Value Controversy* (1981), London: Verso & NLB, pp. 13–14.

24. Geoffrey Pilling, *Marx's Capital: Philosophy and Political Economy* (1980), London: Routledge & Kegan Paul, p. 194.

25. Karl Kühne, *Economics and Marxism* (1979), London: Macmillan, p. 72.

26. Marx used three terms, all of which have been confusingly translated as 'alienation': (1) *Vergegenstandlichung* = objectifcation (English, 'reification'); (ii) *Entfremdung* = estrangement; and (iii) *Entäusserung* = sale of oneself as a commodity (i.e. a worker becomes a thing), has connotation of 'parting with something'.

5 The Market

The concept of a market is widely misunderstood, and the existence of a number of names for the same thing, which are used quite interchangeably, tends to increase the confusion. Nearly everyone engages in market activity, either as a consumer, a producer or the owner of the service of a factor of production, functions which may be found together in a single individual. If market behaviour is common to all individuals, why is it that the principles involved in the operation of markets and what they are capable of achieving (or not achieving) are so little understood? Consider some of the terms used: market economy, free enterprise system, capitalist markets, price mechanism, competitive capitalism, exchange economy, etc. All these terms are often used to describe the same phenomenon and not to accept this fact may seem like a mere verbal quibble. But the trouble with some of the terms is that they employ words such as 'free', 'capitalist', and 'mechanism'. It is not suggested that misconceptions concerning the nature of markets are to be explained simply as disagreements or ambiguities in the words used to describe them, there are much more fundamental sources of misunderstanding. But it is obvious that a word such as 'free', for example, is likely to raise all manner of questions.

One of the most common objections, in fact, to the market as a method of determining how resources are to be allocated rests on the contention that the freedom of 'free' markets is an illusion; that it is not proper freedom because it involves not only freedom to buy and sell but also the freedom to starve.[1] The word 'capitalist' is, if anything, even more confusing than 'free', containing as it does so many overtones of meaning,[2] which vary according to the political philosophy of the person using the word. To some, it signifies simply, 'something undesirable', having no other precise content, rather in the same way as the word 'fascist'[3] has been used. Even apparently innocent words like 'system' and 'mechanism' when used with 'price' may raise unwanted presumptions about the nature of the phenomena so designated. 'System' for example might be taken to imply that markets are social organisations having an institution-like character which have been designed and set up, and the workings of which may be dispassionately and objectively examined and, if desired, improved by the introduction of appropriate modifications. Yet it is a fundamental tenet of the Austrians that markets are quite spontaneous in origin, the product of 'human action but not of human design' (Hayek, 1967, pp. 96–105); markets were not 'invented'. It is not to be denied that the market is properly described as a system[4] in the sense that it possesses orderliness[5] but simply that the use of the word 'system' could have similar connotations as when it is used in 'road system' or 'social security system', that is, something which may be created from scratch and 'supervised' by some outside observer. Hayek states that although he prefers the term 'order', as in 'self-generating order' or 'spontaneous order' to 'system', he 'occasionally' uses the latter 'in conformity with today's predominant usage' (Hayek, 1982, p. xix). The word 'mechanism' might generate a confusion of the market with some type of mechanical structure; 'mechanisms' are things we may try to modify and repair. As with 'system', the usage is widespread and generally understood by economists but does raise the possibility of misunderstanding about the nature of markets. 'Mechanism', for example, might suggest the possibility of 'social engineering', the improving possibilities of which are the object of suspicion by all the protagonists of the market economy, and especially the Austrian wing.

For the purpose of discussion it is difficult, without becoming over-pedantic, to avoid slipping into any of the usages referred to, but in what follows the preferred term will be 'market economy', which is defined as an economy in which there are a large number of markets. It will generally be assumed that a market economy is one in which the non-governmental sector has the dominant role and that private ownership of property exists on a significant scale. But at the same time it should be noted that strong arguments have been advanced which would support the view that markets may not only exist under socialist central ownership of property but that they would indeed flourish. This question will not be pursued here but it is referred to in Chapter 14.

2. THE NATURE OF MARKETS

An important distinction to be noticed in reviewing the various ideas as to the true nature of markets is that which divides those who see markets simply as technical devices and those who regard them as a necessary precondition for the existence of individual freedom. It is not only socialists who are quite happy to regard markets as largely technical devices for the allocation of resources; many mainstream economists appear to ignore the political implications of markets – at least they do in their professional work. For example, throughout two modern textbooks on microeconomics, there is no suggestion that markets have anything to do with liberty (Layard and Walters (1978); Gravelle and Rees (1981)). This is quite reasonable, of course, given the underlying positivist methodology of the neoclassical approach. When considering welfare optima, freedom is not one of the products to be measured. Inside the front cover of every publication of the Institute of Economic Affairs – often regarded as 'right-wing', and hence 'political' – appears a statement of the Institute's aims: the chief emphasis is placed on 'the study of markets and pricing systems as *technical devices* for registering preferences and apportioning resources' (my emphasis).

Not all economists who follow the positive methodology take a neutral view of the market. Milton Friedman, for example, strongly believes that the free market is an essential condition for the preservation of political freedom (Friedman, 1962, pp. 7–21). There are, then, no hard and fast lines to be drawn between those who see the free market as first and foremost an essential ingredient – and perhaps the most essential ingredient – of a free society, and those who see it as a 'technical device'. The Austrian conception of the market is, of course, that the political implications of markets must never be forgotten.

Before trying to identify a distinct Austrian attitude to markets, let us suggest a summary of the essential nature of markets which would be endorsed by most economists, the one given by Assar Lindbeck.[6] He argues persuasively that there are only two ways open to a society for the allocation of resources: a market or a command economy. In both cases the following problems must be solved:

(a) to discover individuals' preferences;
(b) to allocate resources in accordance with these preferences;
(c) to decide between alternative methods of production;
(d) to provide incentives;

(e) to coordinate the wishes of millions of individuals and firms.

The main theme of Lindbeck's book is that the 'New Left', who are opposed to both capitalism and bureaucratic centralism, are searching for a non-feasible alternative kind of system given that the problems which Lindbeck proposes are common to any society. Lindbeck, who is certainly not of the Austrian school, shares this view with Mises, who also rejected the idea of a 'third system' – the market economy and public ownership, according to Mises, cannot be mixed or combined in any way (Mises, 1949).

The most essential condition for the existence of markets is the freedom for individuals or groups of individuals to make exchanges without coercion.[7] This voluntary co-operation of individuals brings about coordination and reconciliation of their desires. Individuals must be free to enter into, or not enter into, any particular exchange. So long as this freedom exists, another important feature of the market is present: it prevents one person interfering with another's freedom.

The consumer is protected from coercion by the seller because of the presence of other sellers with whom he can deal. The seller is protected from coercion by the consumer because of other consumers to whom he can sell. The employee is protected from coercion by the employer because of other employers for whom he can work, and so on. And the market does this impersonally and without centralised authority. (Friedman, 1962, pp. 14–15)

In essentials the Austrian view of what is important about markets is not altogether different from Friedman's, but they do differ on where the emphasis should be in analysing market behaviour.

3. THE AUSTRIAN VIEW OF THE MARKET

All Austrian economists are in agreement on the importance of a market economy as a precondition for individual freedom as are many economists of the neoclassical tradition, but the Austrians take a quite different view of the essential features of markets and contend that mainstream economic theory misses the most important characteristics. These are the importance of knowledge and the process by which equilibrium is attained rather than the conditions for equilibrium. The Austrian stress on the role of knowledge for a proper understanding of markets was stated convincingly by Hayek in his famous essay, 'The use of knowledge in society' (Hayek, 1945).

It is remarkable to what extent, in this essay, Hayek foreshadows many of his subsequent ideas. The economic problem, as it was generally understood in 1945 – and as it is still understood in neoclassical theory – is seen as one of optimisation of given resources.[8] Hayek argues that this 'is emphatically *not* the economic problem' (ibid., p. 77). Dissatisfaction with the way in which neoclassical theory handles the problem of knowledge is by no means confined to Austrians, though they have done a great deal to draw attention to the problem. For example, there are the words of an eminent economist speaking to the American Economic Association, in his presidential address:

the uncertainties about economics are rooted in our need for a better understanding of the economics of uncertainty; our lack of economic knowledge is, in good part, our difficulty in modelling the ignorance of the economic agent. (Arrow, 1974, p. 1)

The real importance of the market is as an information-transmitting mechanism, and the economy of knowledge with which it operates; 'how *little* the individual participants need to know' in order to act correctly (Hayek, 1945, p. 86).

The term 'knowledge' as used by Hayek with reference to markets refers more particularly to non-scientific knowledge.[9] There is a mass of knowledge which is important but not scientific, examples include the knowledge associated with a particular occupation; to know of resources which are not fully employed and of opportunities to put them to work; and knowledge of some better opportunity of doing some job. According to Hayek such knowledge tends to be looked upon with contempt and anyone who gains an advantage through the use of it over an 'expert' is regarded as having done something disreputable. Even economists tend to assume that all knowledge 'ought' in some way to be 'given' and at everyone's disposal. The point is that how knowledge can best be so diffused is the economic problem. One reason why economists tend to ignore the day-to-day changes in knowledge which are so typical of the market economy is their obsession with statistical aggregates and this leads, according to Austrians, to all the folly associated with macroeconomic analysis which ignores the underlying microeconomic structure of an economy. The way in which the price system transmits knowledge to the individual participants is illustrated by Hayek in the following way. Suppose that in some way a commodity, such as tin, has become scarcer. It does not matter why, and this is the significant point; it could be for a 1001 reasons. All that tin users need to know is that they must economise tin. The effects will spread rapidly through the system and influence all the users of tin and its substitutes – and their substitutes. The whole acts as one market because the individual horizons overlap sufficiently to coordinate their actions and because of the fact that there is one price for a single homogeneous commodity in the market (taking into account transport costs). The 'man on the spot' does not need to know *why* tin has become more difficult to obtain. All that is significant for him is how much more or less difficult' (ibid., p. 84) it has become to acquire compared to all the other things he wants to acquire. This is where what Hayek describes as the 'economic calculus', or the 'Pure Logic of Choice' helps us to see how the problem can be solved 'and in fact is being solved by the price system'. The price of a good is seen as a kind of 'numerical index' in which is encapsulated that good's significance in the light of the whole 'means-end' structure.[10] Hayek finds something marvellous in the prospect of a raw material becoming scarce, with only a few people knowing why and then tens of thousands of people (whose identity need not be known) are caused to economise the raw material and its products, i.e. they move in the 'correct' direction. The fact that the system does not always work 'perfectly' is no deterrent to Hayek's admiration. He takes the view that if such a system had been 'designed' it would be acclaimed as one of man's most tremendous achievements. This is one of the reasons why people do not appreciate the market; another, is that even the participants who are themselves guided by the market do not usually grasp the significance of the way the mechanism operates on them.[11] The market may be seen as one of many facets of human activity in which constant use is made of formulae and rules without people having to understand the meaning of them, but through the use of which we draw upon knowledge not known to us individually. The diffusion of knowledge principle is not confined to economics; it is, according to Hayek, the 'central theoretical problem of all social science'.[12]

So far as the nature of markets is concerned one of the main criticisms made by Austrians of the neoclassical picture is with regard to the perfect competition model. Not only Austrians have criticised this model, of course; there has been a constant barrage of disapproval from many quarters, some of it stemming from a misunderstanding of what the perfect competition model is about, or indeed what an economic model in general is about. Friedman defends it on the grounds that, although it has its drawbacks, for many purposes of predicting real-world behaviour of firms it is by no means entirely useless. The wonder is, however, that some version or other of the perfect competition model is to be found in nearly all introductory textbooks in spite of the widespread unease about its validity and usefulness. One reason for this may simply lie in the fact that, in common with other models of neoclassical theory, it lends itself easily to quantification and exposition – it is neatly structured for classroom purposes. Arrow has put this as follows:

one cause for the persistence of neoclassical theory in the face of its long line of critics is precisely that for some reason of mathematical structure, the neoclassical theory is highly manipulable and flexible; when faced with a specific issue, it can yield meaningful implications relatively easily. (Arrow, 1974, p. 2)

One reason why economists are so reluctant to relinquish perfect competition is because of its importance in welfare economics inasmuch as perfectly competitive equilibrium yields a Pareto–optimal allocation of resources, and every Pareto–optimal allocation of resources is a long-run, perfectly competitive equilibrium (Blaug, 1980, p. 153). Another reason is that the perfect competition model simplifies the proof (by Euler's theorem) that factor shares determined according to marginal product exactly exhaust the total product.

The older Austrian school, represented by Menger, were never in agreement with the use made of equilibrium concepts by the Lausanne school of Walras, and Mises and his followers deplored the excessive preoccupation with competitive equilibrium states, both in theory and its application. Much applied economics assumes that markets are already in equilibrium with little regard for the dynamic processes which might produce such a state. Austrians do not deny the usefulness of the equilibrium concept as a tool of analysis, but take the view that without an understanding of market process it leads to unfortunate and wrong conceptions of the nature of markets. Hayek has stated the Austrian view most clearly in a number of essays (e.g. Hayek, 1978c, p. 179ff.; 1982, II, pp. 107–32).[13] The most unfortunate consequences of the perfect competition model are:

(a) That the assumptions on which it is based, if they were true of the real world, would make it 'wholly uninteresting and useless'.
(b) It has lent support to the idea that the 'economy' can, in some way, be manipulated to achieve 'social' ends.
(c) Because of its unreality, generations of students have con-

cluded that in the real world competition does not exist and, therefore,

(d) the whole idea of competitive markets is a fiction probably designed to give support to bourgeois capitalism, by suggesting – wrongly – that the people get what they want through the market.

Neoclassical theory appears to block, right at the outset, any true appreciation of market competition, because it starts from the assumption of a 'given' supply of scarce goods. But the extent and nature of this supply of scarce goods is precisely what can only be discovered by competition. This is why Hayek has referred to competition as a 'discovery procedure' – to begin a study of competition by assuming the facts to be known beforehand is therefore absurd, since it leaves out the activity called competition itself. Although misuse of the concept of equilibrium has led economists astray, the concept has a clear meaning if applied to the actions of a single individual. In a sense, a single individual is always in equilibrium. An isolated person (or a group of persons acting under the direction of one person) can easily be imagined as acting over some period according to a plan. The aims of the plan may not, in every case, be realised since the assumptions on which it is based and the data being employed in drawing up the plan may very well be wrong. But the point is that 'there will always be a conceivable set of external events which would make it possible to execute the plan as originally conceived' (Hayek, 1937, p. 37). However, there is every reason not to draw the same conclusion when considering the possibility of market equilibrium.

Consider a situation in which a number of separate plans are drawn up by separate individuals all acting simultaneously but without knowing anything of each other's plans. First, in order for all these plans to materialise they must be based on the expectation of the same set of external events. This is because, if the individuals' expectations conflicted, there is no conceivable single set of external events which could allow each individual plan to succeed. Secondly, in a society based on exchange, some elements in the plans of individuals will consist of particular expectations of how other individuals will act. Since the 'facts' or data observed by each individual are ultimately modified by each individual's perceptions (i.e. they are subjectively determined), it is entirely misleading to treat them objectively as is the practice of much economic theory. For example, the assumption that information in the form of demand schedules is equally available to all acting individuals ignores the fact that one person's actions are the other person's data and this is circular reasoning. Of course, there is no question but that, in the real world, disparities between individuals' subjective assessments do become reconciled and that there is a tendency for markets to move to an equilibrium. In this respect orthodox theory is not in error. What Hayek and Kirzner wish to emphasise is that equilibrium is not the most important aspect of markets; the process by which reconciliation of plans is brought about should be given greater attention.[14] The question should be asked: for the purpose of making some quite useful predictions about market behaviour does it really matter that economists treat subjectively determined data as if they were objective? After all, simple orthodox supply and demand analysis can be very fruitful in its predictions. The high price of potatoes in early spring or the chronic shortage of houses to rent are explained more neatly perhaps in terms of supply and demand curves than by any other method. 'I cannot really imagine how a Marxian or a neo-Ricardian would even approach the question', as Arrow says, referring to the example of a similar neoclassical explanation of a rise in medical costs in America (Arrow, 1974, p. 2)

It does not appear very obvious that Austrian subjectivism could do any better in regard to this sort of prediction. But the significance of the Austrian approach probably lies elsewhere, since it presents a truer picture of what really goes on in the dynamics of the process. The 'usefulness' of Austrian insights into market behaviour lies in the fact that they argue strongly against the possibility of calculation of market data by a centrally-situated observer; also that the Austrian picture of the market is much more convincing than the perfect competition model. The defence of the free market as an essential institution inseparable from political liberty suffers when it has to rest only on the implausible model of perfectly competitive equilibrium, a concept which it is only too easy to criticise as being non-existent in the real world. Furthermore, once the datum of perfectly competitive equilibrium is seen to be dubious, comparisons and subsequent 'policy' conclusions for 'correcting' the market such as 'monopoly policy' are less convincing also.

4. ECONOMY AND CATALLAXY[15]

The unspoken and dubious assumption that there exists something called 'the economy' which has an existence in some way over and above the seething complexity of individual markets, and which may be 'steered' in given directions,[16] was noticed by Menger who contended that the nation does not work, practise economy or consume; only individuals or associations of individuals do these things. In order to make this distinction clear Hayek redefines 'economy' as used to describe the whole system of interrelated markets which comprise the 'market order'. (By 'market order' he means the same as market 'economy'.) He proposes that the term catallaxy[17] be adopted to signify a whole 'economy' in the sense in which this latter term is used, and 'economy' be confined to stand for 'a complex of deliberately coordinated actions serving a single scale of ends' (Hayek, 1982, II, p. 108). Such an arrangement might apply to a household, a firm, or a centrally-directed state, in which resources are directed with known ends in view. A catallaxy on the other hand is 'a special kind of *spontaneous* order' within which many economies mutually adjust. Apparently, when Hayek first suggested such a distinction he was motivated not only by his desire to oppose the whole idea of central direction of an 'economy', but quite seriously hoped that the derived term *Katallaxia* might replace *economics* to designate the whole subject and thus serve as a constant reminder of this important distinction. This has not happened even among modern Austrian economists.[18]

The distinction between an economy and a catallaxy is most important when considering macroeconomic theory and the role of the state which are discussed in later chapters, but for the purpose of analysing the nature of the market it serves as a useful reference point. In catallactic exchanges, which originated with barter, there is no need for the parties to the exchange to know each other's purposes in making the exchange, whereas in a single organisation (an 'economy'), such as a firm or any other group of individuals, they will work together to a common purpose. The benefits which accrue to individuals in a market economy[19] as a result of exchanges need not be known to each other; and if they were known to any particular individual he may well disapprove of others' reasons for making the exchanges. This is a source of strength for the maintenance of a harmonious free society since it renders unnecessary any collaboration for agreed common purposes. This is the principle of the 'invisible hand' of which Adam Smith is the best-known originator. In Smith's version of the 'hidden hand' its chief virtue lies in its claim to harness the selfish aims of individuals, and its generation of the principle of division of labour. Division of labour, however, is not peculiar to the market economy; it is more like an engineering concept as it occurs within organisations having unified ends; neither is selfishness an essential ingredient of free market behaviour – individuals may, if they wish, behave altruistically.[20]

A quite deeply-rooted fallacy is that market-exchange always involves a loss by one of the parties to the transaction. But this is a misunderstanding; exchange is not what game theory describes as a 'zero-sum game', since *both* parties can gain. However, exchange is a kind of game, which Hayek calls a catallaxy (ibid., p. 115), the outcome of which will be decided by a mixture of skill and chance. It is essential, in the Austrian view, for the successful operation of a catallaxy that the law only protects property rights over particular goods and services, and hence command over their deployment by their owners; it is neither necessary nor desirable for the law to specify or guarantee in any way the prices which these possessions or services should exchange for. The law must not 'assure any one that the goods and services which he has to offer will have a particular value, but only that he will be allowed to obtain what price he can' (ibid., p. 124). The fact that there can be no certainty that market expectations will be fulfilled in all cases ensures 'learning' by trial and error involving frequent disappointment of expectations. This gives rise to the cybernetic concept of 'negative feedback' previously referred to.

It is the basis of many of the arguments for 'control' and intervention in the market that individuals, and especially 'unlucky' ones (those whose expectations of market outcomes are disastrously wrong) should be protected and not left to the 'mercy of market forces'. On this view the market creates grave injustice,[21] and it is argued that it is unfair to let the burden of unforeseeable events fall on individuals who could not possibly have foreseen them. (Such ideas are discussed in Chapter 16.)

In conclusion it should be pointed out that markets do not preclude altruistic behaviour. Both Mises and Lindbeck, as we have noted, speak of there being only two ways in which to allocate scarce resources: through the market or by a centralised bureaucracy. However, there is within a market economy no obstacle placed in the way of individuals cooperating as they do in families, clubs or religiously-based groups. As David Friedman succinctly puts it: 'under any institutions, there are essentially three ways that I can get another person to help me achieve my ends: love, trade and force' (Friedman, 1978, p. 18). The trouble with altruism is its limited range. It is difficult to know enough people to whom you wish to extend your altruistic feelings, and for the cooperation of thousands of individuals who cannot possibly know one another the incentives of the market provide the only practical alternative to the use of force. There has been much discussion of the ways in which markets allegedly fail. Before moving on to this subject we first look more closely at one of the main incentives to market activity known as entrepreneurship, a matter to which the Austrian school has given great attention.

NOTES

1. See Chapter 15 for further discussion of the 'freedom to starve' argument.
2. Mises regarded the terms 'capitalism' and even 'capitalistic production' as 'political catchwords'. 'They were invented by Socialists, not to extend knowledge, but to carp, to criticise, to condemn' (Mises, 1949).
3. The use of 'fascist' simply as a term of abuse was noticed by Orwell as long ago as 1946. The same might be said, of course, of the use by some of the word 'communist'.
4. The market has been described as a *cybernetic* system – a system in which there is adaptive control such as negative feedback.
5. Somewhat paradoxically the use of 'system' is sometimes heard in the same breath as complaints that the market lacks 'order' and where the 'law of the jungle' prevails.
6. See Assar Lindbeck, *The Political Economy of the New Left* (1971), New York: Harper & Row.
7. For the benefit of any reader who is not familiar with the implications of the term 'exchange', it should be noted that it embraces not only barter, but the payment of money in exchange for goods, i.e. money has been given in exchange for other goods or a factor service, such as the individual's labour.
8. As in the famous definition of Lord Robbins: 'Economics is the science which studies human behaviour as a relationship between ends and scarce means which have alternative uses.'
9. Hayek now prefers the term 'information' to 'knowledge' since 'the former clearly refers to the knowledge of particular facts rather than theoretical knowledge to which plain "knowledge" might be thought to refer' (Hayek, 1982, p. xix).
10. What better modern real-world example could there be of

Hayek's account of the information-transmitting role of prices than the world market for oil in recent years? When, as a result of the formation of the oil producers cartel (OPEC), oil prices soared in the mid-1970s, there were heard loud voices advocating price control, i.e. restriction of the price below the free market level. If this advice had been taken, it is very doubtful whether that increase in oil exploration and discovery would have taken place, which, by increasing supply, was the biggest single factor in forcing an eventual *fall* in price, and the virtual disintegration of the producers' cartel.

11. This seems to be shown by the frequency with which businessmen are apologetic on behalf of capitalism and are often poor advocates of the private enterprise system in which they are vital participants. Hence the appearance, no doubt, in recent years of the 'statesman–businessman' type.

12. Hayek quotes from the philosopher, Whitehead: 'It is a profoundly erroneous truism . . . that we should cultivate the habit of thinking what we are doing. The precise opposite is the case. Civilisation advances by extending the number of important operations which we can perform without thinking about them' (in Hayek, ibid., p. 88).

13. The following exposition is drawn mainly from the two sources quoted.

14. 'It is one of the chief tasks of competition to show which plans are false' (Hayek, ibid., p. 117).

15. See ibid., pp. 107–32; Hayek (1968), pp. 28–9; Mises (1949), *passim*.

16. It is a commonplace to hear politicians 'steering the ship of state' (or the 'economy'); or various vested interests appealing for government intervention 'for the sake of the economy'.

17. The term catallaxy is derived from the Greek, and means 'to exchange'. It can also mean 'to change from enemy into friend', which is additionally appealing to supporters of the market, suggesting an inherently harmonious relationship. Mises also uses the term in *Human Action*.

18. Even Hayek himself admits to some lack of resolution in this respect (1982, p. xix).

19. Market economy should from now on be rendered, of course, as catallaxy, but for the sake of avoiding any misunderstanding, tradition prevails.

20. If, however, we construct a model of an economy such as one derived from an ideal of perfect competition in all markets

and hence seek the conditions for a Pareto-optimum, one of these conditions may well have to be profit-maximisation (selfishness) by agents. Any individual who fails to strive for profit-maximisation ('irrationally' gives away something which he could have sold) will be reducing economic efficiency. It is an essential feature of Austrian subjectivism, however, that no observer may pronounce upon an individual's behaviour as being irrational or rational. Only he is the judge of this.

21. The Hayekian view of market transactions assumes the right of any and every participant to break off a transaction if it does not meet with his wishes, whether he is a buyer or a seller, but it may well be objected that transactions should not be regarded as a homogeneous class, i.e. there are real differences between, for instance, 'the rich vain man wondering whether to pay the exorbitant fee demanded by the fashionable portrait painter' and 'a garage charging $100 a gallon for gasoline to a motorist on his way to his dying mother' (Cunningham, 1979, p. 156).

6 Profit and the Entrepreneur

1. INTRODUCTION

Although it might be possible to separate the entrepreneur and profit for discussion purposes, and various schools of economists would give different answers to the question of how separable the two topics are, there is, as will be seen, no doubt in the case of the neo-Austrian school that the entrepreneur and profit must be considered together.

Whenever a word taken from another language appears in common use in English,[1] a frequent explanation is that the word is expressing some meaning for which there is no obvious English equivalent, and this was the original explanation for its acceptance into English. *Entrepreneur* is a term for which there is still no agreed definition. Most of this disagreement is related to deciding what an entrepreneur does, or whether or not entrepreneurship is a factor of production, or indeed whether there is any need for such a concept; and the prevalence of the large joint-stock company in modern economies has made more difficult the task of identifying exactly where the entrepreneurial function (if it exists) is to be found. A very brief survey of the history of the term throws light on the reasons for disagreement.

According to Schumpeter, Cantillon (1680–1734), a Paris banker of Irish extraction, was the first to use the term entrepreneur and seemed to possess some understanding of the possibility that its function might be distinguishable from the other factors of production in the economic sphere (Schumpeter, 1954, p. 555). Adam Smith tended not to distinguish the entrepreneur's role from that of an organiser or manager of labour, land and capital, giving the impression that once these factors are assembled, the business runs itself. J.B. Say, in his *Treatise* (1803), designated the entrepreneur as the one who combined the factors of production, but evidently again failed to distinguish clearly the function from merely that of organiser. For Ricardo and his followers, as well as Marx, the entrepreneur virtually vanishes, to be swallowed up by the 'capitalist', whose main importance arises from the fact of his ownership of the physical means of production. In Marx, especially, with his emphasis on the proper role of political economy as the discovery of objective laws, there was little room for the entrepreneur as distinct from the capitalist. J.S. Mill introduced the term entrepreneur into use among English economists, but failed to see that it might be used to designate functions quite separate from managerial skills. The fact that he and his followers also wished to include risk-bearing as an entrepreneurial function is seen by Schumpeter as pushing 'the car still further on the wrong track' (ibid., p. 556).[2] The question of distinguishing the entrepreneur from the capitalist, and his profit from interest, received some clarification in the work of Marshall but the 'organising' function continued to be subsumed under entrepreneurship.

The older Austrian school and Jevons did not add much to this, according to Schumpeter (ibid., p. 893). However, it is suggested that Schumpeter, in this reference, did an injustice to the ideas of Carl Menger. Kirzner finds it understandable that Schumpeter should take this view given the absence in Menger's work of any deliberate discussion of entrepreneurship (Kirzner, 1979, p. 56), and perceives Menger as deeply aware of the notions of knowledge, error and alertness, yet failing fully to grasp the significance of his own insights as a means of viewing the market as 'a process of social discovery', which was later followed up by Mises and Hayek (ibid., p. 74). Along with the Walrasian concept of general equilibrium appeared the possibility that profit would be eliminated in the perfect equilibrium of pure competition – the model of 'profitless equilibrium'. This analysis of competitive capitalism somewhat paradoxically was later employed to propose the possibility of 'socialist calculation'. The Walrasian model had a double appeal to socialists. On the one hand, it raised the idea of 'planning' perfect competition throughout the economy to attain an optimum allocation of resources – to do deliberately what capitalism, in practice, could not do. And on the other hand, it could be accomplished without the need for the hated profits, associated as they were with having no function other than the enrichment of the capitalist class.[3] It has since been a major concern of neo-Austrians such as Mises, Hayek, Rothbard and Kirzner to analyse the true nature of profit, showing it as an essential part of the market process and not a mere residual or a surplus derived from exploitation.

2. MODERN THEORIES OF ENTERPRISE AND PROFIT

Out of the mixture of ideas from the past which have, because of the constraints of time and space, been given such a necessarily compressed treatment above, there has emerged no general consensus on the entrepreneur and profit; some of this disagreement undoubtedly still has strong ideological roots. In this section we shall first outline the various explanations of profit which are relatively free of political ideology, but which show some measure of disagreement even within the neoclassical school.

At least four explanations of entrepreneurial profit may be discerned within mainstream economics:

(i) Simply to treat it as a 'residual'. This distinguishes it sharply from the payments to other factors of production, the earnings of which are in the nature of prices: the rent of land, the wages of labour and the interest on capital. A residual cannot be a price. The idea of 'normal' profit as employed in economic theory, however, is a kind of price and is regarded as the reward of the entrepreneur which he must receive in order to retain his services in his present productive activity (that is, the profit which he could earn in the next most profitable opportunity open to him). The notion that the income of an entrepreneur is a kind of residual finds a place in neoclassical microeconomics texts even though the explanations of profit involve more than simply this idea, and may be embedded in quite subtle and convincing theories, e.g. 'Factors are hired on a contractual basis, whereas an entrepreneur receives a residual income' (Layard and Walters, 1978) (see also, Lancaster, 1969, p. 232).[4]

(ii) To see it as the reward of enterprise and innovation. In this view, the term profit is to be distinguished from the earnings of managers. Management is still seen simply as a particular grade of labour which firms bid for in the market like any other skill, the services of which they wish to use. Profit is the reward of the innovator – the one who is always searching for new ideas. Such innovators need not themselves be the originators or inventors of the new ideas, but they try to forecast possible ways of using others' ideas. Sir Richard Arkwright, the archetypal entrepreneur of the early industrial revolution, according to one historian, had a very dubious claim to be the inventor of the machine from which he made his fortune, but 'he had fertile brains for devising means of rising in the world and he knew how to drive a good bargain.'[5] If successful, this type of entrepreneur achieves a position of temporary monopoly that results in pure profits being earned until such time as rivals enter the market. This theory of profit is associated with the name of Schumpeter (1950), according to whom the main source of innovation is competition, but not the sort of competition envisaged in the neoclassical model of perfect competition. He had in mind that kind of competition involved in the discovery and introduction of innovations which strike at the very foundations of existing firms and not merely at profit margins. Furthermore, far from seeing the perfect competition model as the ideal for efficiency, he stressed the fact that the incentive for this kind of innovation is the prospect of monopoly power, even if of a temporary kind; the mere existence of these monopoly profits is in itself the incentive to further competitors.[6]

(iii) All true profit is linked with *uncertainty*[7] – a concept particularly associated with Frank H. Knight, the Chicago University economist. Some forms of uncertainty can be converted into *actuarial risk*. Risk occurs when an event is one member of a class of a large set of homogeneous events and there is reasonable certainty of the number of times the particular event will occur in a given period (i.e. the frequency). Thus, a firm making electric light bulbs may know with a fair degree of precision that 2 per cent of the bulbs will be broken in the production process, but without any certain knowledge of which particular bulbs will become broken. Such risks, (other examples are fire risks, or the likelihood of given amounts of rain falling on a particular day), may be pooled, or a specialist firm (e.g. an insurance company) could take over the risk. To the extent that risks can be pooled, the question of profits does not arise. But when risks are taken which are not insurable, entrepreneurs must be paid a premium as a reward for bearing this risk, and, of course, if they guess wrongly they suffer a loss.

(iv) 'Monopoly profit'. It has been suggested that monopoly profits are a separate kind of income that cannot be explained as a reward to one or more of the three factors of production. Suppose a firm has a monopoly based on some advantage peculiar to itself, such as a government charter or licence, or the monopoly of some natural resource. It has the option of selling or leasing its advantage to some other firm, in which case the opportunity cost of not renting the advantage should thus be counted as an implicit cost and not as pure profit over and above all factor rewards. Such profit may be regarded as the reward to the entrepreneur who, seeing an opportunity, exploited it before his competitors. Such profits are always vulnerable to reduction by the latter, unless they are based on some unique advantage as mentioned above. (The subject of monopoly is discussed as a separate topic in Chapter 9.)

So-called 'windfall profits' have not been included in the four types of profit because of the difficulty in giving them any precise definition. The term 'windfall profits' suggests some undeserved gain associated with good luck and without any effort on the part of the profit receiver. This at once calls forth the idea that such profits should be taxed away, a suggestion apparently based on two assumptions: (a) pure envy – what is acquired by luck is undeserved and should be confiscated and perhaps distributed to those who need it badly; (b) removing windfall profit will not affect the allocative mechanism since it cannot have any disincentive effects. In practice it would be difficult to distinguish 'pure' windfall profit from genuinely speculative profit, and so far as the confiscation argument is based on objections to a gain which is entirely 'lucky', this would in equity have to be extended to include other examples of income attributable to luck, the practicality of which is surely out of the question.

These varied theories of profit have been described as all being found within the mainstream of economics but there is a certain illogicality in the inclusion of profit at all in the perfect competition model because of its assumption of perfect knowledge. If the sources of 'profit' are known to firms in advance then it could be argued that the income so gained is no longer profit because it will become expressed as an increase in the value of the firm's assets. The income is then to be seen, not as profit, but as interest on capital. As an example, consider monopoly profit: providing such profit is predictable it will be capitalised in the form of an upgrading of the value of the firm's stock. Thus, all that income which is seen as a 'residual' (profit), would become part of a payment to a factor of production. Only if income results from uninsurable uncertainty can it be properly seen as profit. 'The theory of profit, therefore, has no place in neoclassical analysis because its fundamental theorems rest upon the assumption of perfect certainty' (Blaug, 1968).

Shackle suggests a method of analysing all the possible separate meanings of profit by proposing a list of fifteen questions, and expresses the belief that there is 'a unified conception or scheme of thought in which all necessary meanings and aspects of "profit" can find a place.' This unity is based on the key role of uncertainty and expectations as imagined by the entrepreneur (Carter and Ford, 1972, pp. 195–6).

3. IS THERE AN AUSTRIAN THEORY OF PROFIT AND ENTREPRENEURSHIP?

Some Austrian ideas have in this, as in other branches of economics, simply flowed into the mainstream and not all the ideas about profit which are outside this mainstream are Austrian (even excluding Marxian theories of profit). However, the sharpest division arises out of the Austrian emphasis on the role of the entrepreneur, not as a mere recipient of income which cannot be attributed to a factor of production, nor an 'exploiter', but on the *positive* function of the entrepreneur without which the market economy could not possibly function – 'the prime mover of progress' (IEA, 1980). This concept not only differs greatly from the neoclassical models of the firm, but claims to be significantly distinct from the uncertainty and risk theory of Frank Knight. The name of Israel Kirzner has come to be the best-known of modern economists who have developed a distinctive Austrian theory of entrepreneurial behaviour, but he acknowledges his debt to others, such as Mises, Hayek, Lachmann and Shackle. We begin with a summary of the Kirzner theory and some of its implications.[8]

All economic systems involve decisions and one way of dividing these is into 'entrepreneurial' and 'non-entrepreneurial'. The latter includes calculation, maximising some goal or other, as in the pervasive methodology of neoclassical economics – the constrained maximisation problem.[9] When mistakes occur in such systems they appear as miscalculations But this is not the most important aspect. Much more important is the ability to 'read' the situation correctly. The 'right' decision is not simply a matter of mathematical calculation. This latter type of decision making is seen as 'Robbinsian economising', that is, using known available resources in the most efficient way possible, and it is the preoccupation of neoclassical economics with only this type of decision-making that is criticised by the Austrians. The neglect of other aspects of entrepreneurship arises out of the concentration on equilibrium positions. Robbinsian economising assumes known resources which are to be allocated according to the equimarginal principle, that is, reaching an allocation in which it is impossible to 'improve' the situation by transferring resources between uses. Not only are the resources given but so are the *ends* of action. In this system markets are either in equilibrium or not, and there is no convincing account of how the market is moved from one to the other. (How do market participants change their plans?) This is where, argues Kirzner, Mises' view of human action 'embodies an insight that is entirely lacking in

a world of Robbinsian economisers' (Kirzner, 1979, p. 7.)
However, Mises' position is not always free of ambiguity. Thus in
Human Action he writes: 'Entrepreneur means acting man in regard to
changes occurring in the data of the market' (p. 254). Athough this
fairly general statement could be interpreted in various ways, it could
include 'Robbinsian economising' without contradiction. A view of
the entrepreneur which better supports the Kirzner thesis appears
later on in the same work:

In the market economy it is entrepreneurial action that again and again
reshuffles exchange ratios and the allocation of factors of production. An
enterprising man discovers a discrepancy between the prices of the
complementary factors of production and the future prices of the products as
he anticipates them, and tries to take advantage of this discrepancy for his
own profit. (Mises, ibid., p. 711)

Following this, Mises also stresses, at some length, the unreality
of 'the hypothetical state of equilibrium'. He also emphasises that
men are not equally endowed with entrepreneurial qualities though
they may all strive for the most profit and utility. The entrepreneurs are
not different in their aims from their fellow men, 'They are merely
superior to the masses in mental power and energy' (ibid., p. 336).
This 'alertness to opportunities' is the hallmark of the entrepreneur,
and alertness is to be carefully distinguished from simply possessing
knowledge. Through the operation of the entrepreneur the market
process discovers errors and tries to eliminate them.
  The kind of knowledge which entrepreneurs have is to be
distinguished from the kind of knowledge possessed by the expert in a
particular area of, say, scientific knowledge.[10] An employer may hire
the services of an expert for his knowledge, but it is the employer
rather than the expert who is the entrepreneur. 'Entrepreneurial
knowledge is a rarefied, abstract type of knowledge – the knowledge
of where to obtain information (or other resources) and how to
deploy it' (Kirzner, 1979, p. 8). When a market is in disequilibrium
there must be ignorance, and it is this which is responsible for the
emergence of profitable opportunities. Kirzner gives as an example
the contrast between exploring for oil by weighing alternative ways of
spending a given amount of resources (a 'Robbinsian' procedure)
and knowing before others that a search for oil may be more
rewarding than some other alternative activity; the 'prescient
entrepreneur' is the one who grasps the situation more clearly than
others (ibid.).
  The kind of data or evidence which the entrepreneur requires in

order to come to his decision, or how in fact he goes about obtaining them, is admittedly left a little hazy by Kirzner. Apparently, it simply depends on backing a hunch, and many hunches turn out badly. Professor Shackle's theories involving 'focus-gain' and 'focus-loss' and the subjectiveness of imagined sequels to imagined choices have provided a promising illumination of how entrepreneurial decisions may, in practice, be made (See e.g. Shackle, 1972, pp. 409–21).

Perhaps the most important aspect of entrepreneurship brought out by Kirzner is that not only is the entrepreneur the mainspring of the market economy but that only a market economy produces entrepreneurs. It might be argued that such figures are not needed in a centrally-planned system and so there is no need to worry over their disappearance, along with the market that produces them. This, however, is to miss sight of the fact that the alertness to opportunities of profit is also the means by which consumers' wants are discovered. It is contended by Austrians that there can be no substitute for such a process; such discoveries cannot be thrown up by a computer, no matter how large it is. Kirzner's theory also depicts entrepreneurship as a general case of arbitrage: profit opportunities occur when the prices of products on the product markets are not adjusted to the prices of the resources services on the factor markets. In other words 'something' is being 'sold at different prices in two markets, as a result of imperfect communication between the markets' (Kirzner, 1973, p. 85). An entrepreneur will seek to exploit this opportunity and thus re-allocate resources towards a new equilibrium. The knowledge thus revealed by the alertness of the entrepreneur may also be, at least partly, available to other people, whose ignorance is thereby reduced.

Kirzner sees the prospect of profit as the stimulant to entrepreneurial alertness. This incentive is different from the incentives of the 'Robbinsian' system which may be available in a non-market context. ('The bureaucrat, employer, or official offers a bonus for greater effort.') Profits accrue in market economies from uncertainty 'of the future constellation of demand and supply', according to Mises. Like Knight, Mises distinguishes between insurable and non-insurable uncertainty. The ultimate source of profit is seen by him in the inability of all entrepreneurs to anticipate correctly the future state of the market: 'If all entrepreneurs were to anticipate correctly the future state of the market, there would be neither profits nor losses' (Mises, 1949, p. 293). Kirzner's theory builds on Mises' methodology and extends Mises' concept of profit to not merely taking advantage of opportunities but also discovering where the opportunities are. For Mises the 'ultimate' source of profit is anticipating the future correctly (ibid., p. 664).

From what has been said so far on the various views of profit which are within the neoclassical system's frontiers it will be clear that the question must be asked: does the Kirzner–Mises theory of profit see it as a reward to a factor of production or as a residual? It seems clear that the Austrian theory rules out, if only by implication, the idea of regarding profit as a factor earning. There is no 'demand' for entrepreneurial services and they cannot be hired for example, like capital or managerial skill. Thus entrepreneurship has no price (see Kirzner, 1979, p. 181). It is not a factor of production if defined in the sense of a service for which there exists a market. In the equilibrium models of economic theory profit disappears when equilibrium is attained leaving no problem over whether profit is a residual or a factor reward, but in the Austrian conception of the market, profits exist and have a purpose and cannot be classified as either a factor reward or as a residual. The attempt to fit profits into one or other of these two categories arises from a false picture of the market and the dynamic role of the entrepreneur.

There is an interesting contrast between Schumpeter's and Kirzner's views of profit. Both see profits as the incentive which stimulates entrepreneurship, however, Kirzner's entrepreneur acquires his profit through a kind of arbitrage whereas Schumpeter's is the result of innovation. The latter saw the entrepreneur as a destroyer of existing productive enterprises by his introduction of new products, and the creator of disequilibrium ('creative destruction'). Furthermore, Schumpeter saw monopoly not as an obstacle but as a spur to efficiency. Kirzner's entrepreneur, by contrast, is not a destructive element but more in the nature of a catalyst, in the absence of which the competitive market economy would cease to function properly; entrepreneurial action is viewed as tending to promote equilibrium rather than to upset it, as in the Schumpeter theory.

Neo-Austrian theory often appears at first sight (and sometimes also at second sight) to economists brought up to expect a high degree of mathematical decoration as somewhat vague, and lacking in empirical testability. It is certainly true that Austrians have some reservations concerning the use made of mathematics in modern economics but an interesting essay which suggests a mathematical model of the entrepreneurial process is that by Littlechild and Owen ('An Austrian model of the entrepreneurial market process', *Journal of Economic Theory*, 23, 1980, 361–79). This model embodies some of the key features of the Austrian view of entrepreneurial action including the discovery mechanism. And Reekie (1979) has put forward a reconstituted neoclassical approach to the theory of the firm in the light of Austrian ideas which provides a more realistic and plausible view of firms' behaviour than traditional models.

4. ARE ENTREPRENEURS CAPITALISTS?

The problem of distinguishing the entrepreneur from the capitalist has become more difficult since the joint-stock company has become the dominant type of firm. The larger a firm is, with its growing army of shareholders, the more intangible the entrepreneurial function. Also, it becomes increasingly likely that in large firms the search for profits – or at least, the maximisation of profits – is no longer the top priority in the list of the firm's goals.

Since the owners of the capital of a firm are its shareholders they must be the capitalists if we define capitalist simply as someone who owns assets which, like machines and factories are capable, when employed in conjunction with other factors, of producing goods. Yet shareholders normally have little say in the day-to-day running of the firm. This, however, could be regarded as a non-entrepreneurial function. It has been argued that because the shareholders can always sell their shares then this shows an element of entrepreneurship, but this is not exactly the picture we have of Kirzner's entrepreneur – the *arbitrageur* and discoverer of new knowledge and profitable opportunities. The paid managers, as well as being organisers of production and sales, can be envisaged as carrying out entrepreneurial functions; there is nothing to prevent managers from being 'alert' to new opportunities. But again, this is not quite the Kirzner entrepreneur, who is depicted not as managing but as *employing* managers to implement the exploitation of the profit chances which he alone in that firm perceives. Austrians admit that there is a problem in pinning down the elusive entrepreneur, e.g. 'Is it really at all possible to indicate "the entrepreneur" in a world in which managerial functions are so widely spread?' (Lachmann, 1977, p. 316). Undoubtedly in the real world many managers behave in an entrepreneurial way – they must be innovative and risk-taking – yet they need not supply their own capital. Do these observations render the Austrian stress on the importance of the entrepreneur somewhat vaguely focused? Do we need such a problematical concept in the modern world? After all, many of the current applications of new technology are the product of large firms run by paid managers who seem to innovate[12] with commendable energy. Is not the whole concept of the entrepreneur a bit old-fashioned, being more applicable to the factory-master capitalist of the early industrial revolution? What do modern Austrians have to say on these questions?

One Austrian who apparently sees no problems is Rothbard, who seems simply to assume that entrepreneurs will have to own capital, and who speaks of 'capitalist-entrepreneurs' as 'the men who invest in "capital" (land and/or capital goods) used in the productive process' (Rothbard, 1962, p. 463). The function of these capitalist-entrepreneurs is to 'advance money' to the owners of factors of production in a speculation that the future product will make a profit. There is a streak of Kirzner's entrepreneur in Rothbard's version: 'He is always on the alert . . . for discrepancies, for areas where he can earn more than the going rate of interest' (ibid., p. 464), but in general he is not at all the same.[13] However, a little further on Rothbard seems to see the entrepreneur as bidding for and hiring factors which he reallocates to higher valued productive efforts (ibid., p. 465). Rothbard's entrepreneur appears to be a hybrid of a provider of money for the purchase of factors and an employer of factors; he may also apparently hire factors himself, including presumably the physical capital which he himself owns. Rothbard sees profit as the reward for superior foresight in realising that some factors are underpriced through a general underestimation of the value of their marginal products, and the action of the entrepreneur will tend to eliminate these profits through consequential rises in the demand for the factors, as competitors are attracted in and the factors' prices are bid up. The complement to this will be the fall in price of the product as output expands. Both forces will work together until profits are reduced back to the 'pure interest rate'.[14] The most typical feature of the entrepreneur in Rothbard, whether he owns capital himself or not, is his role in forecasting uncertain future events. In markets where there is no uncertainty (cf. perfect competition) entrepreneurship disappears (ibid., p. 297), but the burden of risking his capital is also seen by Rothbard as an entrepreneurial function (Rothbard, 1970, p. 217).

Lachmann shows a clear awareness of the possible ambiguities: 'If we are clearly to distinguish between capitalist and entrepreneur we must assume that a "pure" entrepreneur, with no wealth of his own, borrows capital in money form, i.e. in a non-specific form, from "pure" capital owners' (Lachmann, 1977, p. 316). If indeed the entrepreneur is to be imagined as a free-floating spirit with imagination but possessing neither physical capital nor 'money capital', then he has the task of first persuading some wealth-owner to lend him some of his wealth, then hiring factors of production including physical capital from 'capitalists'. This possibility throws a slightly different light on the way in which entrepreneurs are regarded as a social class. Although it must be admitted that, in practice, capital-owners are in a better position to decide for themselves on the deployment of those resources which they personally control, it does at least leave a door through which the property-less might enter the ranks of the wealthy. Lachmann seems content not to strain too hard to pin down and isolate the entrepreneurial function from those of organisers of production. He sees the capital-owner deciding to buy new shares in a company and the managers (including directors, works manager and others lower down the scale) as all having in common the fact that they make 'specifying decisions'. The only distinction between them is that the capital-owner (i.e. the one who has decided to buy the shares in the company) makes the 'highest' specifying decision – the highest, because without this primary decision there can be no decisions at the lower managerial level.

On the nature of entrepreneurial profit, Lachmann endorses the Mises view which he claims is remarkably similar to Schumpeter's. Lachmann interprets Mises' view as one in which profit is not only the reward for seeing discrepancies between today's factor prices and tomorrow's goods, as does Rothbard, but that profits are 'signposts of entrepreneurial success' which have to be interpreted. Not everyone has the ability to interpret the signs effectively. The signals, which require judgement and ability to read, resemble the non-scientific knowledge which Hayek regards as the main kind of knowledge which enables the market economy to function properly.

Kirzner himself is not unaware of difficulties involved in sharply defining entrepreneurship, as shown by his response to a comment made by a participant in a seminar held in 1979, the theme of which was the entrepreneur and his function (IEA, 1980). It was suggested by this speaker[15] that entrepreneurial incentive would be stimulated by a tax reform. He spoke of managers 'who are necessarily entrepreneurial' in their initiating and risk-taking but who did not themselves provide capital, and clearly took the view that in order to become a 'proper' entrepreneur a manager must not merely carry out entrepreneurial functions but must also own capital himself. Thus, we are reminded again of the possible fuzziness of the distinction between entrepreneur and capitalist. Kirzner, in replying, acknowledged the difficulty and mentioned the fact that Schumpeter used to ridicule the idea of the entrepreneur bearing risks; he argued that it was the capitalist who bore the risk. However, in what is presumably Kirzner's mature view, it is clear that although he accepts the logic of Schumpeter's comment, he is forced to accept that 'in real life, the entrepreneurial and capitalist functions are inevitably integrated' (ibid., p. 29). He goes on, however, to stress the importance of separating the two functions for 'analytical purposes'. Furthermore, in Kirzner's view, the argument that brilliant entrepreneurs are often frustrated by their lack of, or access to, capital is untenable. This is because he includes the very discovery of how to raise capital among that general set of discoveries which are the business of the successful entrepreneur.[16]

Kirzner's position seems now to be against identifying the entrepreneur as synonymous with 'businessman', for he wishes to distinguish entrepreneur from 'entrepreneurial role'. On this basis, all sorts of people may be entrepreneurial, even trade union leaders and heads of nationalised industries, who apparently engage in 'political entrepreneurship'. There would seem to be no barriers to entry to the entrepreneurial club: 'We are all entrepreneurs' (ibid., p. 146). Such an all-embracing concept as entrepreneur, if used in this sense, is in danger of losing its power as Kirzner has often ably used it as confined to a specific, relatively scarce and essential ingredient of the market economy. Otherwise, we could reach fatuous conclusions such as that countries like the Soviet Union and institutions chosen at random, (e.g. prisons) are teeming with entrepreneurs. It is difficult to believe that Kirzner wanted to leave such an impression. In fact if we interpret Kirzner from most of his other published work it is impossible to define the entrepreneur so broadly. The essential activity of entrepreneurs is not that of economising in a given means–end framework no matter how important this may be. As Kirzner himself has said it represents only one narrow aspect of the human condition, which is an incomplete account of the real nature of choice.

The Austrian view of entrepreneurial choice is subjectivist – choice is made first in the *imagination*. If the entrepreneur merely reacts to objective facts then he is reduced to a Robbinsian economiser. But in the theories of Lachmann, Mises and Shackle, as well as Kirzner, the entrepreneur is not a mere maximiser reacting to objective facts; and totally different possibilities will occur to different individuals when presented with the same objective data. Each individual will have what Shackle calls a different orientation, 'a scheme to exploit in a particular way the economic scene as it presents itself' to him at some moment. These schemes can be innumerable.[17]

Human decisions spring from the pictures of the world that humans paint for themselves, their decisions leap out in pursuit of things imagined, and imagination is no more governed or held prisoner by 'objective' factors than the autumn gale is governed by the leaves it sweeps along. (Shackle, 'Means and meaning in economic theory', *Scottish Journal of Political Economy*, vol. 29, no. 3, November 1982, p. 233)

5. OTHER CRITICISMS OF NEOCLASSICAL THEORY

It is not only Austrians who have expressed dissatisfaction with the neoclassical approach to entrepreneurship. Apart from the Marxist critique which is so fundamental as to merit separate consideration, dissatisfaction has been expressed with the lack of an established theory of the entrepreneur by 'orthodox' economists. Casson (1982) claims that economists have given up the ground to sociologists and psychologists. He develops a theory of the firm in which neglected aspects of entrepreneurship are integrated with neoclassical models, and agrees with the Austrians that the neoclassical picture depersonalises the market process in which the 'invisible hand' becomes merely an assumption of perfectly competitive market equilibrium. But he takes issue with the Austrian theory on a number of points. First, although it takes the entrepreneur seriously, the Austrian commitment to subjectivism makes a predictive theory impossible. Secondly, Austrians fail to recognise the predictive possibilities in statistical aggregation. Casson claims for entrepreneurial behaviour that it can be treated like market demand, i.e. that just as it may not be necessary to know how each individual will behave, so it is not necessary to know how each entrepreneur will behave – the behaviour of a population of entrepreneurs may be quite possible to predict (ibid. pp. 9–10). Thirdly, Casson questions whether there is any guarantee that those engaged in arbitrage will be perceptive enough to 'set the right prices rather than the wrong ones' (ibid., p. 380).

These are serious criticisms and demand fuller consideration than is possible here, but the answers would, it is suggested, be along the following lines. On the question of subjectivist methodology, Austrians do choose to build on this basis for reasons which are discussed in Chapter 1. The limitations to the applicability of frequency-ratio probability were clearly set out by Keynes, and Shackle has shown how many decisions are unique in the sense that by themselves they so alter the available data that it becomes impossible to go back and face the same decision again.[18] With regard to Casson's doubt about whether an *arbitrageur* can be trusted to set the 'right' prices rather than the 'wrong' ones it would appear that there is no problem once the subjectivist view of value is accepted; there is no 'right' price which can be objectively measured, and even if subjectivism is rejected it is not obvious what criteria could be employed to determine the 'right' price.[19]

Finally, we must ask whether the assumption of profit-maximisation is necessary for the validity of the Austrian theory of entrepreneurial profit, and to what extent it fails if we abandon that assumption. The possibility that profits are not the sole, or even the most important, goal of firms has been the subject of a good deal of theoretical and empirical study. W.J. Baumol, for example, advanced several possible reasons why firms might not be preoccupied with profit-maximisation.[20] The starting-point for Baumol's thesis is the separation of ownership from management, which is so common in modern, large-scale business, and as a consequence of which, as we have seen, some serious problems arise in identifying the entrepreneurial function.

For Mises the problems of profit-maximisation are purely imaginary, and based on a fallacy about the nature of 'acting man'. Mises appears, as might be expected, to claim that there is no way in which the outside observer can logically decide whether such and such an action is profit, sales or any other category of maximising behaviour: 'If maximising profits means that a man in all market transactions aims at increasing to the utmost the advantage derived, it is a pleonastic and periphrastic circumlocution' (Mises, 1949, p. 242). According to Mises' interpretation sales-maximisation, if voluntary, is not to be regarded as rendering the market less 'efficient' in some way, since there is no objective way of deciding on efficiency. It is clear from reading Mises that he regards buying in the cheapest market and selling in the dearest as not demanding 'any special assumptions concerning the actor's motives' (ibid., p. 240). If the businessman wishes to behave otherwise – even, for example, altruistically – Mises accepts this as requiring no special modifications of his general assumption that man acts in general to remove 'uneasiness' (ibid.). If Mises' view is accepted then it would appear that the other source of criticism is also undermined. This is the critique refered to by Alchian (1977) as put forward by G. Tintner,[21] which denies that profit-maximisation makes any sense where there is uncertainty, and is regarded by Alchian as the only one of all the attacks on profit-maximisation that 'has been really damaging'. Tintner's proof involves the proposition that under uncertainty each action that may be chosen is identified, not with a unique outcome, but with a *distribution* of potential outcomes. This sounds very like Shackle's concept of the subjective nature of outcomes as 'Sequels imagined and deemed possible by any chooser', which 'must branch and proliferate as he considers times more and more remote from his present' (Shackle, 1979, p. 30).

Lachmann, although appearing to assume that the dominant motive of firms is profit-maximisation, does not follow this line entirely consistently. Thus, 'the firm must [sic] strive to make *a* profit on each transaction', but later he states that 'active entrepreneurial minds [seek] *maximum* profits' (Lachmann, 1973, p. 26). Kirzner evidently sees no special difficulty in dealing with profit-maximisation by taking a similar view to Mises. In discussing the incentive to entrepreneurial action he sees human beings as simply noticing 'opportunities'. Individuals notice 'concatenations of events, realised or prospective, which offer *pure gain*' (IEA, 1980, p. 16). Kirzner defines 'pure gain' as including almost any goal desired by an economic agent. It may include fame, power, prestige, even altruism and the opportunity offered by the observation that something may be bought in one market and sold in another at a higher price becomes simply one among a great variety of goals.

6. THE 'SUPPLY' OF ENTREPRENEURS[22]

Although there is probably little in the idea that entrepreneurial skill may be called forth simply by raising its price as is usually assumed to be true for land, labour and capital resources, and the idea of a supply curve for entrepreneurs seems absurd, this is not to say that there are no determinants of entrepreneurship.

First, if entrepreneurs are those whose acumen enables them to spot opportunities before others, then logically it follows that the largest profits are possible in those societies in which the economy has previously been in an unsatisfactory state in the sense that profit opportunities have been going unnoticed. If profits are the lure which spurs on the entrepreneurs, then one might expect to see a high degree of entrepreneurial vigour in a society in which the economy has hitherto been in a poor state; but in order for the new spirit to function properly, there must also be an appropriate degree of individual freedom.

There has been much discussion of the question of what type of social organisation is most likely to encourage enterprise and a number of theories have been advanced, derived from historical evidence; such as Tawney's famous thesis which sees an important determinant of the evolution of modern capitalism in the development of Protestantism[23] which tended to lend greater social respectability as well as religious sanction to the individualist view of human behaviour. The contrast between the way in which the predominantly Protestant countries, England and Holland, developed the commercial spirit, as compared to Catholic states like Spain has been used to support the theory, but the evidence is not entirely conclusive; there are other reasons which might be adduced to account for these differences (e.g. climate, natural resources).

What does seem an important point to stress is that the entrepreneur should not be looked upon as some kind of inhuman calculating device – he requires the right social context in which to develop. Bentham, in the nineteenth century, aware of the importance of enterprise, was of the opinion that an insufficiency of it should be corrected by the state itself taking a direct hand in business enterprise, indicating that he regarded the latter as being capable of creation, or at least stimulation, by conscious, deliberate policy, and suggesting that Bentham had not realised some of the more intangible characteristics of enterprise.

The climate of opinion in a society may work in favour or against the 'business ethic'. Thus, notably in the United States, the successful businessman was held in high esteem in the nineteenth and early twentieth centuries; and the same was true of Britain though possibly to a lesser extent.[24] Today, it would be unusual for a businessman in either country to state as his *chief* motive the search for profit. In the past, at various times and in various places, the status of the businessman has varied greatly and religious or racial persecution has driven gifted people from one country to another. Barriers to the enterprising spirit have taken many forms. Various types of caste systems segregate people according to religion, colour or political allegiance, and effectively block social mobility.

Furthermore, the attitude of intellectuals to commerce has often worked against the business ethic. The roots of this phenomenon are analysed in *Capitalism and the Historians* (1954)[25], a collection of essays edited by Hayek. This prejudice, which is still very much alive today, can be seen in the way in which school-leavers, especially those who have had a 'good' education, often show a marked preference for the non-commercial sectors of the economy. This has something to do, of course, with the fact that some very attractive careers are available in the civil service, local government and other non-commercial fields, but it seems also to be influenced by avoiding 'mere money-making' and wanting to 'do something for society'.

Much of the prejudice against profit-seeking is traceable to two main confusions. One is the failure to distinguish means from ends. A profit-seeking entrepreneur who sees a gain in marketing more comfortable shoes or a new method of re-lining sewer pipes, although only intent on his own interests, may quite possibly indirectly increase humane welfare by at least as much as the deliberate, conscious efforts of a paid welfare worker. The second confusion arises from the disapproval which is felt from time to time by everyone, varying according to taste, at the prospect of a particular product or service which is offered by unbridled private enterprise. The blame for the supply of the offending commodity or service is placed on the entrepeneurial spirit. But the questions which must be faced in such cases are involved ones concerned with ethics and freedom, not with the entrepreneurial spirit *per se*.

The study of societal influences which encourage or discourage enterprise is clearly a large subject in its own right and only a few of its many aspects have been touched upon. But a short passage from Hayek on the subject is worth quoting as typical of the modern Austrian view:

Competition is as much a *method for breeding* certain types of mind as anything else: the very cast of thinking of the great entrepreneurs would not exist but for the environment in which they developed their gifts: (Hayek, 1982, III, p. 76)

Hayek sees 'unlimited' democracy[26] as fatal to both the original development, and subsequent preservation, of the spirit of enterprise, since the majority will always resist innovation. 'If, in a society in which the spirit of enterprise has not yet spread, the majority has power to prohibit whatever it dislikes, it is most unlikely that it will allow competition to arise' (ibid., p. 77). Furthermore, Hayek contends, unlimited democracy will tend, where there already exists enterprise, to destroy what there is. The source of this flaw in democracy lies in the power conferred on politicians to buy votes, the 'payments' for which inevitably must go to the majority.[27]

The general conclusion is that the Austrian School, and Israel Kirzner in particular, have been influential in regenerating interest among economists as a whole in the importance of entrepreneurial functions in the market economy. One of these functions, which appears often to be misunderstood, is the discovery of new products and techniques. It has been estimated that nine out of ten new goods or services launched, prove to be commercial failures; this is often wrongly depicted as market failure, but the entrepreneur who bears his own business losses thus serves a most useful purpose in identifying demand at his own expense, and with no charge to the taxpayer. Also they have persuasively argued that profits are not necessarily either the undeserved rewards of exploitation or a mere 'residual'. The chief weakness in the Austrian argument lies in the question of whether their view of the entrepreneur is equally applicable to the large corporate firm in which ownership and control are separated between paid managers and shareholders as it is to the small, private enterprise. But if entrepreneurship means any decision making involving risk in the light of special local knowledge then there is no reason to exclude the reality of such activity even in the largest corporate business.

NOTES

1. Although 'entrepreneur' is a French term, a corresponding term in German, *Unternehmer* (lit. 'under-taker'), was in use in the fifteenth century.
2. According to Schumpeter the notion that risk-bearing is to be included in the entrepreneurial function is misguided even though it is often so included by modern economists.
3. J.M. Keynes appears to share this view to some extent. After a passage in which he confidently anticipates the disappearance of the scarcity of capital and the 'euthanasia of the *rentier*, of the functionless investor' he seems to come quite close to equating *rentier* with entrepreneur (*General Theory*, p. 376).
4. Although it is not suggested that the authors of these two books are unaware of this, the 'residual' approach might suggest a somewhat functionless or parasitic role for the entrepreneur.
5. See Paul Mantoux, *The Industrial Revolution in the Eighteenth Century* (1928), London: Jonathan Cape, p. 226.
6. A dramatic example of the 'process of creative destruction'

(Schumpeter's term) is the history of the development of the ball-point pen; see Lipsey (1975) pp. 317–18.

7. Frank H. Knight, *Risk, Uncertainty and Profit* (1933), London School of Economics, Series of Reprints of Scarce Tracts, No. 16.

8. See Kirzner (1973, 1979); IEA (1980), pp. 5–28.

9. In elementary theory, the indifference curves of the consumer constrained by his 'budget line' and the producer similarly presented with isoquants and his 'isocost curve' are examples of this. But see B.J. Loasby, 'The entrepreneur in economic theory', *Scottish Journal of Political Economy*, vol. 29, no. 3. November 1982, 235–45.

10. Cf. Hayek (1945).

11. For his view of the Schumpeter theory, see Kirzner (1979), pp. 111–16.

12. 'Innovation' might well be part of a Kirzner-type entrepreneur's activities, but it is not all of it.

13. The second edition of Rothbard's *Man, Economy and State* was published in 1970, i.e. *before* Kirzner's theory had been made fully explicit.

14. The 'pure interest rate' is described by Rothbard as that rate of interest which would prevail where there is no entrepreneurial uncertainty. There is no entrepreneurial return in the pure interest rate; it is the pure exchange ratio between present and future goods (ibid., p. 299).

15. Dr Ralph Horwitz of the London Regional Management Centre (see IEA, 1980, p. 29).

16. For some very interesting discussion on the entrepreneur, especially concerned with real-world examples in both public and private sectors, by academics and businessmen, *The Prime Mover in Economic Progress* (1980), IEA, is much to be recommended.

17. See Shackle (1972), esp. p. 75, and many other references to the nature of choice.

18. See Carter and Ford (1972), p. viii, and Shackle (1972), pp. 393–408.

19. See Casson (1982), chapter 5, for a theoretical framework which generalises the problem of entrepreneurial uncertainty with considerable ingenuity.

20. For an informative survey of the models suggested by Baumol and an assessment of the results of empirical tests, see e.g. Koutsoyiannis (1979), chapter 15.

21. G. Tintner, 'The theory of choice under subjective risk and uncertainty', *Econometrica*, 9, 1941, 298–304. Other examples are listed in Alchian, op. cit., p. 17, n. 4.

22. For the nature of entrepreneurship and what kind of people become entrepreneurs, see Binks (1983), pp. 12–16.

23. R.H. Tawney, *Religion and the Rise of Capitalism* (1938), London: Penguin.

24. In spite of the favourable image of the entrepreneur as presented in such writings as those of Samuel Smiles in his *Self-Help*, there was in Britain some prejudice against those 'in trade', under the influence of the land-owning aristocracy's mores.

25. Some of the historical roots of the intellectuals' attitude towards commerce are entertainingly analysed by G.J. Stigler, *The Intellectual and the Market Place*, (1963), Glencoe, Ill: Free Press, pp. 85–99; chapter 12 of which is reprinted in *Price Theory* (1971), ed. Harry Townsend, Middlesex and Baltimore: Penguin, pp. 461–72.

26. Hayek's definition of unlimited democracy is a state in which the 'omnipotent and omnicompetent democratic assembly, in which a majority capable of governing can maintain itself only by trying to remove all sources of discontent of any supporter of that majority' (Hayek, 1982, III, p. 138).

27. Hayek's contention that unlimited democracy results in the suppression of minority views does not seem to be well supported by some of the evidence. For example, it seems probable that certain quite far-reaching changes have been introduced by British governments in recent times – changes which it is unlikely would have had majority backing – such as the abolition of capital punishment, homosexual law reform, and 'metrication'.

7 Market Failure I

1. INTRODUCTION

The term 'market failure' implies that the market is a means to desired ends which, if not attained, constitute a deficiency of some sort in the 'system'.[1] The ends – those results which are expected of the market economy – may for convenience be divided into two major categories: technical and social. In this chapter attention is confined to technical 'failures'. These could be described as instances in which the market is not achieving those ends which it is supposed to be 'best' at, irrespective of whether it succeeds in broader aims such as social justice.

There is one category of phenomena which forms the basis of many critiques of the market, subsumed under the general title of *externalities*. This includes collective or public goods and spill-over or neighbourhood effects – in fact, all those cases in which divergences occur between private and social costs. Other instances in which markets are suspected of not always doing what is claimed for them are the 'correct' registering of preferences; the limitations of the market's ability to transmit knowledge; and 'prisoner's dilemma' situations.

Externalities will first be considered, and subdivided into collective consumption goods and neighbourhood effects. (When rigorously defined, these two externalities may be regarded as different aspects of the same phenomenon[2]). One reason for the adoption of this division is the rather noticeable difference in emphasis by Austrians in their references to them.

2. COLLECTIVE CONSUMPTION GOODS

Before defining collective consumption goods it should be mentioned that there could be confusion over alternative names for the same thing. What, in the following section, are referred to as collective consumption goods (or simply collective goods) are sometimes described as 'public goods' (e.g. by Samuelson). As the word 'public' may be confused with 'public sector', which is taken to include all the activities in the economic sphere by central and local government and their agents, it will not be used in this context. Furthermore, as Rothbard and others have pointed out, the term 'public ownership' suggests, misleadingly, that individuals in some meaningful sense have command of a small part of state-controlled property. In practice such 'publicly'-owned assets are at the disposal, not of individual citizens but of bureaucrats (Rothbard, 1962 p. 828). We shall therefore be discussing here only those goods which, it is frequently argued, must necessarily be provided by government ('government' will be taken to include central government itself plus its agents, e.g. local authorities) and which, following the most usual definition, are those goods which create joint benefits but from which individuals who refuse to bear a share of the cost cannot be excluded. The effectiveness of the market relies on the fact that in most cases the suppliers of goods will be able to identify who will pay for the goods and who will benefit from them; if a good can be subdivided so that each part can be sold separately to a different person with no side-effects on some other person, then the market is the appropriate method of allocation.

A collective good, on the other hand, is one which, if it provides benefits to anyone, necessarily provides them to many other people. National defence is a good example of a collective good having the following characteristics:

(a) It gives protection to everyone from external attack.
(b) It protects everyone irrespective of whether each individual wishes to 'buy' any of it.
(c) There is no way in which anyone can 'buy' any more or less than anyone else.
(d) The 'quantity' of national defence produced is decided, not through the market, but by some sort of voting procedures in elected assemblies.[3]

This definition is what most economists mean by collective goods, and would apply also to the provision of such things as roads,[4] public parks, policing, environmental health, etc.

The most important difference between collective goods and other goods is that the service or benefit generated by the former cannot be allocated among the beneficiaries on any economic principle, but is the subject of political decision. The only way in which collective goods' production can be financed is by governments through the power to tax. The recognition of collective goods has respectable roots. Adam Smith considered that, in addition to defence and law, the 'Sovereign' has 'the duty of erecting and maintaining certain public institutions, which it can never be for the interest of any individual, or small number of individuals, to erect and maintain'. And Abraham Lincoln perceived a similar duty for the government: 'The legitimate object of government is to do for people what needs to be done, but which they can not, by individual effort, do at all, or do so well, for themselves.'

Interesting and somewhat different ideas of how to define the limits of collective goods have been proposed by some economists. J.M. Buchanan, for example, argues that much of the basis of the orthodox treatment of collective goods rests on fallacious assumptions which have failed to recognise the importance of the legal structure, which protects and enforces individual rights and contracts. According to Buchanan, much of modern public goods theory as it has emerged from the welfare economics of Pigou proceeds as follows. The economists have assumed that the need for collective goods arises from the failure of the market. The market is assumed to be operating within an efficient protective system of government and thus any 'failure' is therefore attributable to the market. Many of the alleged failures of markets should more properly be explained by the inadequacies of the state, because of its failure to delineate and uphold property rights efficiently. In many cases the need for the state to 'produce' and administer the distribution of collective goods would then disappear;[5] in other words, the law is itself a collective good.

Hayek[6] accepts that there are 'obvious instances' of true collective goods, such as protection against 'violence, epidemics, or such natural forces as floods or avalanches'; but also a wide range of goods and services which are not so obviously collective goods – most roads, standards of measure, information such as maps and land registers, and certification of the quality of some goods or services which are available in the private free market. 'These are the collective or public goods proper, for the provision of which it will be necessary to devise some method other than that of sale to the individual users' (ibid., p. 44). Hayek perceives a problem here for his general principle of non-coercion. The necessity for some form of coercion arises because, in the collective goods case, individuals, however much they may wish that the service should be available, will not voluntarily contribute to its provision unless they can be assured that everyone else is paying their share of the costs. An individual will generally follow his own self-interest and try to avoid paying towards the cost, hence compulsion is the only way of achieving the provision of the collective good.

Hayek's escape from the dilemma posed by his conclusion is to present the compulsion as 'a sort of exchange'. In free markets it is assumed that both parties gain from any voluntarily agreed exchange. Thus, in compelling each individual to contribute to a common pool, 'each may expect to get from this common pool, services which are worth more to him than what he is made to contribute'. Hayek accepts the impossibility of actually measuring the individual's benefit but proposes only that each should think that the aggregate of all collective goods he receives should be worth at least as much as he is paying towards their cost. Although he qualifies this tolerance of government provision of collective goods by emphasising that even though some services must be financed by compulsory levies (taxation), they need not be administered by the government, Hayek appears to be less worried about this type of intervention even than some economists who adopt the neoclassical positivist methodology.[7] But Hayek also warns that in adopting any centralised resource allocation we must never do so in 'a manner which impairs the functioning of the spontaneous market order', and sees great hope in the possibilities of the 'independent sector' as a provider of all kinds of collective goods, but especially those which are wanted only by a minority, such as museums, theatres and symphony orchestras. In these concerns it is far preferable that they be provided by the voluntary initiatives of private benefactors, charities, welfare agencies and the like. Hayek commends the book by R. Cornuelle[8] as showing the merits of this independent sector: 'one of the most promising developments of political ideas in recent years' (ibid., p. 51).

Rothbard[9] regards the very concept of collective goods as 'a highly dubious one'. How, he asks, can a 'collective' want, think, or act?: only individuals can do these things. Examples of collective goods of the kinds discussed above are all dismissed in statements such as 'there is no absolute necessity for a police force to defend *every* inhabitant of an area, or, still more, to give each one the same *degree* of protection.' Even national defence is rejected as automatically qualifying as a collective good, as is the famous 'lighthouse' case. Rothbard argues that there is a fallacy in Samuelson's definition,[10] which states that collective goods are those 'which all enjoy in common in the sense that each individual's consumption of such a good leads to no subtraction from any other individual's consumption of that good.' National defence is not within Samuelson's definition: 'A ring of defense bases around New York, for example, cuts down the amount possibly available around San Francisco' (p. 885). If a good is really 'collective' in the Samuelson sense it would have to be like air – so plentiful that no ownership is possible. Thus Rothbard's conclusion is that only 'goods' like air or the ocean are truly collective and the question of who should allocate these – governments or the market – does not arise.

Another point of departure for a critique from an Austrian-libertarian angle of the conventional view is from a consideration of the nature of costs. As has been noted, one of the characteristics of a collective good is that the market reaches an inefficient solution due to consumption being 'non-rival', i.e. that the costs of excluding any single individual from the enjoyment of the good are high, and that the marginal cost generated by the individual is zero. A common argument for this case is seen in the example of paying for a bridge. The marginal cost of each user as he crosses the bridge is zero. If a toll is levied this would curtail the use of the bridge which makes no sense, given the zero marginal cost involved. It has been quite convincingly argued that, from an Austrian subjectivist point of view of costs, the conventional view is fallacious.[11] The error lies in a confusion over what should be the relevant marginal cost. This is the cost of the bridge at the time of construction: 'When a decision is being reached whether the market or the government should provide the services afforded by a bridge the relevant marginal cost is the cost of constructing the bridge' (Brownstein, op. cit., p. 102). A similar argument is appropriate in the case of pay (or 'cable') television. The fact that the marginal costs of having one extra family tune in on a programme is zero is again irrelevant to the decision as to whether the government or the market should provide the service. There are several marginal costs involved here: when the transmitter is being invested in; when an extra programme is envisaged; and the only time that the marginal cost of an extra viewer is relevant is when the decision must be made whether to provide that viewer with the necessary technical devices for receiving the signal.

The conclusion to be drawn from the Rothbard–Brownstein arguments is that the very existence of collective goods is doubtful. First, because no goods other than things like air can be absolutely non-rival in consumption, and secondly, because even in cases which are approaching complete non-rivalry (e.g. bridges) there is often a failure to recognise the subjectivity of costs. If there is no logical way of showing the existence of collective goods, then arguments about who should provide them are futile.

The conventional approach to the question of externalities is dissected with skill by Rothbard (1962, p. 886ff.). From his basic assumptions about the correct methodology of economic analysis he deduces, quite logically, that no argument for government intervention to 'correct' external effects will bear close scrutiny. For example, take the familiar case for making a compulsory levy on those who will benefit from the productive activity of others where the market fails to extract payment: the 'free-rider' case. Supposing A's actions do benefit B who receives this gift unasked. In a free society A will have acted presumably for his own benefit (he need not have produced what he did); so A is better-off and so, incidentally, is B. 'Are we to be indignant because more than one person benefits from someone's actions? After all, the free-rider did not ask for his ride!' Rothbard also answers the objection that B may not have been able to obtain the benefit he has now acquired even if he had wanted to buy it voluntarily. How, he asks, could anyone 'know' that B would have liked to buy the benefit he has received? By what process could such knowledge have been obtained?[12]

The free-rider argument is often used to support compulsory membership of a trade union, but the free-rider, it may be contended, is merely a competitor to what is, in effect, a state supported monopoly (see Pasour, 1981), and is therefore to be encouraged. Also, there are many organisations which dispense benefits to non-members such as churches and charitable organisations – you do not have to subscribe to the Royal National Lifeboat Institution in order to be rescued from drowning. Furthermore the 'free ride' is of uncertain benefit in the union case. Some unionised occupations are at the lower end of the pay ladder, and others without unions are highly paid.

3. Neighbourhood or over-spill effects

E.J. Mishan has aptly designated over-spill effects as 'bads'.[13] This is derived from the method of calculating a country's GNP as a totting-up of all the 'goods' produced, while ignoring all the simultaneously produced 'bads' – such things as oil on beaches, pollution of lakes and rivers, smoky chimneys, traffic congestion and unwanted noise. When such 'bads' are produced, individuals suffer their effects: they are 'social costs' which receive no compensation. It is as a result of such effects that the free market has been the subject of much criticism with consequent calls for government intervention. There are several conceivable ways by which the market's failure to apportion social costs correctly may be dealt with. The offending over-spill could be banned by law; taxes could be levied on the producers of the nuisances sufficient to compensate the victims; the external costs could be 'internalised' by suitable legislation; or property rights could be extended to cover such things as fresh air or clean rivers.

To adopt a general policy of banning over-spills would be regarded as a crude method by liberal economists, and especially by Austrians. It increases the number of bureaucrats, may be costly, and may tend to 'over-kill' the spill-over. For example, it might involve banning all air travel until aircraft were quieter, or stopping altogether the production of a factory making some useful commodity which is in great demand. A second possible solution is for the government to tax the offending activity – the tax to be sufficient to make good the social damage. One difficulty with this method lies in the problem of acquiring a correct valuation of the disamenity caused, and hence the level of the proposed tax. Cost-benefit analysis has been employed to arrive at solutions to such problems, but some costs are very difficult to quantify. It should be noticed here that some of the greatest offenders in respect of causing disamenity are governments or their agents rather than private enterprise. For example, the decisions to build urban 'flyovers' which prevailed in the 1960s and early 1970s were made with little attention given to market forces. Not only was the demand from motorists never properly assessed, but neither was any attention given to calculating the distress and inconvenience caused to householders living nearby. 'Internalising' externalities includes such things as compulsory exhaust 'cleaners' on motor vehicles, hotels with fire escapes, chimneys with filters, etc. There is no reason why laws should not be passed to enforce such things but similar problems arise as with the imposition of taxes – there is the danger of 'over-kill'. Imposing internalised costs on industries may, it has been argued, put the products out of reach of the poor. The most favoured solutions by liberal economists of all varieties, including Austrians, hinge on the establishment of property rights. For example:

Change the law from being in general permissive of spill-overs to being prohibitive of them and the justly admired market mechanism will tend to a solution that seeks to avoid spill-overs. Under such a law the 'unmeasurable' spill-overs are effectively transformed, in the first instance, into legal claims for damages. And such claims enter directly into the economic costs on a legal par with payments for the use of other people's property and services.[14]

The prevention of the over-fishing of the sea and pollution of the air which nobody owns presents special, but not inherently insurmountable problems. New property rights would have to be created. For instance, it should be feasible using modern electronic equipment to police the sea and hence protect the ownership of each country of part of the ocean. The most difficult part might well be that of agreeing who owns what in the first place.[15]

Some critics of the free market seem to want to include under 'technical failure' what are usually regarded as sociological effects. In other words, it has been suggested that such things as 'want creation' on Galbraithian lines – the fostering by advertising of wants which people left to themselves would not have desired – produce externalities of a very serious kind, such as making people materialistic and greedy. Discussion of such critiques of the market will be regarded as more appropriately placed within the general context of social effects.[16]

Austrian economists do appear to give relatively little attention to the over-spill question, although they devote quite a lot of space in their writings to the related question of collective consumption goods[17] (see above). Austrians see the question of neighbourhood effects not as problems of market failure, but as problems of government failure. Spill-overs are seen as invasions of private property against which it is the job of the government to protect the individual. 'Air pollution, then, is not an example of a defect in a system of absolute property rights, but of failure on the part of the government to preserve property rights. . . . The remedy [in a free society] is *judicial* action to punish and proscribe pollution damage to the person and property of others' (Rothbard, 1962, p. 156). Mises also regarded the whole question of externalities as yet another pseudo-problem in disguise; one of that multitude of alleged problems which, on close examination, turn out to be simply either someone's disapproval of the voluntary choices made by others (and hence not an *economic* problem), or as the consequence of some ineptitude, past or present, on the part of government (Mises, 1949, pp. 650–3). A noticeable feature in comparing neoclassical economists' attitude with that of modern Austrians is that the latter have not devoted anything like as much attention to the problem as have the more orthodox schools.[18] One reason for this difference is that, in neoclassical theory, it is customary to contrast various real-world allocations with Paretian optima whereas the Austrians regard this as misleading because of, among other things, the 'impossibility' of measuring welfare efficiency objectively.

Given that the 'correction' of over-spills should depend on the upholding of property rights it is argued by all liberal economists that such rights are more likely to be established firmly in a market than in a centralised economy. For those who generally condemn the institution of private property this proposition, of course, carries no weight. (For a full discussion see Becker, 1977.)

A common assumption of interventionists is that market failure is correctable by government action. However, it is argued by Austrians, and increasingly by other liberal economists, that the costs and benefits of government action should be evaluated just as are market forces, using similar criteria. An interesting recent study of a case[19] in which allocation depended much more on political than economic forces shows that the result may be quite unpredictable and 'irrational'. Whereas much attention has been given to the externalities thrown up by markets, and possible 'cures', too little attention has been given to the unpredictability and costs of non-market bureaucratic decisions which emerge from political bargaining processes.

4. CONSUMER PREFERENCES

A number of critiques of market efficiency are based on the contention that although economic theory often assumes preferences are capable of being accurately reflected in markets, that this is often a spurious assumption. The most general form of this line of attack is that of the 'New Left',[20] who depict consumer preferences as manipulated and 'created' by 'big business'. Since this critique raises much wider questions than what could reasonably be called 'technical' market failure discussion will be deferred until Chapter 8.

Some serious criticism of markets as devices to register consumer preferences have come from F. Hirsch (1977), who has argued that an important market failure arises from the nature of what he terms 'positional goods'. The subject is one of some complexity and cannot be adequately discussed here, but two features of Hirsch's critique will be mentioned. First, many sources of satisfaction or utility, in the modern world, depend upon the relative positions of individuals. For example, having access to a crowded beach – one's ability to enjoy the beach depends on being *ahead* of others. Secondly, there is little scope for the market to increase the availability of such goods and anyway such goods are either not marketed or are non-marketable. A rather more subtle and potentially more important example of a 'positional good' is to be seen in some of the consequences of educational expansion. Educational qualifications convey information to employers about the innate or acquired ability of the individual; but 'more education for all leaves everyone in the same place' (ibid., p. 49). In this model, expanding educational opportunities means that one person's higher qualifications devalue the information content of another's – it is rather like everyone in a crowd standing on tiptoe to get a better view. Such 'positional goods' raise the possibility of conflicts which are not resolvable through the market. Hirsch contends that such conflicts are likely to increase with economic growth. If we look for the Austrian response to Hirsch's critique it is difficult to find any specific examples. However, it may be that the conflicts generated by Hirsch's positional goods would have some feedback effects. For example a *crowded* beach is a different good from an uncrowded one: the consumer is on a different demand curve.

That preferences are sometimes inadequately dealt with by the market is exemplified, according to Sir Roy Harrod, by the problem of where to site a third London airport.[21] Two questions occur: how do we know we even need a third London airport? and if market data cannot reflect preferences very well, what alternatives would be better? This question should, for a reasoned appraisal, always be asked in such circumstances.

5. PRISONER'S DILEMMA SITUATIONS

The prisoner's dilemma has been used to argue that self-interest behaviour may be unavoidably self-defeating.[22] It can be shown in principle that, given certain initial conditions, where each individual has pursued his own self-interest there would have been an improvement in total welfare if they had each pursued some strategy other than that of self-interest. From this it is then a short step from what is an abstract theory of behaviour to conclude that individuals should, in some way, be manipulated by a 'policy-maker' in the direction of their own best interests. The market is seen as 'failing' in this type of dilemma, and this proposition seems to be widely agreed upon in neoclassical welfare economics. However, the Austrian approach is to argue that there exists a fallacy at the heart of the jump from the theoretical 'game' situation to policy prescriptions. This is the assumption that the actual choice-maker in the real world behaves strictly as the pure economic man of the theorist's model. The policy-maker and observer of the pay-off matrix of the prisoner's dilemma can thus propose appropriate taxes and subsidies in order to direct the choices of the 'players' (in the real world, economic agents) so that the 'best' collective outcome is realised. However, this policy depends on assumptions about individual economic behaviour which, according to Austrian concepts, are unfounded. The Austrian attitude is that there are no circumstances in which some outside policy-maker is able to pronounce upon an individual's behaviour as 'irrational'. In this extreme form the Austrian position would prohibit all attempts at improving collective welfare by manipulation of consumers and producers in desired directions; subjectively-based choices cannot be questioned. This does not however rule out the possibility of improving communication and the dissemination of knowledge between market participants by suitable institutional changes. These might then modify decision-makers' choices.[23]

6. WELFARE ECONOMICS

Welfare economics is the branch of economics which tries to evaluate alternative economic arrangements or systems using some criterion of social well-being. It has been a fruitful source of propositions which carry implications of free market failure and the need for state intervention.

Jeremy Bentham's criterion was that welfare was maximised when the 'greatest good is secured for the greatest number'. Another way of expressing this is to say that if we add together the utility functions of all the individuals in a society we have a total welfare function. This concept, however, assumes measurable utility and takes no account of the distribution of income.

It was later proposed that the principle of diminishing marginal utility should be used as a criterion of welfare and, incidentally, that progressive taxation was thereby logically as well as ethically justified.[24] Essentially, the idea was that a given increase in income gives less satisfaction to a rich man than to a poor man. However, this involves interpersonal comparisons of utility, and there is no objective basis for deciding between conflicting views on the needs of different individuals. It seems very doubtful that the concept of decreasing marginal utility applied to income has any clear meaning. Utility is a relative concept, and therefore we can only say that something has more or less utility than something else. If income is defined as all the benefits (i.e. goods and services) derived from it, then in order to speak of marginal utility of income we should have to leave out something to compare it with.

The best-known approach to questions of social welfare is the Pareto optimum, which is based on the appeal of the idea that if one could make one person better-off without simultaneously making someone else worse-off, then this must surely be 'better'. This is, of course, ultimately an ethical judgement but it is argued that it is one that most people would be bound to agree with. The Pareto-optimal state could prevail in any one of an infinite number of patterns of income and wealth distribution, and any particular optimum may coincide with a very equal or a very unequal distribution of resources as between individuals. One argument against free markets is that although they may result in efficiency in production (i.e. a Pareto optimum in factor allocation) and distribution in a Pareto sense, the existing distribution may be unjust. This involves judging between alternative distributions or social welfare functions involving inter-personal comparisons. This raises some quite complex problems[25] which cannot be discussed in detail here, and we shall simply point out the obvious difficulties and then go on to note the typically Austrian reaction.

Suppose we ask two individuals to choose between alternatives, such as how a cake should be divided between them. They might very well have conflicting preferences. It is difficult to see on what basis their preferences could be compared. Arrow supported this by asking: Can there be any rules which would tell us how to rank different states of the world from an ethical point of view if the only information we have relates to individual preferences?[26] He showed that there was no such rule, and that this was so both for majority voting and the market. The central conclusion of his argument is that these ordinary decision-making systems do not produce rational choices. The question of majority voting lies outside our present scope,[27] but Arrow's conclusion on the market was no surprise to Austrian economists since, from the subjectivist point of view, there is no possibility of an outside observer being able to rank various states. Furthermore, there is no way of judging the rationality of an individual's decisions. Of course, an individual could be wrong in choosing a certain course of action, but this is irrelevant, since he is the only judge of his own 'better-offness'. This is, of course, itself a value judgement and it is 'the value judgement upon which western liberal society has been founded' (Buchanan, 1979, p. 152). Also, not only can an outside observer not determine an individual's utility function, neither can the individual; therefore there is no way in which he could communicate it to an observer.[28] The identification by welfare economists of optimal welfare states has led to the discovery of market 'failures' which it is sometimes suggested could be remedied by some agency such as the state. The recommendations of welfare economists might be appropriate for a centrally-administered economy or a benevolent despotism, but not for a liberal market economy in a democracy. As Austrians see it, the proper way forward from sub-optimal states is to extend individual freedom not reduce it.

Neoclassical welfare economics is concerned with Pareto-type concepts of efficiency. The Austrian view is that 'efficiency' consists of acting individuals who alone are the arbiters of what they consider as failure.[29]

In this chapter the Austrian solution to what we have designated technical market failure is seen to comprise varying degrees of tolerance of government intervention, from Hayek who is willing to accept government provision of a wide variety of services, to Rothbard who argues for almost complete non-intervention. In general however, the Austrian position rests on two propositions: that many types of market failure turn out, on careful examination, to be caused by non-market institutional failure; and that even where there is 'true' market failure there is no reason to assume that the situation will not be made worse by government intervention. Many criticisms of the market economy are not based wholly on its inefficiencies but more on its morality. These questions are the subject of the next chapter.

NOTES

1. This is to express rather too simply and crudely what would be stated more precisely as: 'market failure' means the failure to sustain 'desirable' activities and prevent 'undesirable' ones. The desirability of an activity is judged relative to the achievement of some end such as a Pareto optimum.

2. For a formal and rigorous analysis of externalities, see Buchanan and Stubblebine, 'Externality', *Economica*, November 1962,

pp. 371–84. For a subjectivist approach see S.C. Littlechild, 'The problem of social cost', in Spadaro (1978), pp. 77–93.

3. At least this is the case in parliamentary democracies, but even then the long 'chains' transmitting political decisions from above to the local level result in quite far-reaching actions by non-elected officials whose accountability is often slight.

4. Roads, although commonly supplied 'free' by governments, are not, like defence, considered entirely out of the question for supply by the market. This applies to other services which, it is often assumed, mainly through unthinking habit, the government must supply, e.g. refuse collection, which has lately been handed over to private firms in some places, with beneficial results.

5. J.M. Buchanan, 'Public goods and natural liberty', in T. Wilson and A.S. Skinner (1976), pp. 275–6. See also reference cited in note 11 (ibid., p. 276).

6. Hayek (1982), II, pp. 43–6.

7. Milton Friedman points out that the government, when it intervenes, itself produces 'neighbourhood effects', the most important of which is the limitation of the area of individual freedom. An individual's assessment of this is according to a version of diminishing marginal utility. 'If, for example, existing government intervention is minor, we shall attach a smaller weight to the negative effects of additional government intervention' (Friedman, 1962, p. 32).

8. Richard C. Cornuelle, *Reclaiming the American Dream* (1965), New York: Random House. See Hayek, op. cit., p. 186.

9. See Rothbard (1962), pp. 883–90.

10. From Paul A. Samuelson, 'The pure theory of public expenditures', *Review of Economics and Statistics*, November 1954, 387–9.

11. Barry P. Brownstein, 'Pareto optimality, external benefits and public goods: A subjectivist approach', *Journal of Libertarian Studies*, vol. IV, no. 1, Winter 1980, 93–106.

12. It is remarkable that it is almost impossible to discover in any of the vast number of introductory textbooks any awareness of most of the awkward questions posed by Rothbard on this subject (as on some others). It is doubtful that this omission is only because Rothbard's views are regarded as too 'extreme'.

13. Mishan is notable for his critique of economic growth which he sees as a crucial factor in the production of 'bads'. see, e.g., 'The spill-over enemy', *Encounter*, December 1969.

14. Mishan, ibid.
15. See Lepage (1978), pp. 148–50. For a good example of the problems associated with the alternative of trying to measure social costs of pollution (in this case, oil on beaches) by direct methods, see Paul Burrows, 'Nuisance: the law and economics', in *Lloyd's Bank Review*, January 1970, 41–3.
16. See Chapter 8.
17. Not only Austrians seem to see the spill-over problem as relatively trivial, see, e.g. Brittan (1979), p. 66, in which the author is satisfied that appropriate taxes and subsidies are all that is required.
18. In the work of Hayek and Rothbard, for example, although there is detailed analysis of the 'externality' of collective consumption of public goods, there is no comparable space given to the problems associated with neighbourhood effects. See also Brownstein note 11.
19. See Rosalind Levačić, 'Political bargaining: bricks, bluff and blackmail', *Journal of Economic Affairs*, vol 3, no. 2, January 1983, 116–21.
20. The term 'New Left' signifies those modern Marxists who, unlike the traditional communist Left, are highly critical of the Soviet system as well as of capitalism.
21. Sir Roy Harrod, review of *Roads to Freedom*, in *Economic Journal*, March 1970, 105–7.
22. For exposition of the prisoner's dilemma, see e.g. Derek Parfit, 'Prudence, morality and the prisoner's dilemma', *Proceedings of the British Academy* (1981), London; Oxford University Press.
23. For a formal analysis of the prisoner's dilemma from a subjectivist point of view, see Buchanan (1969b), pp. 56–62.
24. For a critique of the principle of progressive taxation, see Hayek, 'Progressive taxation reconsidered', in Sennholz (1956), pp. 265–84.
25. See, e.g. Amartya Sen, 'Interpersonal comparisons of welfare', in Michael J. Boskin (ed.), *Economics and Human Welfare*, New York: Academic Press.
26. K.J. Arrow, *Social Choice and Individual Values*, 2nd edn., Edinburgh: Oliver & Boyd, 1970.
27. See Buchanan (1959) and (1979, pp. 143–60), for a defence of majority voting and a refutation of the idea that it is comparable with markets on rational choice criteria.
28. 'most economists seem to begin to see that the whole of the so-called "welfare economics", which pretends to base its

arguments on interpersonal comparisons of ascertainable utilities, lacks all scientific foundation' (Hayek, 1982, III, p. 201, n. 35).

29. For a survey of the Austrian view, see Cordato (1980).

8 Market Failure II

1. SELF-INTEREST

Human conduct, according to Adam Smith, is based on six motives, the first of which is self-love. If an individual is left to pursue his own interests driven by self-love, not only will he attain his own best advantage, but he will also achieve the best outcome for others (i.e. for society at large). Not only that, but Smith believed that any explicit attempt to 'do good', usually resulted in less benefit than would selfishness. This is the classic defence of the free market and is summed up in Smith's well-known statement: 'It is not from the benevolence of the butcher, the brewer, or the baker, that we expect our dinner, but from their regard to their own interest.' This became the basis of nineteenth-century economic liberalism. The reaction which appeared later was actuated by the view of an increasing number of people that the problems of poverty, degrading toil and inequality were the outcome of this economic philosophy, which appeared to extol the virtue of selfishness. By 1890, even Alfred Marshall, although setting his economic theory on foundational assumptions of utility and profit-maximising behaviour, evidently felt a little apologetic about the morality of accepting selfishness without reservation: 'The term "competition" has gathered about it evil savour, and has come to imply a certain selfishness, and indifference to the well being of others.'[1]

Such mild qualms concerning the basis of private enterprise capitalism seem very innocuous compared with other critiques, as the full tide of collectivism began to sweep in and the 'constructivist' mentality gained influence over the intellectuals. For example, Bertrand Russell, in 1917 wrote: 'Material possessions, in fact or desire, dominate our outlook, usually to the exclusion of all generous and creative impulse.'[2] And called for 'institutions which will diminish the sway of greed'. These could only be created 'through a complete reconstruction of our economic system' (ibid.).

Although all 'free market' economists share the assumption that an economic system should be judged by the extent to which it yields individual satisfactions, there is one important distinction which most Austrians would appear to make. This is that there is no method by which these satisfactions can be objectively measured. This has an important consequence for the selection of standards by which to judge the efficiency of particular behavioural patterns. An example will make this point clear. Suppose an individual owns shop premises for which the free market rent is £100 per week. The neoclassical theory of the market would accept that the rent of £100 is being offered by the would-be tenant who has the best expectation of profitability and hence is (in his estimation) likely to offer the greatest value of goods or services. In other words, in order to best serve the wants of society (other individuals) the shop should be let to the entrepreneur offering the highest rent. The owner, in acting selfishly to charge the highest rent he can get, is thus instrumental in achieving the greatest benefit to others. If, however, he had chosen instead to let his shop at a lower than market rate, this would be reducing the allocative efficiency of the free market, which is likely to make the community worse-off. Also the recipient of the altruistic action is seen as not 'deserving' his benefit, in the context of the smaller value he is assumed to be able to contribute to the national product. But on one interpretation of Austrian methodology no outside observer is entitled to pronounce upon the ethical content of action: 'A man's ends may be "egoistic", or "altruistic", "refined", or "vulgar".' Economics is not concerned with their content, and its laws apply regardless of the nature of these ends (Rothbard, 1962, p. 63). Apparently, the only criterion of efficiency is whether individuals are free to act without coercion; we are not entitled to enquire into the reasons for a given action. Inefficiency, for Austrians, only arises when means are chosen that are inconsistent with desired goals. Austrians do not envisage society as having goals over and above the individuals comprising it.

Although the Austrian view of individual action may be open to criticism as being rather unsatisfying in its implications for the ability to *measure* economic efficiency compared to the neoclassical Pareto-optimum approach, it has the advantage of including all kinds of behaviour as consistent with free markets. For example, the success of the Japanese economy may owe a good deal to what has been called 'the Japanese ethos' which fosters loyalty, a sense of duty and public spirit.[3]

Since the Austrian attitude is based on subjectivism, it only requires that *free* choices are available, i.e. absence of coercion. One of the virtues of free market exchange in Hayek's view is that the participants need have no regard for each other's interests; this has been questioned as not being a true picture of market reality. Sometimes people, it has been suggested, do take some pride in serving the needs of others in market transactions: life is not all hard bargains; exchanges are often not competitive in nature, but include co-operative elements also. (Lucas, 1979). Although this view is open to the accusation of vagueness, Lucas sees the Hayek view as too restrictive and more vulnerable to attack, but he concludes that men will often act selfishly and then the market is preferable to all available alternatives (ibid., p. 157).

> Speculators who build office blocks and then keep them empty . . . are far less a threat to my happiness than Jew-baiting commissars or empire-building civil servants. . . . Better legitimise the profit motive and have some people honestly out to maximise their own profits than have them feather their own nests dishonestly in the course of official business. (ibid., p. 159)

Hayek's view is seen however as insufficient to 'strike responsive chords in men's hearts', which unfortunately has caused it to appear callous. This reaction perhaps overlooks that neither Hayek, nor any of the Austrian school, insists that men need to be selfish; merely that they need not be unselfish.[4] In spite of his reservations, Lucas concludes that the market is the system under which bad men can do least harm,[5] (using the phrase coined by Hayek in *Individualism and Economic Order* (1948) in his praise of the system advocated by Adam Smith and his contemporaries).

2. CONSUMER MANIPULATION

An important attack on market allocation is directed at the way in which consumer preferences are formed: that in various ways the individual's 'true' needs are not known to him or that they are 'manipulated' in some way by 'big business,' through the power of advertising. Typically this view is held by the New Left and has been publicised by that master of lively and persuasive prose, Professor Kenneth Galbraith. It is also characteristic of this critique of markets that wants are 'created', in the sense that many of the products people buy are things which they would not have thought of until presented with them by producers, who then persuade them that they need them. One way of looking at this is then to conclude that demand adjusts to supply, rather than the reverse, as seems to be implied in the conventional textbooks. Hayek's answer to Galbraith's critique runs as follows.[6] He accepts that many of our wants are created in the sense Galbraith means: 'we would not desire any of the amenities of civilisation – or even of the most primitive culture – if we did not live in a society which provided them.' Apart from our basic desires for food, clothing and shelter almost every other of our wants are derived from the example or influence of others. 'To say that a desire is not important because it is not innate is to say that the whole cultural achievement of man is not important.' Practically all cultural and artistic 'products' would fall into the category of 'manipulated' wants. For example, much political activity (e.g. attempts to change the capitalist system) and philosophical speculation are attempts to change people's tastes and are not peculiar to capitalist systems.[7] The trouble with assertions like: 'consumers do not know their true needs' is that they invite simple questions which may be quite unanswerable, such as: how can you tell what a given individual's true needs are? Hayek concludes his essay with the following:

for a hundred years we have been exhorted to embrace socialism because it would give us more goods. Since it has so lamentably failed to achieve this where it has been tried, we are now urged to adopt it because more goods after all are not important.

Part of Galbraith's critique falls on the consumer who is buying goods simply to 'keep up with the Jones's'. The Austrian view on this ancient chestnut is to the effect that, if one of a consumer's wants is emulating others then he should be allowed to do so.[8]

It has been argued that Hayek's reply to Galbraith misses the point, in that the important thing is 'not that the wants which are created are those which any specific producer desires to create, but merely that in general wants are "deliberately" created.'[9] The writer holds that producers 'purposefully synthesise wants in order to sell commodities in general, not necessarily the product of their own work'. It is not obvious in what way this disposes of Hayek's critique. One response to Hayek is to accept that the alleged need for consumer goods is real enough (i.e. the consumer himself originates the demand), but that these demands stem from the nature of the society in which the consumer finds himself. This may well be true but it would apply to any conceivable type of social system. If, for example, the society were to be dominated by some kind of hair-shirted puritanism, presumably most consumers would only want hair shirts.

Rothbard (1962) repeats the main critiques of Galbraith by Hayek and adds some of his own. Galbraith, he argues, fails to distinguish between satisfying a new want and inducing new wants (p. 843). This implies a curious view of business. Why should firms go to the expense of finding a new want for consumers when it is far easier to satisfy those wants that consumers already have. The fact that firms spend a great deal of money on market research suggests that they try to find out what consumers really want; if want-creation was their main aim there would be better ways of spending their money. One is bound to point out here, however, that it is not unknown for firms to try to create 'brand loyalty' by persuading consumers that their particular product possesses some unique characteristics, which claim may well be trivial, or possibly untrue. A much more convincing refutation lies in the comparison of the persuasion exercised by the business world with that of governments. 'Apparently, Galbraith has never heard of, or refuses to acknowledge the existence of, *governmental* propaganda' (p. 845). Government 'commercials' are not considered by Galbraith as want-creating. Furthermore, this is a field in which consumers have no market test of the product. Rothbard finally sees Galbraith's thesis as the product of his alleged élitism. 'Everyone will have to give up his tailfins so that all may be compelled to . . . read books (like *The Affluent Society*, for example?).' It is assumed that this comment is not intended to be taken too seriously, since there is no evidence that Galbraith seeks other than to persuade people to his point of view, even though he does enjoy the advantage of easy access to the information media.

Attacks on the free market based on the assertion that consumers do not always know their own 'true' interest are wide of the mark because the justification of the free market does not rest on the assumption that everyone knows his own interest best; it merely asserts that 'everyone should have the right to be free to pursue his own interest as he deems best' (Rothbard, 1970, p. 206). However, there are some goods and services in respect of which it is difficult to see how a consumer can know his own best interest; for instance, where the product in question is technically advanced and complex and for which the layman cannot possibly himself judge on safety aspects. Even the most libertarian-minded consumer could hardly object to being reassured that an electrical appliance will not be likely to cause his sudden death, and the same reasoning would apply to hundreds of goods in advanced economies. A 'straight' libertarian would argue that the consumer can always hire expert advice in the free market and that such experts will be kept up to the mark by the natural selection process of the market; the ones who give what subsequently is discovered to be poor advice will simply not be patronised again. This is the view of Rothbard, who sees no advantage in government intervention as an attempt to show people their true interest, since there is no market test of its effectiveness. The contrast is between consumer advice organisations of private origination and state-provided consumer advice bureaux.

It is interesting to note that Hayek's position on this question is by no means dogmatically libertarian. He accepts that, for example, the certification of the quality of goods or services must be done through a non-market agency and that such a service is a true example of a collective or public good,[10] but admits that this raises problems for his general principle of non-coercion.

3. THE ALLEGED IMMORALITY OF THE PROFIT MOTIVE

The widespread, long-standing, and extraordinarily persistent feeling that the seeking of private profit is in some ways immoral is derived from Aristotle and medieval Christian doctrines of the 'just price' through Hegel and Marx to our own times. Even now, in an almost wholly materialistic society phrases such as 'production for use, not for profit' are quite commonly used, whilst to say something is being done 'for purely commercial reasons' is to invest the deed in question with a shady air of immorality. The sense of outrage against the prospect of private profit reached a peak in the early years of the twentieth century when widely-read intellectuals such as Shaw, Wells, Orwell and Russell raged against the capitalist system and managed to spread their ideas to a wider audience than had the more analytical, but more difficult, Karl Marx. Of course, the sight of the rich enjoying huge incomes apparently without labour, side by side with the most degrading poverty was bound to provoke a reaction from all but the most insensitive observers. But amidst all the shouting and indignation there was little attempt to educate the public in the true nature of the problem. Two principal issues stand out: that of the private ownership of property, and the question of its just distribution. If 'society' is to be changed these important questions need to be answered and it must not be airily assumed that fundamental changes will not introduce new and hitherto unimagined evils, as even Bertrand Russell, though at the time a ferocious critic of capitalism, had begun to think about as early as the first world war, in his essay 'The Pitfalls of Socialism'.

Three major misconceptions concerning the nature of profit seem to have originated with Aristotle.[11] First, the idea that trade is exploitation. George Orwell put this view in the form: 'The trouble with competitions is that somebody wins them.' He saw competition as the equivalent of a boxing match or a race.[12] John Ruskin had expressed similar thoughts: 'Whenever material gain follows exchange, for every plus there is a precisely equal minus.' Obviously, however, trade is not a zero-sum game: both parties who freely enter into an exchange may gain from it. Aristotle's objections to any return from a loan has had enormous influence, mostly for the worst.[13] Yet the objection to interest is really invalid. When we lend money we are, in a sense, in receiving interest, getting paid for the use of goods we might have bought with that money; the absence of money would not change our desire to possess goods. The third part of the Aristotelian doctrine explains the 'production for profit, production for use' distinction. The false antithesis is exposed when it is realised that the buyers presumably want to use their purchases and that there is no point in anyone producing something with a view to selling it if no one wants to buy it.

Income from investment is 'probably the most powerful of the sources of this revulsion against "the profit motive"' (Flew). In this revulsion two possibilities may be distinguished: either the objection rests on opposition to income from any kind of (private) ownership or, more narrowly, against income accruing to the individual arising from private ownership of the means of production (e.g. capital). Assuming there exists a right to the private ownership of property then there is no practicable way, in a free society, of preventing owners from charging for its use by a payment which may be regarded as rent. But suppose property were to be collectively, instead of privately owned: why is this more moral than private ownership? The objection is not to 'acquisitiveness, or to excess, or even to exploitation. It is to what is individual and private rather than public and collective' (Flew).

A variant of the 'production for use, not profit' is that many of the goods and services from the sale of which profit is gained are undesirable. The Austrian position on this point is that in order to make a profit, entrepreneurs must be providing something that buyers want, and that it is not their business to enquire into the 'goodness' or 'badness' of the commodity.

It is not the business of entrepreneurs to make people substitute sound ideologies for unsound. It rests with philosophers to change people's ideas and ideals. The entrepreneur serves the consumers as they are today, however wicked and ignorant. (Mises, 1949, p. 300)

Mises would reject any coercion by the state to forbid the sale of 'bad' things, even for example guns, and presumably (though he is not specific on this) addictive drugs such as heroin. His attitude is that the entrepreneur who, tempted by the opportunity of profiting from the sale of a 'bad' thing, refrains from seizing his chance, is to be admired for his superior ethical stance but that even if all other entrepreneurs were to follow his example, governments 'would produce weapons in their own arsenals and drinkers would distil their own liquor'. Mises does not tell us whether he would look favourably or not on state-provided educational propaganda campaigns to persuade people to give up harmful practices, such as cigarette smoking.

Hayek's defence of the morality of profit-seeking is derived from his ethos of the open society.[14] This he traces to the trading towns of medieval Italy, where it first became accepted that it was better to benefit a multitude of unknown people rather than to meet the needs of a few neighbours. The individuals or groups who followed this precept prospered the most and it became, in consequence, elevated to a moral principle in the sense that it became a duty to pursue a self-chosen goal without paying too much attention to the part the action might play in the whole web of human activity. This ethos or 'spirit of capitalism' has come to be associated with Protestantism, especially in its Calvinist variant, but Hayek cites evidence to the effect that it was taught by the Spanish Jesuits during the same period. This view of the morality of private profit-seeking was confined, until the recent past, to small groups mainly in the towns, and its acceptance in the western world is a comparatively recent development, so that the egoistic striving for gain is still viewed with suspicion and seen as unnatural. In the older tribal societies which existed for thousands of years, the most socially respectable and admired behaviour is that which is governed by needs as perceived by the individual to be of benefit to other particular individuals. Hayek sees the acceptance of the new values of the open society as a step towards a superior moral code, since it involved the concept that it enlarged the circle of other people in relation to whom one had to obey moral rules. The persistence of opposition to the pursuit of private gain is seen as being due to the reluctance of human beings to shed 'moral views developed for the tribal society'. Even Adam Smith had harmed his own cause when he gave the impression that striving for known ends is altruistic, whereas the search for private profit is simply egoistic.[15] On the basis of this view, Hayek sees socialism and the striving for 'social justice' as throwbacks to tribalism which can only threaten his ideal of the free society. This, however, raises some much broader questions than simply explaining prejudice against the profit motive.

As an example of some of the objections to the alleged beneficence of free market allocation the reader is recommended to consult recent essays by two eminent 'mainstream' economists, one of which[16] throws some interesting light on the profit motive, and the other which among other things discusses the tendency of politicians to act on the basis of economic theories which they may assume (wrongly) to fully support their actions.[17]

The outstanding element in the Austrian view of market morality is not simply that individuals are the best judges of their own interest (a belief which is shared by other free market advocates) but that, in addition, there is no way in which an outside observer may assess whether or not a particular individual's action increases or decreases that individual's welfare. One important corollary of the Austrian position is that the freedom of the individual within a market order includes the freedom to behave altruistically if he wishes to. Suppose, however, that freely-acting individuals are unwilling to provide voluntarily through charitable organisations the means to support the sick, the old or any other individuals who are regarded as being unfairly handicapped in market competition with others. On ethical grounds does this justify state intervention to correct the balance between the fit and the unfit? The answer to this question depends ultimately on what attitude one takes to the morality of coercion: forcing people to do good to others. This matter is discussed at greater length in Chapter 15, but there is one aspect of altruism which may as well be referred to now. One criticism of the foregoing argument for 'leaving it to the market' is that it misses out an important limitation on the scope of altruism. Let us accept that, left to their own devices, individuals will, either singly or in groups, combine to behave altruistically. This may well be true of small groups, such as immediate neighbours or the people of a local church or a village, but as the size of the group becomes larger and more scattered so, even though the individual may *wish* to show kindness and generosity, the scale of the problem poses insuperable difficulties in the way of his freedom to act thus. Therefore, it has been argued, in a society of small groups within which there is altruism, there is a need for a third party to organise the desired degree of altruism in a wider setting; this leads to the conclusion that there is a natural demand by individuals and small groups for the creation of a 'third party' which serves to link the small groups. This third party might well be the government (see Bosanquet, 1983). This is a persuasive argument for the need for one type of government intervention, but it still leaves questions concerning coercion as a moral issue partly unresolved. For example, what happens to small groups who refuse to behave altruistically? Are they to be punished? There is also the point that, in fact, there are many non-state agencies which give scope for individual or small-group altruism on a wide, often on an international scale, such as numerous charities, and organisations of the Oxfam type.

Possibly the most familiar of all the arguments against the free market is that competition, if left to evolve freely, contains the seeds of its own destruction and has often ended in monopoly. This topic obviously merits a separate chapter.

NOTES

1. Marshall (1890), 1916 edn, p. 10.
2. Bertrand Russell, *Political Ideals*, 1963 edn, London: Unwin, p. 24.
3. See Amartya Sen, 'The profit motive', *Lloyd's Bank Review*, January 1983, p. 14.
4. There is a passage in Mises' *Human Action*, however, which somewhat contradictorily seems close to regarding selfish as 'rational' (pp. 725–6).
5. Keynes took a similar view of the comparative innocence of self-interested market behaviour as in his often-quoted dictum: 'It is better that a man should tyrannise over his bank balance than over his fellow citizens' (*General Theory*, chapter 24).
6. See F.A. Hayek, 'The non-sequitur of the dependence effect', *Southern Economic Journal*, vol. xxvii, no. 4, April 1964. Reprinted in Hayek (1967), pp. 313–17.
7. Only open societies, however, offer the real possibility of freely advocating a complete change in the system, and using any lawful means of persuasion to this end. At the moment of writing this, it is reported that a professor in Yugoslavia has been sentenced to five years' imprisonment for stating that capitalism is 'better' than the Yugoslavian system.

8. This is a convenient point at which to draw attention to a short, but brilliantly executed polemic against Hayek's liberal philosophy, which could serve as the basis for not joining any sort of uncritical Hayek admiration society. See Donald Winch's review of Hayek's *Studies* in *Economic Journal*, December 1968, pp. 903–5. In view of the fact that Hayek's reply to Galbraith was included in this book it is somewhat puzzling to read Winch's remark that 'the *only* person with whom he [Hayek] engages in direct attack is a contributor to an obscure journal whose views are more libertarian than his own.'

9. James O'Connor, 'Scientific and ideological elements in the theory of government policy', *Science and Society*, vol. 33, 1969. Reprinted in Hunt and Schwartz (1972).

10. See Chapter 7.

11. See Antony Flew, 'The profit motive', *Ethics*, vol. 86, no. 4, July 1976, 312–22.

12. George Orwell, review of F.A. Hayek's *The Road to Serfdom*, *The Observer*, 9 April 1944. Reprinted in Sonia Orwell and Ian Angus, *The Collected Essays* (1970), vol. III, Harmondsworth: Penguin, pp. 142–4.

13. It is possible that one element in anti-semitism is derived from the fact that the medieval Church frowned upon usury and that as a consequence non-Christians (i.e. Jews) became the principal money-lenders.

14. See Hayek (1982), II, pp. 144–7.

15. Hayek's preferred equivalent to Adam Smith's expression that everyone should be free 'to pursue his own interest in his own way' is 'each being allowed to use his own knowledge for his own purposes'. The reason he gives for preferring this version is that 'to the modern ear Smith's phrase suggests a spirit of selfishness which is probably not intended and certainly inessential to the argument' (Hayek, 1982, II, pp. 153–4, n. 7).

16. Amartya Sen (see note 3).

17. Frank Hahn, 'Reflections on the invisible hand', *Lloyd's Bank Review*, April 1982.

9 Monopoly

In the *Constitution of Liberty*, there is a short section with the significant sub-heading, 'Monopoly and Other Minor Problems'.[1] The reason Hayek gave for classing monopoly as a 'minor' problem was that its importance seemed to him to have been exaggerated. Although he had earlier urged positive action against monopolistic business enterprise as a necessary prerequisite to the removal of trade union monopoly, he later formed the opinion that the latter posed more of a threat to liberty; furthermore, he became convinced that although monopoly is undesirable, the character of much government anti-monopoly legislation may, in itself, be more harmful than private monopoly.

If we were asked to sum up briefly the Austrian view of monopoly it is that much of the energy devoted to the analysis of monopoly models in economic theory and most anti-trust policies are misguided and harmful both to economic efficiency and individual freedom.

1. THE 'MAINSTREAM' PICTURE OF MONOPOLY[2]

In all their varied forms the monopoly models of the textbooks have in common certain features: control by firms over price or output, and divergence between marginal cost and price. Monopoly is contrasted with perfect competition as in various ways reducing consumer welfare: non-optimal welfare equilibrium; 'excessive' profits leading to an unacceptable distribution of wealth; 'cut-throat' competition to exclude competitors; and reduction of freedom consequent upon the monopolist's power of coercion.

The conventional view is that monopolies originate from such things as ownership of some important natural resource (e.g. oil), patent rights or other legally-backed protective measures such as customs barriers. However, the most important cause of monopoly is seen in the increasing size of the optimum firm brought about by economies of scale. This in itself then constitutes an important barrier to the entry of competitors because of the amount of finance capital required; and in the Marxist version there is allegedly an inherent tendency in the free market towards 'monopoly capitalism', which provides a powerful justification for state intervention to 'control' monopoly.

2. THE AUSTRIAN CRITIQUE OF ORTHODOX MONOPOLY THEORY

The perfect competition model, which is often used as a yardstick by which to judge monopoly, is itself seen as flawed (see Chapter 5). The presence of monopoly in a market does not extinguish what Austrians see as the most important aspect of markets – the process of discovery. Monopolists must find out what their customers will buy and at what prices. There are no 'given' data which the firm can use as the basis of the demand curve for its product.[3] The perfect competition model implies that many familiar features of the real world, such as product differentiation and advertising, are associated with monopoly, whereas they are more realistically to be regarded as part of the competitive process. One consequence of viewing monopoly as an aberration of the free market is to suggest that it should be 'corrected' or 'controlled' by government. Even those economists who, in general, favour free markets over collectivism, advocate that government should adopt a positive policy of reducing monopoly. The distinctive Austrian approach is sceptical of government intervention to 'control' monopoly and suggests that government, could, with benefit, do two things: encourage competition and put its own house in order by abstaining from creating monopolies. In fact the state is seen by Austrians as the most important cause of monopoly.[4]

3. THE AUSTRIAN DEFINITION OF MONOPOLY[5]

It is possible to reduce definitions of monopoly to three.[6] The first is derived from the word monopoly – the only seller of any given good. The trouble with this is that it is too broad. It means that all products which differ in any way are monopolised. This definition regards all distinctions made between individual products as establishing monopolies. Anyone becomes a monopolist who sells anything which is not identical in every respect (e.g. with regard to packaging, after-sales service or location), with what everyone else sells. If we are to use the single-seller definition of monopoly then we have to be able to lay down criteria for deciding whether or not two goods are identical, but since such decisions must ultimately depend on the subjective assessments of consumers, there is no way in which an economist can decide the question.

The second possible definition of monopoly is that it is present when 'monopoly prices' are being charged. This is the definition favoured by Mises[7] and may be identified as existing when a seller can, if the demand curve is inelastic at the point of competitive price, restrict sales and raise the price and thus maximise revenue. One advantage of this definition is that there is no need to be concerned with whether or not the seller is the sole producer. Rothbard rejects the monopoly-price definition for several reasons, the main one being the impossibility of identifying the 'competitive price'. The definition depends on the assumption that a seller can, by restricting his sales, increase the price to the point on his demand curve above which the curve becomes elastic. But there is no 'competitive price' which is established elsewhere with which the monopoly price may be compared. The notion that economists can stipulate objectively what the competitive price would be is seen by Austrians as an illusion. Similarly, using 'monopoly profits' as the criterion for identifying monopoly price is seen as failing (Rothbard, ibid., p. 608).

The third definition, and the one thought to be the most realistic by Austrians, is that 'monopoly' is properly applied only to governmental grants of privilege, direct or indirect.[8] This was the original understanding of the meaning of monopoly as understood by English common law. If the state is the creator of monopoly it is clearly seen as absurd for the state to pursue an anti-monopoly policy; all it need do is to abandon its own creations.

4. ORIGINS OF MONOPOLY

The Austrian explanation of the originating causes is implicit in the favoured definition. The crucial point is that there will be no invulnerable monopoly unless it is protected in some way by the state.[9] Most of the other alleged causes for the emergence of monopolies in hitherto competitive markets can be seen as of a temporary nature in the absence of state protection. The venerable

Marxist contention that monopoly is an inevitable feature of 'late' capitalism is regarded by Austrians as unsupported by the evidence, since most instances of monopoly are the result of government intervention, not capitalism. If technological advance leading to increasingly large-scale production has led to 'monopoly capitalism', then monopolies might have been expected to appear first after the industrial revolution in countries which had the most advanced economic systems.[10] In fact they appeared first in the United States and Germany, two countries which were at a comparatively early stage of industrialisation. Especially in Germany, cartels and monopolies were the direct result of state policy, and protectionism had similar effects in the United States. But Britain remained comparatively free of monopoly until the 1920s when it was encouraged by the government's policy of 'rationalisation' – a euphemism for reducing competition.

'Collusion' is often given as the explanation for collective monopolies or cartels. Collusion is not seen as being particularly sinister by Austrians. Firms co-operating to increase their incomes are viewed as no different from any partnership or joint-stock company. Also, experience shows that cartels are inherently unstable; the most efficient producers are likely to be the first to become restive.

Apart from those barriers to the entry of competitors sustained by the state it has long been accepted in mainstream economics that the logic of large-scale production tends to decrease the number of competitors in an industry and at the same time to make it more difficult for new entrants by reason of the greater capital required to start up.[11] This argument loses some of its force if it is remembered that although firms have become larger, so has the average wealth of individuals; and individuals can pool their resources through the medium of pension and insurance funds, but there does appear to be a reluctance on the part of these fund managers to be adventurous in any way. 'Why is it that some unions or groups of workers don't start their own business?', asks Nozick (1974, p. 253), a question to which he offers the answer that it is risky starting a new firm and in a capitalist system specialised investment institutions develop to run just these risks.[12]

5. Oligopoly

The essentials of the treatment of oligopoly in conventional theory are to be seen in the concept that in an industry with a few producers, each individual firm has some influence on the market price. This has led to a proliferation of hypothetical models but no unique theory of equilibrium, as with perfect competition and pure monopoly. The general approach of Austrians to oligopoly might be accused of not taking the subject as seriously as it merits. Rothbard regards some of the concern about oligopoly as creating pseudo-problems. All the talk of strategies, 'warfare', etc. as depicted in games theory is viewed as fairly pointless. Shackle has commented that '[Games theory] *assumes away* the whole of that aspect of business, science, art and contest which allows originative genius to exist.' It assumes that oligopolists can knowingly survey all the possibilities open to them and leaves out '*surprise*, the supreme achievement of the tactician'.[13] Rothbard regards the difficulties allegedly surrounding the theoretical study of oligopoly as exaggerated. His solution to the 'problem' of the indeterminacy of oligopoly behaviour is simply to treat the demand curves facing the firm as including the expected behaviour (action and reaction) of other firms.

6. MONOPOLISTIC COMPETITION

Dissatisfaction with the perfect competition and perfect monopoly models led, in the 1920s, to the proposal of a more plausible model: monopolistic competition. Since this model is now regarded as of dubious value even among orthodox economists[14] it will be dealt with only briefly. The theory predicts product differentiation and unused capacity. The former, Austrians see merely as a typical feature of the competitive process not as monopolistic behaviour, and how, in practice is it possible to distinguish product differentiation from those desirable quality improvements which constantly occur? Sir Roy Harrod has drawn attention to the paradox that in the monopolistic competition model a firm is supposed to foresee that its profitable output should be limited to $(X-Y)$ units but actually plans to build a plant that will produce X units at its minimum cost point.[15] Rothbard plausibly explains the paradox as 'hinging on a mathematical technicality'. The habit of drawing cost curves as continuous smooth functions prevents us from drawing the downward sloping demand curve tangential to the lowest point on the average cost curve. In the real world such functions are discrete and represented by a series of angular lines. Once the continuous function is replaced it is seen that the 'excess capacity' prediction vanishes (Rothbard, 1962, pp. 643–4).

7. ARE MONOPOLIES HARMFUL?

The answer given to this question by Austrians is that it is not monopoly as such but only the prevention of competition which is harmful. Monopoly which has emerged as a result of superior performance is to be welcomed. But it would be harmful if a monopoly were able to protect and preserve its position after the original cause of its superiority had disappeared. For example, a monopolist might use his power to exclude competition by offering discounts to only those people whose custom might be sought by a potential competitor.[16] There are difficulties in dealing with this type of discrimination because certain kinds of discrimination can be quite justifiable (e.g. in transport pricing). Hayek is rather sceptical concerning the possibility of framing beneficial rules covering all cases and would, typically, tend to leave such things to civil procedures – e.g. claims for damages (1982, III, p. 85). In general, the Austrian view is that so long as the possibility of substitutes exists, there is no fear of coercion by monopolists. If free entry is not blocked then no coercive power can be long lasting.

The bogy of 'excess' profits is not a problem from the Austrian point of view. Even if the monopolist does make large profits, the important point is that as long as his prices are sufficiently competitive to deter entrants he must be at least as efficient a resource user as any potential competitor.

'Cut-throat' competition is often alleged to be a common practice in which a big firm drives out a small one by deliberate undercutting. But how is it proposed that this phenomenon should be identified? One suggested criterion has been 'selling below costs', but costs are irrelevant once the goods have been produced. Price cutting may equally be due to inability to sell at a higher price as to cut-throat competition, and it is impossible to distinguish the two elements.[17]

8. MONOPOLY AND THE STATE

Austrians, as we have noted, view anti-monopoly legislation rather differently from many economists. As well as for the reasons mentioned above, there is always present a danger of 'unintended consequences', which are not always immediately obvious. The Hoffman–La Roche company was condemned by the Monopolies Commission for making excessive profits from the drugs Librium and Valium. The company agreed to repay a large sum of money to the national health service and to lower the prices of the two drugs. As Littlechild observes, although this may appear a beneficial act of government, if such control became common it might inhibit the necessarily expensive research into new drugs (1978, p. 46). There are, however, a few simple steps the government could take to encourage competition. Those services in which today governments often have a legal monopoly such as are to be found in transport, communications, postal services and various public utilities such as gas, water and electricity supply, could be opened up to legal competition. (Hayek would include the issue of money in this list.) It might turn out that the existing state monopolies would prove to be the most efficient, but it is important that the possibility of competition should exist. Reform of taxation is another way in which competition could be encouraged. The effect of heavily progressive income tax and capital transfer taxes is often to deny to individuals and small firms the opportunity to accumulate the capital needed to break into markets. The result is that accumulation by the large corporate (perhaps monopolistic) enterprise is favoured, at the expense of individual new enterprise.

Finally, it should be noted that the Austrian view of monopoly, so far as government policy is concerned, is not very different from that of those other economists who strongly favour free market allocation, such as the Chicago school.[18] The most important difference lies in the stress Austrians place on the state as the main, if not the sole, creator and protector of monopolies.

9. TRADE UNIONS[19]

Labour unions are seen by Austrians as monopolies of a special kind different from, and more dangerous to liberty, than enterprise monopoly. There are two obvious differences. When a monopoly producer of goods or services restricts supply he does it hoping that the increased price per unit will more than compensate him for the reduction in the number of units sold; this will, of course happen if he has forecast the elasticity of demand correctly. There is a built-in check on the extent to which he can reduce supply – the loss of revenue may not be compensated for by the increased price. In the case of a union, however, the consequences of withholding supply are not borne by the individuals in work. If a union achieves a wage higher than each individual could get by himself, the loss of 'revenue' will be borne by those excluded from the market. These may consist of the unemployed or would-be entrants, for instance, who are not now able to enter the trade or profession.[20]

The second difference lies in the privileges enjoyed by unions. These immunities take two forms: those which are backed by the force of law, and those which result from the fact that the authorities, often supported by public opinion, are generally unwilling to enforce the law against violent picketing and other forms of unlawful coercion. In Britain the Trade Disputes Act 1906 conferred on unions unique privileges: immunity from prosecution on the ground of tortious acts (civil wrongs) committed by their agents. The reason for this legislation was partly due to a feeling that in disputes with employers the dice were unfairly loaded against unions. Thus unions have achieved their present position, not merely by exercising the free right of association, but through the law. Hayek views union coercion as being mainly directed not at employers, but at fellow workers, and regards their present power as resting largely on their unique position in law. This seems to underestimate the strength of the desire of workers to form unions quite freely without the backing of the law, as in the nineteenth century. Nevertheless, the legal immunities possessed by unions are impressive: it puts them in a position enjoyed by no other institution: 'This measure [The Trades Disputes Act 1906], in fact resigned to the trade unions part of the authority of the state.'[21] Legislation in the United States through various Acts and Supreme Court decisions conferred similar privileges. Underlying all these measures seems to have been a presumption that privilege conferred on unions was beneficial to people in general.

The Austrian view is that trade union monopoly is the most dangerous form of monopoly because of the powers of coercion that accompany it. One type of coercion has been mentioned – that which results from tolerance of the breaking of picketing laws. Another is the closed shop. Hayek would treat closed shop agreements as 'contracts in restraint of trade'. He sees them as no different from the practice of prohibiting an individual worker from joining a union and thus denying him work. It has been pointed out[22] that Hayek's proposed outlawing of closed shop agreements may conflict with his general aim of reducing coercion to a minimum. If a closed shop agreement is freely agreed by an employer and a union, then to forbid it by law would be coercion by the state. To some extent it depends on how we define 'freely agreed'. Perhaps some voluntary closed shop agreements are rather like paying protection money – the employer buys freedom from industrial unrest. On the other hand, it is difficult to see how a contract to which both parties admit they freely agreed could be questioned within the Austrian minimal coercion principle.

The aggrandisement of unions can also be seen as dangerous in reinforcing the recent tendencies towards the 'corporate state'. One of the ministers in Mussolini's fascist government contrasted 'the ephemeral value of the individual with the indefinite life of society'. He saw as a desirable ideal unions and employers' organisations joining together within each industry, collaborating to achieve common aims: 'We should abandon the rigid dogma . . . that wages and systems of labour are determined by supply and demand.' The corporate state rests on the fallacy that the national interest is the sum of the interests of trade unionists, employers, shopkeepers, the professions and other groups. It ignores the interest everyone has as a consumer.[23] The importance accorded to collective bodies may be the result of an erroneous belief that the larger is the group the more it will, in some undefined way, represent everyone's interest best. The term 'collective' has become one of those 'good' words like 'social'. The Austrian view is that, as a 'rough approximation', individual selfishness will lead to the preservation of spontaneous order and is in the interests of all; the closed group works in entirely the opposite direction.[24]

To sum up: the Austrian view is that the major problem is not private enterprise monopoly but those monopolies either directly run by the government or indirectly fostered and protected by the government. Absence of competition is the real problem and government should confine its activities to changing the economic environment so as to encourage competition rather than enacting anti-monopoly law. If there is free entry to industries then coercive power will not persist for very long. The record of anti-monopoly legislation both in Britain and the USA tends to support the Austrian view that it has not been effective in increasing competition and some of the side effects have produced unintended and unwanted consequences. Also many myths are still believed; such as the alleged wickedness of the so-called robber barons of America's developing period, and how they had to be tamed by wise government anti-trust laws.[25] Labour unions are seen as potentially more dangerous to individual liberty than enterprise monopoly when backed by laws having the effect of empowering them to prevent an employee from working, as in some closed shop situations. Austrians are wholly in favour of the principle that individuals should be free to combine together for the purpose of collective action, but only without coercion. A dilemma for libertarians comes when an employer and a voluntary collective of workers mutually agree on a closed shop agreement. Both parties may well have been making free non-coerced choices but the result may be ultimately coercive for the individual employee.

Notes

1. Hayek (1960), pp. 264–6.
2. 'Monopoly' is to be understood in the following discussion as including all departures from perfect competition, unless otherwise stated.
3. See Littlechild (1978), p. 33.
4. The very word 'monopoly' was used originally to describe a special privilege granted by the monarch, e.g. the Trade and Navigation Acts, the attempt to enforce which was a contributory cause of the American revolution.
5. See Rothbard (1962), pp. 587–93; and Mises (1949), pp. 277–9.
6. Rothbard (1962), p. 590, asserts that most definitions of monopoly are hopelessly confused.
7. See Mises (1949), pp. 357–63, for his theory of monopoly price.
8. See Rothbard (1970), p. 79 and (1962), p. 591.
9. For the view that the government has been the main cause of monopoly in the USA, see Machan (1974), essays by Yale Brozen and D.T. Armentano, pp. 149–76.
10. See Hayek (1944), pp. 34–5.
11. It is, of course, a well-known and elementary error to equate the size of firm with a monopoly. But compare the motor car industry (few, but competitive) with, say, solicitors (many, but having common scales of fees for conveyancing).
12. When *The Times* newspaper was recently for sale it would seem to have been a good opportunity for the trade unions to have bought it and provided themselves with a national friendly press voice.
13. See Shackle (1972), p. 422.
14. E.g. Chamberlin, himself one of the inventors of the model, in 'Monopolistic competition revisited', *Economic Journal*, 1952. D. Laidler writes: 'it would appear that the notion of the monopolistically competitive industry adds nothing to our ability to understand firms' behaviour that is not already inherent in the theory of pure monopoly' (*Introduction to Microeconomics* (1974), Deddington: Philip Allan, p. 167.

15. Roy Harrod, *Economic Essays* (1952), New York: Harcourt Brace, p. 149. Cited by Rothbard (1962), p. 642.
16. The famous case brought against Standard Oil had a strong influence on subsequent American anti-trust policy. In this Rockefeller was accused of price discrimination to drive out competitors. It was subsequently shown that the evidence against him was fabricated by unsuccessful competitors. (See Lepage, 1978, p. 36.)
17. See Rothbard for this and other aspects of 'cut-throat competition' (1962) pp. 600–4.
18. See Friedman (1962), pp. 119–36.
19. See Mises (1949) pp. 376–7, 777–9; Hayek (1982, III), pp. 89–90; Hayek (1960), chapter 18; Rothbard (1962), pp. 620–30.
20. The workers excluded from employment may well include ethnic minorities; to discriminate costs the employer nothing. For example, in the USA, following federal regulation and unionisation in the nineteenth century, blacks were totally excluded from work on the railroads in which many had formerly been employed. (See Sowell (1981), pp. 40–8.)
21. Schumpeter (1950), p. 321.
22. See, for example, Barry (1979), pp. 74–5.
23. See S. Brittan, *The Economic Consequences of Democracy* (1977), London: Temple Smith, who quotes Mancur Olson, *The Logic of Collective Action* (1965), Harvard University Press.
24. See Hayek (1982, II), p. 90.
25. For a concise recent account which takes a strongly Austrian view of anti-monopoly legislation, see Arthur Shenfield, *Myth and Reality in Anti-Trust*, (IEA, London: 1983).

10 Macroeconomics

1. INTRODUCTION

The purpose of this chapter is first to discuss the general outlines and origins of that large division of the subject which is familiarly known as macroeconomics; how and why it has become so important, and in what ways the neo-Austrian school is in disagreement with the general orthodoxy (in so far as one exists).

Although in recent years there has been an ever-rising tide of criticism and disillusionment among economists who, increasingly, have felt impelled to question Keynesianism which dominated the academic and political scene in the immediate aftermath of the second world war,[1] there is little doubt that J.M. Keynes will remain, for good or ill, the outstanding pioneer of the use of aggregation in economic theory. A simple indication of the extent of his influence is to compare principal textbooks before and after the publication of *The General Theory* (1936). Marshall's *Principles*, for example, might well, if published today, be entitled simply *Microeconomics* or *Price Theory*, without doing it much injustice; and Philip Wicksteed's admirable *Commonsense of Political Economy* (first published 1910; last reprint 1948) is similarly taken up largely with *individual* consumers, firms and markets. Nowadays it is, of course, the conventional practice to divide economics quite sharply into 'micro' and 'macro' and syllabuses and books tend to be drawn up along such lines. The influential figure of Keynes was the chief agent in this transformation of the subject, and the process has been called the 'Keynesian revolution' so often as to be now almost too banal to mention. Not everyone agrees that the modern approach has been an unqualified advantage, and modern Austrians especially regard it in many ways as having been disastrous in terms of its influence on policy,[2] not to mention the fact that it has been suggested that Keynes himself might be horrified by the results of his disciples' endeavours.[3]

2. KEYNESIAN ANALYSIS: A GENERAL VIEW

In this section we shall first sketch the general outlines of how the Keynesian view created the scaffolding of what has since become the structure of macroeconomics. Why the Austrian school are critical of these developments will then be explained.

In the *General Theory of Employment, Interest and Money* emphasis is on the economy *as a whole*; the variables analysed are such aggregates as total national output, the general level of employment, and the general price level. Whereas much of economics before Keynes involved the study of individual markets, Keynes wrote about *aggregate* demand and supply. In his theory of the determination of national income, he put forward probably his most powerful and subsequently most influential insight – the possibility that equilibrium national income might not be at a level consistent with full employment. He also attempted to show that money could not simply be regarded as a medium of exchange but that it has certain special characteristics which, in themselves, are an important factor in the determination of income and employment. From these theoretical considerations he argued that it might often be necessary for governments to intervene in a market economy in order to ensure full employment and, what was equally important, such government action might confidently be expected to be successful.

Such a message of apparent hope, in the midst of a world-wide depression of unprecedented severity, naturally had a strong and wide appeal, particularly for socialists or collectivists, and served to provide formidable intellectual backing for a political philosophy which had hitherto justified its beliefs more by an appeal to morality than to logic. Keynes showed that capitalism had a fatal defect which could only be remedied by state intervention in the market. Somewhat paradoxically, it has been said that Keynes 'saved' capitalism by showing that it could be made to work and need not be overthrown by revolution, thus his appeal was also to conservatives in some respects – those whose consciences were affronted by the consequences of unemployment, yet who did not want to see a revolutionary solution to the problem.

3. THE AUSTRIAN CRITIQUE OF MACROECONOMICS

Much of the neo-Austrian view of the method of macroeconomic aggregation has been a reaction against the assumptions of

Keynesianism.[4] The basis of Austrian dissent is composed of several elements. In summary these are first, that many aggregates (or grand totals) of monetarily-valued quantities tend to cause the underlying microeconomic and subjectively determined valuations to be lost sight of; secondly, human action is not driven by macro aggregates, and to assume that it is leads to misguided policy prescriptions; thirdly, that the preoccupation with aggregates fosters undesirable tendencies to bureaucratic management of the 'economy' and 'social engineering', which tendencies are ultimately a threat to individual liberty.

Although attention has been drawn to the fact that most pre-Keynesian economics was concentrated on price and distribution theory, there was an exception: the theory of money and the general price level. Money had tended to be treated as if a separate compartment and since the study of it involves the general price level this was the thin end of the macroeconomic wedge. Price theory dealt with individual action – the microeconomic level. But the theory of money and the mythical (as the Austrians put it) concept of the price level was regardless of individual components – it was on the macroeconomic level. The Austrians were anxious to apply their marginal utility theory to the valuation of units of money and this raised the problem of circularity in reasoning. This unsolved problem was the reason for the treatment of money as a separate commodity. Mises developed further a solution which had first been put forward by Menger, which was simply to regard money as having developed spontaneously out of the discovery that indirect exchange (i.e. via the use of money) had advantages over direct exchange (i.e. barter). The point of mentioning this view of money is to show that the Austrians were instinctively opposing macroeconomic methods even before the hey-day of such methods had been reached.[5]

In looking back on the late 1930s, the impression is sometimes given that Keynes' ideas were at once almost universally accepted due to his persuasiveness, as well as the 'obvious' correctness of his methods and diagnoses. The fact that Keynes had eminent critics, and that although with hindsight their subsequent defeat may appear inevitable, has tended to obscure some important aspects of the debate which preceded his triumph. One reason for the virtual collapse of opposing views was that economists in general became persuaded on intellectual grounds – Keynes' ideas simply appeared to be generally right. Lord Robbins, for example, in his autobiography, now acknowledges that he was wrong in supporting Hayek's theory as applied to the 1930s, and writes that he would willingly forget his own advocacy of it in the 1930s. Another reason was that the euphoria and optimism generated by Keynesian ideas (i.e. that governments could, by their actions, banish unemployment) tended to make Keynes' opponents appear not only old-fashioned and wrong, but even immoral since they seemed to be arguing against doing anything about unemployment. The slogan, particularly after about 1944, was: 'We are all Keynesians, now.' It was largely true.

Among the dissenters from the general consensus right from the start was F.A. Hayek, and he was to remain almost a lone voice[6] – apart from his teacher Mises, and his student Lachmann – when many other economists had come round to accepting Keynesianism. In the years following the end of the second world war, Hayek's critique of the methods of macroeconomics has continued and become both more relevant to the times and convincing to a growing number of disciples, which has surely given him some compensation for his 'wilderness' years.

He gives a short, but interesting account of the debate which took place in the early 1930s between himself and Keynes, in 'Personal recollections of Keynes and the "Keynesian Revolution"' (*New Studies*, pp. 283–94). Although the two men were on friendly terms, they seldom agreed on economics. In 1931, Keynes' *Treatise on Money*, published the previous year, was the subject of two review articles by Hayek in *Economica*[7] into which he 'put a great deal of work'. These articles, and the subsequent replies and rejoinders which followed between Hayek, Sraffa, Keynes and others[8] with shorter contributions from Hawtrey, Pigou and Robertson, were described by Sir John Hicks as a 'drama' in which the leading characters were Hayek and Keynes (Hicks, 1967, p. 203). Keynes replied to Hayek's criticisms by a counterattack on his *Prices and Production* (1931).[9] Hayek declares that 'though he had great admiration for the many profound but unsystematical [sic] insights of Keynes', he considered that he 'had largely demolished his [Keynes] theoretical scheme' (*Personal Recollections*). All the more disappointed was he, therefore, when Keynes told him 'that he had in the meantime changed his mind and no longer believed what he had said in that work' (ibid., p. 284). This, when the *General Theory* appeared, was one reason why Hayek did not return to the attack, since he was afraid that before he had completed his analysis 'he [Keynes] would again have changed his mind'. Furthermore, Hayek evidently found it difficult to accept the designation a 'general' theory which Keynes used. Far from being general in its applicability, it seemed to Hayek, though being full of profound perceptions, specifically relevant to the rather unusual conditions of the period ('a tract for the times').[10]

But Hayek's decisive reason for not taking on Keynes for a second time was because he questioned the very basis of Keynes' method – the *validity of macroeconomic analysis*. The obvious question arises: since Hayek was at this time sceptical as to the very foundations of the Keynesian approach why did not this act, as one might well imagine it would, as a spur to reply to Keynes rather than the opposite? His failure to do so is regarded by some Keynesians as puzzling. A recent view by an economist who is sympathetic to the Keynesian viewpoint of the Hayek *v.* Keynes controversy also argues that Hayek's criticism of Keynes was too harsh: specifically, that Keynes was not as unaware of microeconomic factors as Hayek argued, and that Hayek, in his later writings, pays too little attention to recent work in developing the micro foundations of macro theory. (The work of Patinkin and Tobin[11] are cited as examples); also, that Hayek underestimated Keynes' opposition to inflation (Gilbert, 1982, pp. 95–7). He concludes that Hayek's view of Keynes' economics is 'both false and dangerous' (ibid., p. 95), but concedes that Hayek's 'general attack on monetary inflation is salutary' (ibid., p. 97).

Hayek has recently indicated other reasons which he has subsequently come to regard as more decisive to account for his initial reactions to the *General Theory*. When the *General Theory* appeared in 1936 Hayek was already at work on his *Pure Theory of Capital*, which was intended to demolish all belief in the dependence of employment on aggregate demand. This work took longer than he had expected and the second part, in which he had planned a definite refutation of all final demand theories, was never written, as he had turned his attention to other matters. Furthermore, by the end of the second world war, Hayek believed that he and Keynes would be on the same side in the fight against inflation.[12]

The debate between Hayek and Keynes is not only of historical interest. In the light of our experience in recent years during which we have seen, as most economists now agree, some grave weaknesses in the Keynesian system, it does appear that the astonishing, almost unanimous acceptance of its assumptions owed more than was desirable to a preoccupation with the contemporary scene. The fact of unemployment led to a somewhat uncritical acceptance of Keynes' theories. Today, when a much greater scepticism prevails as to the beneficence or wisdom of government, such ideas would undoubtedly be scrutinised more closely. If it is true that Keynes has been a major influence on the course of economics and politics since 1945, it is interesting to speculate on what difference it would have made if Hayek's warnings had been heeded at an earlier stage. Whether, if this had happened, the 'sum total of human happiness' would have been greater or less is only a matter for guesswork, but one thing does seem fairly certain; that we might have been spared such high rates of inflation and all the consequences which have flowed from them.

Mises' attitude to Keynes and Keynesianism was made only too clear in an essay entitled 'Stones into bread, the Keynesian miracle', first published in 1948,[13] in which he showed his quite passionate disapproval of the whole of Keynesian theory and implied throughout that the (by then) widespread acceptance of Keynesian ideas owed more to Keynes' sparkling wit and 'cheap rhetorical tricks' than to logic. The multitude of Keynes' disciples, including Samuelson, who were by then portraying the opposition as old-fashioned, are soundly rebuked by Mises for their over-susceptibility and abandonment of their critical powers. Although this essay is full of sharp and perceptive criticisms it is perhaps somewhat marred by a tendency to over-earnest reactions as shown by the author's failure to be even slightly amused by Keynes' Cambridge-reared sense of humour.

Mises' attitude to macroeconomics derives first from his basic opposition to holism – that is, that the macroeconomic approach looks upon the 'nation' as if it were a single unit. In fact, the nation is a quite arbitrary segment of the market economy. Although within a nation the actions of millions of individuals are coordinated through market processes, there is no justification for regarding these individual actions as the result of the 'operation of one macroeconomic magnitude upon another such magnitude' (Mises, 1962).[14] Secondly, he contrasts the relationship between the macro/micro distinction as found in physics with that of economics. In physics the study of 'microscopic' systems at the atomic level is seen as the field of proper study for the attainment of knowledge about the fundamental forces governing the behaviour of aggregates (molecules). The transition in physical study from molecule to atom (from macro to micro) is seen as progress; but in economics the reverse holds; the move to macroeconomics from microeconomics has been regarded as an improvement (ibid., p. 84). Thirdly, Mises is critical of national income accounting, and the political implications of the concept. The idea of national income implies that there is something over and above the activities of individuals which changes the quantities of goods available.

This mysterious something produces a quantity called 'national income', and then a second process 'distributes' this quantity among the various individuals. The political meaning of this method is obvious. (ibid., p. 85)

The political danger of national income accounting is that it provides a justification for the Marxian idea that goods are 'socially' produced and then 'appropriated' by individuals. This is to put things upside down. Mises proclaims his firm belief that production is the outcome of individuals' voluntary co-operation and that the resulting 'distribution' is simply explained as being a reflection of the perceived value to others of each individual's contribution (ibid., p. 86).

The whole basis of the macroeconomic approach is yet another example of what Hayek has described as the fallacy of 'conceptual realism' which the philosopher A.N. Whitehead has referred to as the 'fallacy of misplaced concreteness'. Macroeconomic aggregates such as national income, in other words, should not be regarded as things we can recognise through our senses such as flowers or light rays, they do not stand for definite things in a concrete sense but for *patterns* in which different things may be related to each other (Hayek, 1952, pp. 95–7).

Lachmann has developed his own particular critique of macroeconomics based on Mises–Hayek methodological principles. He has in particular stressed two points: the way in which macroeconomic aggregates 'seem to lead a life of their own'; and the dubiousness of the assumption that output and income flows can in reality be objectively measured. The difficulty with measurement is that ultimately all such measurement is dependent on subjective valuation by individuals (Lachmann, 1976). Lachmann is not convinced that there are any real signs of enlightenment among economists in general, in spite of recent acknowledgements that macro variables have micro foundations and that the latter must be understood.[15] Lachmann has also attacked both of two prominent and rival schools of economics, the Cambridge and the neoclassical, for something they have in common; what he has described as the method of 'macro-formalism' – 'a style of thought according to which abstract entities are treated as though they were real' (Lachmann, 1973). The 'Cambridge School' refers to that group of economists in Cambridge, England, which includes Professor Joan Robinson, who have developed their ideas under the influence of the original theories of Piero Sraffa; they have the support of a substantial number of economists, including those who find Marx's economics convincing. Although the New Cambridge School's theories have wider implications, the feature of their teachings which is of immediate relevance is that they wish to repudiate subjectivism and regard marginal utility theory as an unfortunate diversion from the correct path. It is not surprising, therefore, to find Cambridge (England) quite at home with macroeconomic aggregates, the objective measurability of which causes them no problems. Although Joan Robinson has claimed that the Cambridge School is neo-Keynesian, this claim is weakened by a good deal of evidence which seems to show Keynes himself as very much alive to the ultimately subjective nature of economic behaviour; this surely follows from his stress on the uncertainty of expectations of the future. 'The outstanding fact is the extreme precariousness of the basis of knowledge on which our estimates of prospective yield have to be made' (Keynes, 1973, p. 149). Where expectations are uncertain, they are going to differ greatly as between individuals; and Shackle has more than once stressed Keynes' fundamental subjectivism.[16] The Cambridge School's conclusions on capital theory have damaging implications for the neoclassical theory of production and a controversy has continued for two decades between the rival protagonists, (Cambridge, England *v.* Cambridge, Massachusetts). But although Austrians find themselves on the neoclassical 'side' in the argument, the latter are regarded (e.g. by Lachmann), as being equally hopelessly out of touch with the foundations of economic analysis, in that they too, embrace the style of 'macroeconomic formalism'.

In the two presidential addresses reprinted in the same edition of *The Economic Journal* March 1972 (see Chapter 2, notes 10 and 11) neither of the two eminent speakers, although amazingly critical of much of current economic methodology, seemed to show any scepticism towards economic aggregation as it has been practised since the *General Theory.*[17] But for the Austrians this is one of the main areas of economic theory in which illusion persists:

Precisely because it has divorced itself from the central proposition relating to human behaviour, modern macroeconomic theory is really no theory at all. It has evolved, and remains, a set of models for the workings of economic aggregates, models that have little predictive value. (Buchanan, 1979, p. 121)

One of the most pernicious results of the use of macroeconomic aggregates, in the Austrian view, has been the growth of pretensions to measure social welfare and not only to measure it, but to manipulate 'the economy' in ways which will maximise it.[18] This aspect is referred to in Chapter 7.

In this chapter the fundamentals of the Austrian view of

macroeconomics in general have been set out, but the different applications of macroeconomics, such as the business cycle, growth, inflation and the rest, automatically come under suspicion as 'unsound', from the Austrian point of view. If the methodological foundation is faulty then its application to any particular topic might be seen almost as futile or at least yielding misleading predictions. Nevertheless, some of these applications are now of such widespread interest and importance that we shall consider, in what follows, a few of these 'macro' topics and the neo-Austrian position with regard to them.

When considering these topics, the relevant Austrian methodological preferences and their application should be kept in mind. These are, first, the scepticism concerning the usefulness of holistic magnitudes; secondly, the idea that there exists a national income to be 'distributed'; and thirdly, the difficulty in measuring quantities which are subjectively determined (note Keynes's own sympathy for subjectivism). The macroeconomic models which are constructed from aggregates have been described by Austrians as having little predictive power, but this is surely overstating the position. Some forecasts have been reasonably accurate, considering the nature of the data, although others, it cannot be denied, have been misleading and have resulted in wrong policies being followed.

NOTES

1. There is now, for example, a whole genre of books to be read which juxtapose in their titles, 'Keynesian', 'Crisis', 'Economics', 'What's Wrong' and the like, in various combinations, e.g. Hicks (1974), Buchanan and Wagner (1978). The focus of criticism is usually Keynesianism. 'If there is a crisis in economic theory, it is a crisis in Keynesian economic theory. Most economists, even Keynesians, seem to agree that there are at least some defects in this theory' (Mark. H. Wiles, in Bell and Kristol, 1981). Some economists however regard all the current criticism as a sign of a healthy discipline.
2 .It has been pointed out, for example, that Keynes himself was aware of certain dangers and drew attention to the famous statement attributed to Lenin that the best way to destroy capitalism is to debauch the currency: 'it will be largely due to

Keynes' influence if this prescription is followed' (Hayek, 1967, p. 347).

3. Evidently Keynes was well aware of the inflation danger involved in the injudicious application of his policy prescriptions as interpreted by his disciples, but was characteristically quite confident that if the situation got out of hand he would again be able to swing public opinion round to support appropriate corrective measures, just as he had done before the war. Unfortunately, by the time the situation had become potentially dangerous, he was dead (Hayek, 1967, p. 348).

4. The term 'Keynesianism' is used here to designate all those developments in macroeconomic theory and policy attributable to the disciples of Keynes, although the latter, were he alive today one suspects, might well have wished to declare himself not a 'Keynesian', just as Karl Marx is reported on one occasion to have declared himself no Marxist. Apparently Keynes did say something of this sort. (See E.A.G. Robinson, 'J.M. Keynes: economist, author, statesman', *Economic Journal*, June 1972, p. 541.)

5. For the Austrian view on money, see Chapter 12.

6. For other critics of Keynes, see Hazlitt (ed.) (1960).

7. F.A. Hayek, 'Reflections on the pure theory of money of Mr. J.M. Keynes', *Economica*, Part I, 11, 1931; Part II, 12, 1932.

8. Shackle, for example, in his first published work, and written only two years after his first graduation, contributed a thoughtful essay to the debate in 'Some notes on monetary theories of the trade cycle', *Review of Economic Studies*, October 1933, pp. 27–38.

9. Keynes complained of Hayek that he 'evidently has a passion which leads him to pick on me, but I am left wondering what this passion is', and described Hayek's *Prices and Production* as 'one of the most frightful muddles I have ever read'. See *The Collected Writings of J.M. Keynes*, vol. XIII, 1973 edn, London: Macmillan, pp. 243–66. This book also contains the interesting correspondence which ensued between Hayek and Keynes.

10. It is possible that too much has been read into the term 'general'. E.A.G. Robinson thinks that Keynes would have 'hated to be judged, as he so frequently is . . . as if he had sought to write an economic bible, to serve as the verbally inspired truth for all time' (Robinson, op. cit., p. 539).

11. D. Patinkin, *Money, Interest and Prices*, 2nd edn, 1965; J. Tobin, *The New Economics One Decade Older* (1974).

12. I am grateful to Professor Hayek for the foregoing clarification of his position (in correspondence October 1982).

13. The title of this essay is a reference to a report written by Keynes in 1943, in which he extols the virtues of credit expansion as being able to perform the 'miracle . . . of turning a stone into bread'. Mises' general tone in this essay is not merely one of disagreement but one of quite violent denunciation, not only of Keynesian theory but of Keynes' particular style of exposition. His disciples are accused of name-calling as a substitute for reasoned discussion. A second essay by Mises followed in 1950 in which he prophesied that Keynesianism would result not in the turning of stone into bread but in the not at all miraculous procedure of eating the seed corn ('Lord Keynes and Say's Law'). Both essays are reprinted in Hazlitt (1960).

14. Hayek had also frequently pointed out that averages and aggregates cannot conceivably be regarded as acting upon one another, e.g. (1931b), pp. 3–5. See also Ramsey (1977).

15. This was written by Lachmann before the publication of recent work, such as that of Weintraub, *Microfoundations* (1979).

16. See, for example, Shackle (1967), p. 130, and (1972), chapter 37.

17. The pattern of gloomy presidential thoughts on the state of economics was cheerily broken by D. MacDougall. See 'In praise of economics,' *Economic Journal*, December 1974.

18. Keynes makes a rather significant comment in the Preface to the German edition of the *General Theory*:

the theory of output as a whole, which is what the following book purports to provide, is much more easily adapted to the conditions of a totalitarian state, than is the theory of production and distribution of a given output produced under conditions of free competition and a measure of laissez-faire. (*General Theory*, 1973 edn, p. xxvi)

This, of course, is the very thing about Keynes' theory which particularly worries Austrians. Whether Keynes is meaning in this extract to praise totalitarianism for its ability to implement his theory is not clear, but it is difficult to believe that such was his intention.

11   The Business Cycle

1. DEFINITION

Although output of goods and services and living standards, have shown a rising trend during the period since the industrial revolution in many countries, such changes in economic activity have not proceeded along a smooth curve. For example, if we take the level of unemployment in countries such as Britain or the United States as a rough indicator of business activity in general over the period 1850 to 1914, the cyclical variations are quite noticeable and fairly regular, with a duration from peak to peak of between seven and ten years. Such regularity demands an explanation. Similar cyclical variations in other economic indicators, such as output, prices, exports, imports, saving and investment, are what we mean by the business or trade cycle.

2. HISTORICAL BACKGROUND

The first recognition and preliminary study of business cycles, coinciding significantly with the development of the factory system and the growth of commerce in the early nineteenth century, was apparently made by writers such as Tooke and Overstone, and especially by Malthus,[1] who appeared to realise, unlike most of their predecessors, the cyclical character of business fluctuations. J.S. Mill gave the subject considerable attention, but his thoughts are scattered over various parts of his *Principles*, and it is thus difficult to see in his work any concentrated and clear analysis of the cycle. Marx, of course, had a great deal to say on the subject and precisely what he intended to say has – and continues to be – the soil in which seemingly endless scholarly exegesis flourishes. Available space and a wish to move on to later developments render impossible anything but a brief and inadequate mention of Marx's theory of the business cycle and the interested reader is recommended to sample the now extensive literature on the subject.[2] Suffice it to say that Marx saw the business cycle as mainly a phase in the process which must end in the breakdown of the capitalist system and therefore, to him, the analysis of the cycle was subordinate to his main theme. Furthermore, implicit in Marx is the notion that there can be no question of taking counter-cyclical measures (cf. Keynes), since the cycle is inherent in the nature of capitalism; to get rid of booms and slumps, capitalism must first be replaced – by Marx's system.

3. KEYNES AND THE AUSTRIANS IN THE 1930s

A number of writers had offered explanations of the business cycle before the publication of the *General Theory* but there is no question but that Keynes is almost invariably given the overwhelming role in engineering, or influencing others so to engineer, the long period of 'full employment' following the second world war. His work is seen as the chief influence in causing governments of the post-war period to follow full employment policies. It is possible, it might be noted, that the long post-1945 boom which lasted until the 1970s might have occurred with minor modifications if the Keynesian revolution had never happened. Certainly, if that unprecedented period of full employment and growth was mainly because of Keynes' business cycle theory it would be a remarkable vindication of his famous dictum about the superiority of ideas in the shaping of men's actions. Professor R.C.O. Matthews has suggested[3] that various non-Keynesian factors which were in operation at that time may have been of greater importance in maintaining full employment. If there is any validity in his thesis, and there is some reason to think there is, then Keynes has been given too much credit for the post-war boom; but equally it follows that his ideas have been credited with too much blame for the rising tide of unemployment which began in the 1970s.[4] This would tend to weaken some of the recent critiques which seem at times to be blaming Keynes for most of our problems.

Between the two world wars, the business cycle, of course, took a novel and much nastier form than at any time during the Victorian period. Unemployment was chronically high and this led to much greater interest in the question among economists. Not only was there much more attention given by academics to discovering the causative process of boom and slump, but because of the obvious human misery resulting from unemployment it was natural to seek for remedies; something *ought* to be done about it.[5] Keynes contrasted the comparative blindness of orthodoxy to the true nature of the problem in the 1930s with the correct intuition of the mercantilists and even 'cranks' such as Major Douglas, whose under-consumption theories showed that 'he at least has not been wholly oblivious of the outstanding problem of our economic system' (*General Theory*, p. 371). Hayek remarked rather cuttingly that he found it no surprise 'that Mr. Keynes finds his views anticipated by the mercantilist writers and gifted amateurs: concern with the surface phenomena has always marked the first stages of the scientific approach to our subject' (1941, p. 409). It seemed to Keynes and his followers quite natural that governments were the only possible agents who could do anything about unemployment. It was around the question of the wisdom and even the validity of such intervention that much of the disagreement between Austrians and Keynesians revolved in the debates of the period.

The foundations of Austrian trade cycle theory lay in Mises' application of his theory of money to Wicksell's theory of cumulative expansion.[6] The essence of Wicksell's theory was that if the commercial banks keep the market rate of interest below its 'natural' level, there will be an increase in the demand for loans which will force up commodity prices. Wicksell asked the question: are there any built-in forces which will tend to push the interest rate up again and hence to put a brake on the credit expansion? He concluded that in a pure fiat system of money, the expansion could continue indefinitely. Mises was not satisfied with this and wanted to suggest reasons why the credit expansion would automatically be brought to a halt. In his *Theory of Money and Credit* (1912) he put forward a theory to explain how the process might work. It is interesting to note that Keynes credited Mises with being the first to introduce the distinction which Keynes had made between savings and invest-ment, and that Mises' theory was 'fairly close' to his own as set out in his *Treatise* (1930).[7] The importance of Mises' theory is that it was upon it that Hayek developed his theory of the trade cycle which has become almost synonymous with the neo-Austrian approach.

Mises' explanation is, in brief, as follows: he assumes first that following a lowering of interest rates by the banks, additional long-term investments become realisable by entrepreneurs; this lengthens the 'period of production'. Now no additional planned saving has occurred, but the investors (i.e. the entrepreneurs) are enabled, being armed with additional money borrowed from the banks, to bid resources from the consumer goods industries into the capital goods industries. This results in a rise in consumer goods prices in order to generate the 'forced savings' needed to finance capital goods creation. Further credit has to be sought by entrepreneurs in order to finance their raised resource costs. If this process continues without hindrance, as Wicksell had suggested, the eventual result is hyper-inflation and a collapse of the monetary system. But before this happened the banks would be impelled to restore equality between the natural and the money rate of interest with the consequence that capital projects would have to be abandoned and resources transferred to other parts of the economy. The essence of Mises' theory is that it predicts that only 'artificial' credit expansion is responsible for the business cycle. Without this the process is self-correcting by the operation of market forces:

it remains inexplicable how they [entrepreneurs] could go on in the absence of credit expansion. The striving after . . . additional investment raises the prices of the complementary factors of production and the rate of interest on the loan market. These effects would curb the expansionist tendencies very soon if there were no credit expansion. (Mises, 1949, p. 586)

All Mises' writings on the business cycle are pervaded by two central propositions. First, that cycles are a monetary phenomenon (all non-monetary explanations being futile), caused by interference with the natural rate of interest, and that government intervention cannot help; secondly, that the self-acclaimed freedom of socialist systems from depression is only achieved at the cost of complete loss of choice by citizens over the allocation of resources.

in a socialist economy it is only the government's value judgements that count. . . . A dictator does not bother about whether or not the masses approve of his decision concerning how much to devote to current consumption and how much for additional investment. (Mises, 1949, pp. 565–6)

Before proceeding to consider how Hayek developed Mises' theory we need a preliminary note on Hayek's particular view of the relation between money, credit, capital theory and cycles.[8] Many economists would treat these subjects separately and this plan, as far as possible, will be the approach we shall for convenience follow here, but Hayek's own view appears to be that the four subjects should be treated together. This is entirely logical given the nature of his cycle theory: starting with an increase in money through credit expansion, firms use the money to finance (mainly) capital goods. This changes the capital structure and this may result in booms and slumps.

Although the debate on capital theory was of long standing, it was to some extent eclipsed by the novelty of Keynes' ideas. But Hayek synthesised the Austrian theory of capital and the business cycle in order to show that rising consumption must, after a certain point, reduce rather than increase the level of investment. This produced what Hayek called the 'Ricardo effect' and what Kaldor called the 'concertina effect' (i.e. that the length of the period of production falls in the upswing and increases in the downswing).[9]

In the 1920s, Hayek had already shown the future direction of his thinking and also a certain ability to make accurate prophecies, in articles in German. In these he opposed the orthodox view that the stability of prices in the USA would ensure the continuation of the boom. He detected a significant expansion of credit leading to over-investment which would eventually force a painful readjustment. (Some account is given in Chapter 10 of the prolonged controversies surrounding the ideas of Keynes which engaged the attention of Hayek and others in the 1930s.)

Theories of business cycles may be divided into two types: those which seek their explanations in 'real' forces, such as changes in technology, investment, or the state of business expectations; and those which rest on variations in monetary phenomena. Hayek's theory is, to some extent, a hybrid of the two.[10] The first thing which at first sight appears rather curious, or even perverse, is that Hayek begins by assuming full employment (this, at a time in the early 1930s when unemployment was unprecedentedly high). It may have been this single fact more than anything else which was the cause of the 'bad press' which his ideas subsequently received and why, by contrast, Keynes' *General Theory*, which started from an assumption of unemployment, appeared the right message for the times. The explanation given by Hayek for his assumption (in *Prices and Production*, 1931 edn) is that he is enquiring into the 'immediate' causes of variations in industrial output as a preliminary to understanding the influence of prices on the amount of goods produced. He rejects the idea of explaining variations of production simply by changes in the amount of factors employed, because although he accepts that bringing unemployed resources into use will undoubtedly increase output, the existence of such unused resources is not a necessary condition for an increase in output: 'The existence of such unused resources is itself a fact which needs explanation' (1935, p. 34). A further advantage of the assumption is that it enables him to direct attention to those changes in output brought about by changes in the structure of production – by a transition to more or less 'roundabout' methods of production: 'For, in my opinion, it is only by an analysis of this phenomenon that in the end we can show how a situation can be created in which it is temporarily impossible to employ all available resources' (ibid., p. 35). Hayek's theory also differs from the traditional quantity theory of money in that money is not regarded as neutral in its effects. Although it is accepted that a change in the quantity of money will affect prices, this is not the whole story: changes in the quantity of money also affect the structure of production. Furthermore, that even when prices are stable money can influence production.

The starting-point for Mises' theory (as derived from Wicksell)[11] was that the banks had the power to initiate a cumulative movement away from equilibrium by lowering the interest rate below the 'natural' rate (i.e. the rate that would ensure equality between saving and investment).[12] Hayek made two amendments to this (see Machlup, 1977, p. 19). First, the credit expansion need not originate from the banks; it could happen through the advent of novel opportunities for investment, e.g. changes in 'real' factors such as technology or expectations. As a result, the natural rate of interest would rise, but the banks would not have changed money rates. Secondly, Hayek's view was that price stability was not guaranteed even when money rates of interest were equal to natural rates. Suppose an economy is experiencing an increase in business activity: the rate of interest must fall if credit is to expand corresponding to the increase in activity, and this rate of interest will be less than that required to call forth the sufficient voluntary saving. A typical 'disturbance' following an expansion of money or credit might proceed as follows: the increase in the quantity of money will not be neutral, it will not simply affect the general level of prices; it will have different effects on successive stages of production. Suppose, for instance, there follows 'over-investment' in capital goods (i.e. investment exceeds savings). Sooner or later investment would have to fall unless bank credit continues to expand with accompanying inflation. Unemployment would follow in the capital goods industries.[13] It should be noticed that this process is almost the exact opposite of Keynesian theory in which the trade cycle is due to *under*-investment. Whether recessions are due to over- or under-investment is a question which can only be settled by empirical studies. What then, was Hayek's prescription for the 1930s unemployment? It really amounted to 'do nothing', and it is not surprising that in the turmoil of the times it found little favour, and that Keynes' theory of under-investment and under-consumption triumphed over Hayek's explanation.

However, Hayek's views on the trade cycle, in recent times, and with the collapse of the Keynesian system have begun to be seen in a somewhat different light: 'I suspect, indeed I confidently believe, that the most loyal followers of Keynesian views, if they now [writing in 1977] re-read Hayek's criticisms, would accept many of them partly or fully' (Machlup, 1977, p. 25). Hayek's reputation as a prophet has been enhanced by the traumatic failure of interventionism as seen in the events of the 1970s. The unemployment problem returned, accompanied surprisingly (to Keynesians) by inflation. Long before this Hayek wrote: 'Are we not even told that, "since in the long run we are all dead", policy should be guided entirely by short-run considerations? I fear that these believers in the principle of *après nous le déluge* may get what they bargained for sooner than they wish' (1941, p. 409). Sir John Hicks, who had gone over to the Keynesian 'side' from his LSE 'stronghold' of anti-Keynesianism by 1934, later on had second thoughts. Writing on Hayek's theory in 1967 he found it much more appropriate than Keynes' theory as an explanation of the inflationary conditions of our time. In such conditions Hicks found Keynes as irrelevant as Hayek was for the 1930s.

One aspect of Hayek's trade cycle theory is that he rejects price stabilisation as a policy aim. The idea that money affects prices and production only if the general price level changes, is called by Hayek the 'naive quantity theory'. This is based fundamentally on the Austrian mistrust of aggregates. Instead of looking at the 'general' price level they prefer to stress the fact that it matters where the money enters the system because this can affect *relative* prices. It may cause capital goods to rise in price relative to consumer goods, or vice versa, and it is these kinds of microeconomic changes which, in practice, determine people's behaviour, not macroeconomic aggregates. Even if prices are stable, if an economy is growing with accompanying increased business activity, then money supply must increase if price stability is to be maintained. This new money may then alter the structure of production with consequent 'disturbances'. The policy impli-cations of Hayek's theory are quite clear. In a depression it would be wrong to support investment as Keynes advocated – over-extension of credit and consequent investment were the cause of the problem. The depression must be allowed to run its course as any intervention would do more harm than good.

Some of the differences and misunderstandings between Hayek and Keynes owe something to the great differences in their temperaments. Hayek was painstakingly scholarly where Keynes was brilliantly intuitive. Evidently Hayek found Keynes puzzling from the beginning, to judge from some of his comments in a review of *A Treatise on Money*:[14] 'unusually difficult and important book'; 'The difficulty [between himself and Keynes] may be only that Mr. Keynes has made it so extraordinarily hard to follow his reasoning'; and 'countless obstacles which the author has put in the way of a full understanding'. Hayek complains of 'Mr. Keynes' choice of symbols which makes it particularly difficult to follow his algebra'.[15] In a later essay,[16] he has explained at some length both what he admired and what he disliked about Keynes' methods, and it is clear that he admired most Keynes' non-economic activities and skills: 'He was so many-sided that when one came to estimate him as a man it seemed almost irrelevant that one thought his economics to be both false and dangerous.'

Although, as we have noted, there was a substantial flow of letters and articles between the rival schools following the *Treatise*, in the *General Theory* Keynes does not take up cudgels directly, apart from a few passing references to Hayek's ideas, the most noteworthy of which is the claim that 'as a result of confusing the marginal efficiency of capital with the rate of interest, Professor von Mises and his disciples have got their conclusions exactly the wrong way round' (Keynes, 1973, p. 193). There is also a criticism of the Austrian concept of 'forced saving' (ibid., pp. 80–1).

4. THE DISSOLUTION OF THE KEYNESIAN CONSENSUS

Of what importance are these controversies for today? Keynesian economics left a legacy, first, of optimism concerning the power of governments to 'fine-tune' the economy so as to avoid a repetition of the 1930s. In academic economics, through Samuelson *et al.*'s synthesis, in which Keynesian theory was linked to the Marshallian neoclassical tradition, many loose ends seemed to be satisfactorily tied up. The Austrians, chiefly represented by Hayek, were derided as 'dinosaurs'. By the 1970s it was becoming obvious that both governments and many economists were beginning to pay for their hubris, and the works of Hayek (other than *The Road to Serfdom*, his only book to claim much attention) started to attract more notice. One can only observe that it might not have been altogether a bad thing if Hayek's essentially careful, subjectivist approach had been more influential in time to swing the consensus away from some of the worst of the policy-makers' illusions. Hicks pointed out that Keynes' victory was partly due to luck, as well as genius. The economic phenomena of the 1930s favoured Keynesianism 'because the working of the price-mechanism was largely suspended by Depression', and it was succeeded 'by the world of the 'forties which was Keynesian for quite another reason – because the price-mechanism was superseded by controls.'[17]

Of course, Hayek's was not the only dissenting Austrian voice in the Keynesian chorus; throughout the post-war period Lachmann had been a continual contributor to the Austrian view of the business cycle, and Shackle had constantly stressed, in his own unique way, that much of Keynes' theory depended on subjectivist assumptions – a fact which had conveniently been forgotten by his disciples. On business cycle theories in general Shackle has, among other things, pointed out their tendency to 'give men little credit for any capacity to learn from experience' (Shackle, 1972, p. 56).[18]

For a long time after the 1930s a powerful and widespread belief was that the deficiencies of capitalism had been responsible for the Great Depression. Government intervention, therefore, was the only possible corrective. Only in the last decade or so, in the face of 'stagflation', has the Keynesian consensus become shaken to its foundations with the proliferation of disturbing new ideas: Friedmanite monetarism; the rise and fall of the Phillips curve; the post-Keynesians; the revisions of Clower and Patinkin; the New Cambridge School; the rational expectations theorists; and of course the Marxists. (The latters' beliefs were, like those of the Austrians, based on some fundamental axioms about the nature of the human situation, and were even older in their origins.)

This chapter has mainly relied upon Hayek's theory as representative of the modern Austrian position,[19] and reasons of space have precluded any detailed account of the ways in which other members of the Austrian school vary in their views. Other Austrians, such as Rothbard, should be consulted for confirmation of the assumption that Hayek is fairly representative (see e.g. Rothbard, 1962, pp. 854–77). The only noticeable difference in approach is that Rothbard believes governments, through their power to expand bank credit, to be the sole cause of cyclical movements in the economy.

NOTES

1. Keynes expressed admiration for the perceptiveness of Malthus 'the first of the Cambridge economists' (*Essays in Biography*, p. 101).
2. See, for example, H. Smith, 'Marx and the trade cycle', *Review of Economic Studies*, June 1937; and R.M. Goodwin, 'A growth cycle', in C.H. Feinstein (ed.), *Capitalism and Economic Growth* (1967) Cambridge: Cambridge University Press, pp. 54–8.
3. R.C.O. Matthews, 'Why has Britain had full employment since the war?', *Economic Journal*, September 1968. Sadly, events have rather upset a confident prediction in this essay, namely that low unemployment, as well as not being wholly explained by Keynesian policies, 'can confidently be expected to persist' (p. 568); not that Professor Matthews was alone in believing this at the time.
4. Much neo-Austrian criticism is directed at Keynes' policy suggestions for dealing with unemployment as themselves a major cause of the ultimate inflation and consequent unemployment.
5. It has since become something of an article of faith among Keynesians that both the neoclassical and Austrian schools were so blinded by their belief in the efficacy of the market that they paid little attention to the real problems of the period until Keynes came along to shake them up.
6. See Moss (1976), pp. 36–8.
7. Ibid., p. 10, for this and other aspects of Keynes' initial reaction to Mises' theory.
8. For a concise account of Hayek's business cycle theory which explicitly adopts the principle of showing the connections between the four subjects, see Machlup (1977), pp. 16–24.
9. See Hayek (1978c), pp. 165–78; and Blaug (1968), pp. 543–9 for a full summary.
10. The Hayek theory of the business cycle will be regarded in this account as representative of the modern Austrian school in general. It is drawn largely from Hayek (1933; 1935).
11. Characteristically, Hayek gave generous credit to Wicksell, to whom there are twenty-five page references in the *Pure Theory of Capital*.
12. The 'loanable funds' theory of the role of interest rates is a major aspect of the classical theory which was on the defensive following Keynes' totally different explanation.

13. Hayek's analysis of the origin of trade depression, curiously enough, resembles that of Marx, although his policy recommendations are almost completely opposed (see Karl Kühne, *Economics and Marxism* (1979), London: Macmillan. Hayek himself admitted that his analysis of the trade cycle strongly resembled Marx's analysis in the 1949 edition of *Prices and Production* (p. 103).
14. F.A. Hayek, 'Reflections on the pure theory of money of Mr. Keynes', *Economica*, August 1931.
15. In a letter to Keynes, H.O. Meredith, then Professor of Economics at Belfast, expresses his surprise at Hayek's complaints concerning Keynes' algebra: 'I am no mathematician, but I can find, so far as the *algebra* goes, it's easily explained to a pass class' (J.M. Keynes, vol. XIII, pp. 266–7) Actually, Hayek's difficulty was the symbols chosen, not their relationships.
16. Hayek (1978c). pp. 283–9.
17. See Streissler (1969), p. 248. In this essay Streissler argues that Hayek's ideas had more relevance for growth theory than for the trade cycle.
18. Compare Shackle's view that men learn from experience with the now increasingly fashionable 'rational expectations' hypothesis.
19. An excellent detailed analysis of Austrian cycle theory is O'Driscoll (1978), chapters 4 and 5.

12 Money and Inflation

1. WHAT IS MONEY?

For almost anyone under the age of forty-five, personal experience of a period of stable or falling prices would be, in most cases, a great novelty. Inflation, or generally rising prices, has been the rule in many parts of the world since about 1939. All schools of thought are agreed that changes in the absolute level[1] of prices have something to do with money, even though there exists wide disagreement on the precise role of money in the causal chain of events leading to inflationary conditions, or even on how the latter should be defined.

Although elementary textbooks make a tidy list of the functions we should expect of money – a medium of exchange, a store of value, and a unit of account – and this seems to serve, as far as the ordinary business of life is concerned, the question is evidently not so simple, to judge from more sophisticated enquiries into the nature of money. The trouble is that although we can easily characterise money in this way, it is more difficult to lay down rules to govern what things in the real world should be assumed to have these characteristics. In practice, there are many financial assets which perform similar functions and there appears to be no clear-cut basis in conventional theory for distinguishing between monetary and non-monetary financial assets. One of the main examples of disagreement, for example, is whether time deposits in banks should be considered as money. If such deposits are included, what of things like building society deposits? In practice, conventions are adopted, such as the British M_1, the narrow definition of money (notes and coin outside the banks plus sterling current account deposits of UK private-sector residents with the banking sector, and deposits at call or placed overnight). But from the point of view of modern economic theorists definitions by themselves are not of much value; what they insist upon is a theory of monetary phenomena.[2] This is important for the success of a central authority's monetary policy: for instance, whether the volume of credit will move in the same direction as a given change in the money supply.

2. ORIGINS OF MONEY

The foundations of the Austrian view were laid down by Carl Menger using the praxeological method which traces all phenomena back to the actions of individuals. It has sometimes been argued that money could only have come about through state intervention, but the Austrian view is that even if it could be shown that 'one day, rulers or citizens assembled in convention were suddenly struck by the inspiration that it would be a good idea to exchange indirectly and through the intermediary of a commonly used medium of exchange',[3] this is merely an incomplete explanation. Money was an unintentional outcome of the actions of individuals who discovered that indirect exchange was superior to barter and that commodity which would exchange for most other commodities became money; money is the most marketable of all goods. The alternative explanation of the origin of money – that it was invented and given its value by the authority of the state – implies that governments must control money as a necessary part of economic policy. It is an easy step from this to the assumption that governments should have a monopoly of the supply of money; this carries with it the strong possibility that governments will abuse their privilege by over-producing paper money, and this has been the case in many different countries as the historical record plainly shows.

The earlier Austrians such as Menger and Mises, although agreed on the origins, left unsettled some questions on exactly what should be counted as money. One way of defining it is to try to ascertain those financial assets which correlate most closely with movements in national income or some other variable for which statistics are available, such as wealth. The trouble with such statistical correlation approaches is that the two magnitudes which correlate most closely might not be the most interesting or useful and may also be question-begging.[4]

Rothbard has suggested some clear criteria which might be used in defining money and which, although not all modern Austrians would agree on, clear away some of the conceptual difficulties.[5] In the case of demand deposits there is no problem for Austrians even if the deposits are only fractionally backed by cash. If the public regard them as cash, then they are. The usual objection to including savings deposits in the money supply is that they are not redeemable on demand. This objection fails because a depositor thinks of them as cash. The fact that they cannot be used directly for payment (not chequable) is also an objection which Rothbard considers to be without substance: 'even within the stock of standard i.e. notes and coins money, some part of one's cash will be traded more actively or directly than others'. Some of it may be kept under the floorboards. A commonly held view is that there is no hard line to be drawn between money and other liquid assets such as Treasury Bills (i.e. 'credit instruments'). Rothbard rejects this approach; the fact that Treasury Bills can easily be sold cannot be a reason for counting them as money – 'blue chip' stocks can likewise be easily sold, yet no one would include them in the money supply. Thus Rothbard's definition of money is all 'entities' which are redeemable on demand in 'standard cash' at a fixed rate. This includes total cash (cash in banks plus demand deposits); total savings in commercial and savings banks; time deposits at current redemption rates; total policy reserves of life insurance companies and savings bonds at current rates of redemption. This list, whilst being broader than M_1 avoids the inclusion of all liquid assets, thus avoiding blurring the distinction between money and other commodities.

3. THE DEMAND FOR MONEY

Mises' explanation of an individual's demand for money[6] is that it depends on his estimate of its purchasing power in the market in terms of 'yesterday's' prices. The money we are referring to here is fiat or paper money which has no other use, unlike gold, for example, which can be made into jewellery. Each individual has to decide how much of his wealth to hold in the form of 'useless' cash, and must therefore estimate the marginal utility of money or its exchange-value; he must therefore have some idea of the purchasing power of money in order to determine how much cash to hold. But the purchasing power of money is itself dependent to a large extent on the size of the cash balances individuals decide to hold. There is thus the problem of 'circularity'. This problem does not arise with a commodity such as bread because the marginal utility of bread depends on the physical nature of bread and its power to satisfy wants. But pure money has no value other than its ability to purchase goods. This characteristic may, however, be shared by any goods bought with a view to later re-sale, such as antiques or stamps, so that, the distinction between money and other goods may have been exaggerated (Moss, 1976, p. 19). Mises' view that the demand for money is based on its purchasing power depends on knowing 'yesterday's' prices, seems to go against a basic principle of the Austrian school (cf. Menger), namely that prices depend on an assessment of the future not the past. Moss (ibid., p. 21) argues that Mises' view is 'quite mistaken', and cites Patinkin's demonstration of the possibility of deriving a demand curve for money without involving past price behaviour. But Moss manages to reconcile Mises' view with Patinkin's since both assume that the demand for money is really a disguised demand for a certain number of units of purchasing power.

The most obvious distinction between Mises' explanation of the demand for money and the Keynesian theory lies in the concept of liquidity preference. Although it seems fairly obvious that an individual's cash balance is paid for by the interest he forgoes, Mises appears not to have recognised the full significance of this to judge by the little importance he attaches to the speculative demand for money. Not only that, but he regarded the idea of linking this speculative demand to the rate of interest on bonds as leading to dangerous confusions. People would 'confound the notions of money and capital and believe that increasing the quantity of money could lower the interest rate lastingly' (Mises, 1949, p. 403).

4. THE MEANING OF INFLATION

Although the term 'inflation' was once used principally only within the covers of economics books, it is now on everyone's lips and most people know what it means. This is not the place to go into all the different definitions and kinds of inflation, but a few brief points must be made. 'Too much money chasing too few goods' is the most often heard definition, and one that misleads. More accurate would be 'too much expenditure chasing too little output'. The point is that money not being spent cannot exert any upward pressure on prices. Inflation could exist without rising prices because of price controls – this is known as 'suppressed' inflation. At the other extreme is hyperinflation when money becomes entirely worthless. For present purposes, we shall define inflation as a process in which all prices are rising over a sustained period of time with the corollary that a unit of currency is buying less and less of the same commodities, i.e. money is losing its value.

5. EFFECTS OF INFLATION

Some of the effects of inflation are well known: that debtors gain and creditors lose; that an inflationary country's exports become uncompetitive; and that wealth is redistributed in a purely arbitrary way. Most economists have viewed inflation as a phenomenon to be avoided, though a few argue that a 'bit' of inflation can be beneficial. The Austrian view is that this is a dangerous fallacy.

There are some effects of inflation which are not so widely recognised as those mentioned. First, a fundamental function of a price system, as Hayek has often emphasised, is the transmission of information through the structure of relative prices.[7] But with inflation, the 'noise' of the general rise in absolute prices drowns out this information effect and the market system's efficiency is thereby impaired; if the inflation becomes very volatile and rapid the whole system will break down. Another effect which, in the long run, is equally harmful is that continuous inflation has the same effect as the confiscation of the assets of individuals by the government. 'By a continuing process of inflation, governments can confiscate, secretly and unobserved, an important part of the wealth of their citizens.' This was written by Keynes in 1920.[8] There is some irony in this, for there are some reasons for regarding Keynes' policy prescriptions as being one of the chief causes of the inflation of the past forty years, even though Keynes himself may not have approved the use made of his advice.

6. A GENERAL VIEW OF AUSTRIAN MONETARY THEORY[9]

Austrians agree with the Chicago school ('the monetarists') that it is monetary policy that is the cause of inflation and nothing else. Mises, for example, had a great fear of the consequences of the money-creating power of modern governments and even saw it as a great threat to democracy.[10] Austrians also agree with the Friedmanites on the effect of trying to reduce unemployment below the 'equilibrium' level: that the result will be ever-accelerating inflation. The difference between Austrian and Friedmanite monetarism stems from the former's insistence on micro foundations. The Austrian view is that, for example, an increase in money is not uniform in its effects on production, this extra money will raise incomes in those sectors where it first enters the system, thus changing 'artificially' the allocation of resources between sectors. Those sectors in which the demand for factors of production (e.g. labour) has fallen will suffer unemployment, and attempts to reduce this unemployment through further injections of money will produce chronically accelerating inflation.

There are some indications that recent developments in macro theory are now influenced by certain aspects of Austrian theory. For example, a large amount of work has now been done on the theoretical and empirical aspects of rational expectations theory,[11] with which the names of Professors Lucas, Sargent and Wallace are chiefly associated. In its simplest form, RE theory suggests that any systematic macroeconomic policy measures will be anticipated. 'The dominant post-Keynesian macro theories are susceptible to RE critique, which restated somewhat loosely, argue that policy makers cannot fool all the people all the time, certainly not with the same policy' (O'Driscoll, 1979). One implication of RE theory which tends to support the Austrian emphasis on the importance of the micro effects of any government policy is that not taking account of the differential effect of money expansion upon relative prices overlooks the possibility that market agents may not be able to distinguish between changes in demand which are confined to certain industries, and changes in demand due to aggregate demand changes (the latter 'drown out' the former). If expectations about the future course of prices are subject to 'learning' by market participants as RE theory implies, then it is predicted that interventionist monetary policies, are unlikely to succeed, unless the authorities behave in a random and unpredictable manner (Burton, op. cit., p. 22). No Austrian has suggested that governments should behave in this way, but the conclusion tends to support their general suspicion of the power of governments to act beneficially.

To conclude this account of Austrian monetarism the ideas and policy suggestions of Hayek will now be summarised.[12]

It is sometimes said that it was only after the publication of the *General Theory* that 'Keynesian'-type thinking appeared. It has been pointed out by Hutchison (1968), that several university economists had opposed the 'Treasury view' that it was impossible to create very much additional employment by state borrowing. (e.g. Pigou in 1908 and Robertson and Hawtrey in 1929, as well as Keynes himself), but there were few voices warning of the dangers ahead apart from Hayek although, as we have already noted, Keynes was not himself unaware of the dangers. In his essay *How to Pay for the War* (1940) he wrote of the possibilities of strong trade unions 'hustling someone out of the queue if they were to demand wage increases to compensate them for every increase in the cost of living'.

Hayek's analysis of the impact of inflation is that it shifts the structure of production, and in particular shifts the structure of relative prices in favour of capital goods of long gestation periods. The production process becomes lengthened artificially, that is, into a pattern which is not a true reflection of the real underlying preferences, resources and knowledge of market participants. This cannot continue without accelerating inflation, to sustain the new artificially-induced pattern. In the absence of such a force-fed acceleration of inflation there will be a painful readjustment involving unemployment. The recession is the price which must be paid for the subsequent correction of the dislocation caused by inflation.

Commenting on Hayek's theory, evolved in the 1930s, the authors of *The Consequences of Mr. Keynes* (1978) (London: IEA) point out that, while it was the case that Hayek's excessive expansion began in the capital goods industries, today, now that politicians' power to increase spending has increased so much, the increased spending could be directed anywhere in the economy, e.g. to public services and spending in a marginal constituency is by no means unknown. But the resulting dislocation would be similar wherever the money first entered the system. A further implication of Hayek's theory is that if output and employment are made dependent on inflation, as the economy gets used to a particular rate of inflation, this rate must be constantly increased in order to avoid recession.

7. AUSTRIAN POLICY RECOMMENDATIONS

Anyone looking for magic touches like the 'fine-tuning', which for a time after the second world war appeared attractive, should look elsewhere than to the Austrian school. Since most of the trouble is the result of past government action of various kinds, the Austrians tend to be pessimistic concerning any good which might emerge from positive government policies. Their general advice is along the lines that governments should avoid over-confidence. To those many people who have deeply absorbed the idea that governments are not only more capable but generally more benign than capitalists, the Austrian view on policy seems disappointing, if not immoral. The idea that governments should strive to do less, not more, strikes many people as unacceptable and is often criticised as 'harking back to the nineteenth century'. This shows a touching and old-fashioned belief that new ideas must be better than old ones.[13] The Austrian policy prescriptions, therefore, tend largely to consist of things governments should avoid doing. Prices and incomes policies, for example, are thought to be harmful in their effects; price controls will produce the usually associated phenomena of queueing, or other methods of rationing out the excess demand, and eventually some more formal rationing scheme is likely to be introduced. Prices will now no longer be able to adjust so as to reflect changing preferences and technology and because the process is self-accelerating: 'the transition to a centrally directed economy seems inevitable' (Hayek, 1978a, p. 116).

Hayek had put his finger on what he regarded as a weak point in the Keynesian system in an article written in 1958.[14] Although he had expressed similar views in previous writing, it should be recalled that the late 1950s was still a time of considerable optimism with regard to the power of governments to manage the trick of full employment without inflation; at this time Hayek was apparently backing a lost cause. The Keynesian proposition which he attacked was the assumption (which had been so influential since 1939) that it is impossible to reduce the wages of labour in general without causing unemployment; thus, if wages have become too high to be consistent with full employment, the necessary adjustment must be made by reducing the value of money. 'A society which accepts this is bound for a continuous process of inflation' (ibid., p. 295). The result of Keynesianism is obscured by the fact that it works with aggregates (in this case, the general wage level) whereas the result predicted by Hayek is based on thinking in terms of relative wages of different groups of workers. Relative wages are bound to change as the economy changes its pattern of production activities.

But if the money wages of no important group is to fall, the adjustment of the relative position must be brought about exclusively by raising all other money wages. The effect must be a continuous rise in the level of money wages greater than the rise of real wages, i.e. inflation. (ibid., p. 296)

Hayek rejects incomes policies for similar reasons to those for which he rejects price controls. Because of the growing menace of inflation, incomes policies of various types (voluntary and statutory) were tried in quick succession by the 1960s. What most had in common was that they worked more or less while the policy was in force, but were followed by a surge of money wages. For example, the record for the last three incomes policies in Britain between 1972 and 1979 is that before each was imposed money wages were growing at rates of 20–30 per cent; during the time they were in force there was a sharp fall in these rates; and when they ceased, wages continued to rise at much the same rate as before (see IEA, 1983, p. 38). All had the common feature that they tended to 'freeze' relative wages; in other words they did not look into the microeconomic structure of wages, and they distorted the allocative function of the market.

Austrians would say that only freely-operating market forces are able to adjust relativities in accordance with reality, but there are still eminent post-Keynesians who retain faith in some non-market method of operating an incomes policy so as to avoid its worst consequences: 'At the micro-level it [an incomes policy] would lead to an explicit discussion of income distribution, "fairness", differentials and the like'.[15] However, this economist also declared that free collective bargaining had made life too easy for the unions, 'enabling them to make claims without saying who gets less if they get more', and adding that the cry 'the capitalists will pay' is no longer true (ibid.). The root of the problem of inflation, as seen by Austrians, lies in the wider context of fallacious notions of what governments are capable of, fostered so much by Keynesian aggregative theories. The acceptances of Keynes' proposition that real wages are 'sticky downward' has meant the acceptance of a rigid structure of relative wages so that no wage could ever be lowered (in money terms). This had the consequence that total money expenditure had to be raised sufficiently to make it possible for the whole supply of labour to be employed at whatever wage rate prevailed. Thus the trade unions were absolved from responsibility for any unemployment which would have arisen in the absence of the expansionary monetary policy. There is much evidence that unemployment can always be *temporarily* reduced by monetary expansion but this politically easy way out ends up with the need for ever greater doses of inflation. The reason for this is that if there is only a modest rate of inflation it comes to be expected and loses its stimulating power; thus the rate needs to be increased.[16] One effect of inflation is that any misallocation of labour between industries is preserved; some firms which manage to stay solvent would have failed without the inflation.

Although the Austrians agree in some respects with the monetarists in the matter of reducing the money supply, they regard as an illusion 'The idea that maladjustments in the allocation of resources and *relative* prices can be cured by a manipulation of the *total* quantity of money is at the root of most of our difficulties' (Hayek, 1978a,

p. 118). A market economy cannot work properly if relative wages are not determined by market forces. The chief obstacle to this is trade union monopoly – unless this problem is tackled a monetary policy is not enough. It does not come from the side of money, and an over-reliance on monetarist aggregates merely diverts attention from the underlying problems. Of course, monetary policy, if wrong, may itself become one of the problems, but by itself it cannot do much about those which come from other sources. So far as trade unions are concerned, apart from measures such as removing any legal privileges which support their monopoly in a particular industry, Hayek has tentatively suggested, surprisingly, the introduction of profit-sharing, ensuring that workers would share in the output of growing industries (1978a, p. 117). This represents almost a complete reversal of his view on profit-sharing some years before, when among various objections he spoke of the danger in giving the corporation (firm) increasing power over the employee (1967, p. 302). Even his later view includes the warning that it raises many difficult problems and that it is 'only mentioned to indicate the need to consider more radical changes than have yet been contemplated' (ibid.).

A suggestion of Hayek's which at first sight seems a contradiction of his general belief in free markets is that foreign exchange rates should be fixed, i.e. that governments should undertake to maintain fixed rates between trading countries (Hayek, 1975). Because governments cannot be trusted to control inflation by limiting the money supply, there is a strong temptation for them, if rates are freely floating (i.e. determined by market forces), to let the value of the currency drift downwards with the consequence that the balance of payments will not suffer. A free exchange system thus allows governments a way through which they can avoid the penalty of their domestic irresponsibility. But if rates are fixed, the deterioration of the balance of payments, with the consequent drain of foreign currency and gold reserves, will act as a discipline on governments. Writing in 1977, Trevithick thought that there were preferable methods of bringing governments to heel such as the proposals for a legally enforceable framework in which all government control over the money supply is completely eliminated. He also suggested that Hayek had underestimated the public hostility to both domestic inflation and the depreciation of the currency (Trevithick, 1977, pp. 116–17). The mild public response to the downward drift of the pound sterling compared to the constant grumbling about inflation since 1977 would surely go against this view.

The fact that the nub of the inflation problem is seen by many as deriving from the aim of maintaining full employment by governments and of their power to increase the money supply in pursuit of that aim, has naturally brought forth suggestions as to ways in which a government's power could be limited. For example Rowley and Peacock (1975) suggested that all government control over the money supply could be eliminated by the creation of a legally enforceable framework; and Peter Jay (*The Times*, 15 April 1976), who proposed the setting-up of a Currency Commission which would be empowered to control the growth of the money supply within specified limits related to the growth of productive potential. Schemes such as these, however, are not as radical, nor as controversial, as Hayek's proposal that the government monopoly of the supply of money should be broken. To understand this proposal to 'denationalise' money requires the removal of ingrained habits. The immediate reaction is to recoil in horror at the prospect of several competing currencies circulating, but this in itself might be an improvement on government monopoly, 'which without exception has been abused in order to defraud and deceive the citizens' (1982, III, p. 57). One objection to the idea is that governments are needed to 'protect' the currency, but the chief threat to a currency is from the government itself.[17] Another popular bogy with politicians is the exporters of money (capital) who are no threat to the citizenry only to the government in its attempts to provide dishonest money. The whole of the assumption that there must, within a particular territory, be only one uniform medium of exchange is, argues Hayek, a state of affairs which has arisen from the assumption of totally unjustified powers by rulers. The technical details of Hayek's proposals are set out in two *Institute of Economic Affairs* pamphlets[18] and referred to more briefly in Hayek (1982, III). One possible criticism of Hayek's denationalisation proposals is that because the central bank is banker to the government it would be difficult to displace it by encouraging competition among private banks to decide which particular bank should carry out the banking business of the government. It would be difficult to lay down criteria for the government to decide how to allocate its business between banks. (It is not obvious why this differs in principle from the awarding of other government contracts.)

A more fundamental criticism, which undercuts Hayek's strong approval of institutions which have arisen spontaneously – 'the result of human action rather than human design' – is to argue that the monopoly of money by governments is, as a matter of historical record, the result of such a spontaneous process.[19] Support for the logic of Hayek's proposals is given in an essay by Richard E.

Wagner[20] who argues that macroeconomic discoordination is a predictable result of the pursuit of self-interest by politicians, which is made possible by the monopoly over money enjoyed by governments. This monopoly has been the cause of the inherent expansionary bias. If money were neutral in its effects it would not affect the allocative mechanism, but if the Austrian view of fluctuations is correct, money is not neutral, and, as explained above, an inflation-induced boom initiated by government credit expansion, contains the seeds of its own reversal into depression and unemployment. Although governments' monopoly of money grew up slowly, and possibly may be regarded as an outcome of spontaneous action, the Keynesian revolution is seen by Austrians as having conferred on the practice an invulnerable sanctity. This, according to Hayek, has had the effect of blinkering a whole generation of economists to the true nature of the problem:

One of our chief problems will be to protect our money against those economists who will continue to offer their quack remedies, the short-term effectiveness of which will continue to ensure them popularity. It will survive among blind doctrinaires who have always been convinced that they have the key to salvation. (Hayek, 1978c, p. 221)

The extent to which Keynesianism has rendered Hayekian ideas apparently unworthy of much consideration is indicated if we choose at random some recent writing on inflation. From a selection of *Readings* (Harmondsworth: Penguin, 1969), *Inflation*, Hayek is not even mentioned; in Flemming (1976) there is a similar gap; and in a very comprehensive survey by Laidler and Parkin (1975), which provides an extensive bibliography with commentaries, apart from a brief reference to Hayek's *Monetary Theory and the Trade Cycle* (1933), and a nod in the direction of Shackle's emphasis on the importance of uncertainty, no reference is made to Austrian ideas on inflation.[21]

To sum up: the Austrian explanation of inflation is derived from methodological individualism, distrust of macroeconomic aggregation which ignores microeconomic foundations, and a disbelief in governments' 'pretence of knowledge'. From the Austrian point of view trying to 'mop up' unemployment through government-initiated credit expansion is to compound the worst errors of 'constructivism' (Hayek, 1978c, pp. 3–22). In the dominant current theories of inflation, according to the Austrians, much of the error is derived from over-attention to the absolute level of prices when what matters is the structure of relative prices. Both post-Keynesians and

Friedmanites concentrate on the effect of money supply changes on a price index. But this index is calculated historically (i.e. it is made up of an average of prices which are known); the acting individual, however, is motivated by his judgement of the changes in the prices of particular goods which precede the formation of the price index. Individual price changes determine production and employment. When prices change because of monetary change the underlying real determinants of prices (i.e. market supply and demand, which are ultimately subjectively derived) may not have moved in the same direction. The consequent readjustments following such upsets cause unemployment.[22] In the usual textbook analysis of inflation and economic policy the economy is regarded as if it were a balloon: 'Blow and the economy[23] expands; suck and it contracts.' A more realistic simile would be that the economy is like a complex system of interlocking prices and sub-systems such that changes made at one point will transmit effects throughout the system, but with varying time delays. No one person will be able to apprehend the entire apparatus, quite unlike the case of the balloon.

Once the damage caused by past inflation becomes visible in terms of increased unemployment, the best way back to economic health, as advocated by the Austrians, is by the 'fast lane' i.e. to achieve price stability by appropriate reduction of the money supply as quickly as possible, even if this means very high levels of unemployment. Hayek thinks that even a high level of unemployment (e.g. 20 per cent) is feasible for six months but that a level of, say, 10 per cent for three years would end in the defeat of the governing party at the polls. (Friedman, by contrast, has advocated a much more gradual deceleration.) Also, in the Austrian view, it is not sufficient simply to get inflation down to a low annual rate; the beneficial effects only become evident when inflation is down to a zero rate. There is then a good prospect of a new upturn: 'The boom may even come very quickly.'[24]

Those who, in a period of inflation-induced unemployment, beg for more 'reflation' by the government are seen by Austrians as being like a patient who begs a doctor for more of the medicine which caused his illness. The idea that governments have a choice between curbing inflation or reducing the level of unemployment is seen by Austrians as completely confused. The record tends to confirm this view. During the last thirty years both the rates of inflation and unemployment have been on a long-run rising trend. Whether or not inflation caused the unemployment is a matter for dispute but what does seem certain is that it is possible, and indeed highly probable, that rising inflation will, in the long term, be associated with rising unemployment. There are, however, at the time of writing, no clear signs that a falling inflation rate will result in falling unemployment. Hayek's view is that a zero rate of inflation should be the aim; only then is there a good prospect of a new upturn.

Unfortunately, the long-term prospects of governments restraining their power to inflate are not promising. Politicians have always tended to abuse their monopoly of the creation of money. This may be seen simply as one further example among many which tends to undermine the idea that governments are endowed with some kind of benevolence which distinguishes them from capitalist entrepreneurs.[25]

NOTES

1. A change in the absolute level of prices means that the value of a unit of currency has fallen in terms of the 'basket' of goods, which can be exchanged for it. A change in relative prices is possible in an exchange economy in the absence of money. In practice, a consumer considering price changes in particular goods cannot easily directly distinguish between the two kinds of price change.
2. For amplification of this point see, e.g., the Introduction to R.W. Clower (ed.), *Monetary Theory* (1969), Harmondsworth: Penguin. For an example of this way of defining money, see Morris (1979), p. 341.
3. Mises (1949), p. 407.
4. See L.B. Yeager, 'Essential properties of the medium of exchange', *Kyklos*, vol. 21, no. 1, 1968, 45–68.
5. See Rothbard, 'Austrian definitions of the supply of money', in Spadaro (1978); and 'The Austrian theory of money', in Dolan (1976).
6. See Mises (1934), and (1949), pp. 401–5.
7. Cantillon, in the eighteenth century, had shown his awareness of the fact that the effect of an increase in the quantity of money depends on how the money enters the economy. He grasped that the structure of prices will alter (See Blaug, 1968, p. 22).
8. J.M. Keynes, *The Economic Consequences of the Peace* (1919), *Collected Writings*, vol. II. On the 'taxation' element in inflation, see Rothbard (1962), pp. 875–6.

9. For a comparison of the different aspects of monetarism, see J. Burton, 'The varieties of monetarism and the policy implications', *Three Banks Review*, June 1982.

10. See Mises (1934), pp. 435–57.

11. The rational expectations hypothesis was originally suggested by J.F. Muth ('Rational expectations and the theory of price movements', *Econometrica*, 1961). For an analysis of RE and its connection with Austrian views, see O'Driscoll (1979), pp. 153–76; also D. Laidler, *Monetarist Perspectives* (1982), Oxford: Philip Alan.

12. An excellent summary of Hayek's long critique of Keynesianism and its inflationary dangers is *A Tiger by the Tail*, 2nd edn, 1978, comp. and ed. Sudha R. Shenoy, IEA. See also Hayek (1960) chapter 21.

13. In this context how curious it is that Marxism (of nineteenth-century origin) enjoys such widespread support.

14. F.A. Hayek, 'Inflation resulting from the downward inflexibility of wages' (1967), pp. 295–9.

15. Professor Maurice Peston, *Catch 76* (1976), London: IEA, p. 40.

16. This, of course, is a point of agreement between Chicago monetarists and Austrians.

17. See Hayek (1982, III), p. 58, for his account of how government monopoly has developed historically and why governments cannot be trusted not to abuse their power.

18. *Choice in Currency* and *The Denationalisation of Money* (both London: IEA, 1976).

19. Both these criticisms are contained in a paper given by T. Congdon in Oxford, April 1981, read to a conference on 'Liberty and Markets', sponsored by the Liberty Fund. ('A critique of Hayek's proposal for the denationalisation of money'.)

20. Richard E. Wagner, 'Comment, politics, monetary control, and economic performance', in Rizzo (1979).

21. See R.J. Ball and Peter Doyle, *Inflation* (1969), Harmondsworth: Penguin; John Flemming, *Inflation* (1976), London: Oxford University Press; D.E.W. Laidler and J.M. Parkin, 'Inflation – a survey', *Economic Journal*, December 1975, pp. 741–805. It should perhaps be pointed out that in a later work Laidler has recognised the rational expectations approach as being influenced by the neo-Austrian school (see Laidler, 1982).

22. For a detailed exposition of this Austrian theory, see O'Driscoll

and Shenoy, 'Inflation, recession, stagflation' in Dolan (1976),
   pp. 185–211.
23. The very notion that there is some entity called *the* economy is, of
   course, regarded by Austrians as a typical holistic fallacy.
24. See 'Friedrich Hayek on the crisis', *Encounter* May 1983, in which
   he gives his opinion on the Thatcher and Reagan governments'
   economic policies.
25. See H. Geoffrey Brennan and James M. Buchanan, *Monopoly in
   Money and Inflation* (1981), London: IEA, Hobart Paper 88. This
   study considers how conditions might be created which would
   remove a government's monopoly of money creation.

13   The State

Generally speaking, economists do not enquire too closely into the nature of the state although they are quite used to speaking of policy-makers or about economic theories which have this or that policy implication. They also tend to divide into two categories: those who accept, and even regard quite favourably, an active positive role for the state in a society, and those who think that the state should be confined to a role similar to that of a referee. Underlying such attitudes may be unspoken ideas about the nature of the state. We must hasten to add that, of course, what now follows can only be a mere glance at a subject of ancient lineage and enormous extent, the sole purpose of such a glance being to form a reasonably sound basis from which to discuss the relationship between the state and the economy, and in particular the basis of the neo-Austrian attitude to such matters. One reason for this is that in the various discussions which go on, concerning what might roughly be described as public policy, the speaker's fundamental concept of what a state consists of is commonly not made explicit, though disagreements concerning policy may sometimes boil down to underlying and quite marked differences of view on what a state is. Economists, in general, quite naturally leave the study of political philosophy to political philosophers and there are good reasons for this, given the extent of the subject, but if we are to make some sense of the evident presuppositions of economists and politicians it is necessary at least to set out, if only in outline, some possible theories of the state. To take a simple example, which illustrates how fundamental views on the nature of the state may show through, there is the interesting contrast between people considering how a government might act in regard to some problem, such as, urban decay. One person might say 'what *we* should do . . .', whilst another will put this as 'what *they* should do. . .'. Too much should not be made of this – the distinction could turn out to be trivial; but it could reflect a quite deep division between the speakers as to the very nature of the state.

In the neoclassical economics textbooks there is usually very little said on the theory of the state; it is simply taken for granted that it exists and that it may or may not be the best agent for achieving given ends in the economic sphere. It is customary for economists to look upon the state as a sort of tool for tackling certain economic 'problems' such as arise in connection with economic efficiency, or social justice. This can lead to unnoticed but implied shifts in underlying presumptions concerning the nature of the state. For example, the view went almost entirely unchallenged, until recently, that civil servants and politicians could, in various ways, act in a kind of god-like disinterested manner to set right some of the imperfections of the market, and it was implied that, unlike businessmen, they could act without self-interest.[1] The disinclination of orthodox economists to mix any political philosophy with their economics is not without exceptions. Milton Friedman, for example, in spite of his positive approach to economic theory, has not let this prevent him from having strong views on the subject of the state. At the other end of the spectrum, political economy has become more common as a subject of study in higher education, though the presumptions which it carries with it concerning the nature of the state are often only too explicit and committed to a statist stance. And, of course, Hayek is an outstanding example of an economist who has ventured far into the realm of political philosophy. But usually the neoclassical textbook will have sections with headings such as 'Macroeconomic Policy' which do not pretend to ask whether there should be a policy, who should carry it out or whether non-economic factors might render a given policy proposed by an economist totally unrealisable.

Two fundamentally different theories have been proposed concerning the nature of the state. One is that the state is 'natural' and superior to the individual; the other that the state is artificial and whose only value lies in the capacity to serve the individual. The idea that the state is 'natural' and that it takes precedence over the individual has been described as the 'organic' view; the opposite view, it has been suggested, might be described as the 'mechanical' hypothesis,[2] or the 'machine theory'. The terms 'collectivist' and 'individualist' have also been used to distinguish the two concepts, but they at once tend to raise the prospect of partisanship for one or the other view, much more so than do 'organic' and 'machine theory'.

The usefulness of these descriptions is that they suggest the important distinction between the concept of the state as something for which man exists and its opposite – that the state exists to serve the purposes of man.

The organic state theory envisages the state as being not merely as real as but *more* real than are the individuals who live within its bounds. It follows that the state has a real, unified interest in its own right; the individual is subordinate to the state. Furthermore, in assessing whether a particular state is just or unjust, happy or unhappy, it is entirely consistent with the organic theory to assert that the happiness of a whole society is not merely the sum of the different degrees of happiness of its members. The general interest of a community is not necessarily, therefore, simply the sum of the interests of its members; there is a higher interest, that of the state. State is sometimes misleadingly translated as society, and so we hear phrases such as 'the interests of society' used in the context of claiming that some overriding of individual interests is justified.

No one, today, will need reminding of what a useful idea this becomes for a government which wishes to exterminate its political opponents. It is thus easy to see the repellent consequences of the organic theory and ultimately the preference for a particular type of state is a moral question, but there are also logical difficulties for this theory. For example, why should the state be *the* supreme kind of organised human community. The organic theory of the state would regard all organisations within a state, such as trade unions, as inferior, in the sense that the individual's loyalty is to the state. This view is, of course, quite arbitrary and is defeated by the question: why should my superior loyalty not be to the United Nations or the human race? Also, although there are difficult questions concerning the place of individual conscience in any conceivable type of state, the organic theory simply ignores the problem. Pushed to the limit, in the 'machine' view, if it is held that the individual takes precedence over the state, then it becomes something of a problem to support any ultimate authority as residing in the state; the individual conscience must be the final arbiter of any conflict between the state and the individual. In the organic theory this difficult and important practical question is simply assumed out of existence.

The origin of the organic theory is to be found in the work of Plato whose 'criterion of morality is the interest of the state' which Karl Popper has described as 'the collectivist, the tribal, the totalitarian theory of morality' (1945, vol. I, p. 107). Aristotle adopted this belief, although critical of it. Rousseau's conception of the 'General Will' in the eighteenth century also owes much to the organic concept of the state: i.e. the idea that the state embodies the will of the community as a whole; and history since Rousseau's time abounds with examples of the use made of this concept by tyrants who claimed to know the nature of the General Will. In the philosopher Hegel we have the full flowering of the concept of the state as superior to the individual. In order to give some idea of his idolatry with regard to the state it seems worth quoting some examples: 'The State is the Divine Idea as it exists on earth'; 'The State is the march of God through the world'; 'The State must be comprehended as an organism'; 'The State . . . exists for its own sake.'[3] It is only too easy to dismiss this as mythical, grandiose speculation which is best ignored, yet it came to influence, for good and bad, all manner of political and social philosophy in the nineteenth century. The most obvious influence was on Karl Marx, but although he accepted Hegel's dialectic and his historicism he did not accept Hegel's idealisation of the state.[4] The anti-liberal bias of Hegel's political philosophy is, however, plain to see.

The 'machine theory' of the state may be sub-divided into two varieties: the state may be seen either as the product of consent or of force. But whichever it is, it involves this fundamental distinction: unlike the organic theory it regards individuals and the state as separate entities, and that the state is created by humans, it did not, in some mysterious way, just happen. Since individuals are the component parts of society, then it follows that in the machine theory there is also a clear distinction between the state and society. Today, there is some danger that this distinction may sometimes become blurred, and if we start speaking of the 'good of society' it is easy to slip into endowing the state with knowing what that good consists of; then we are back with the organic theory. An important element in this theory, especially for our present purpose, is that it contains no assumption that the state is the embodiment of some common purpose; the only time this might be true would be in time of war.

The machine theory includes all manner of states which may have arisen by different methods. It is thought likely that the origin of the state was an outcome of the need for wider organisations which could lay down rules as mankind became settled in agricultural communities.[5] The theory of democracy is that the state governs only with the consent of individuals – a social contract theory. The individual agrees to obey the state up to carefully defined limits as prescribed by the law to which the state itself is also subject. The 'force' theory of the state is that states arose from the use made of the state machine by a ruling class or élite. Marx's view was that the state serves the purposes of the possessors of economic power (the bourgeoisie at the time he was writing); this is not same as an organic theory, since the state, in these circumstances, has no rights against the individual. The Marxist revolution would substitute one ruling class for another and would still be a state based on force, although this is envisaged as a transitory phase before true socialism. Finally, two very important distinctions should be noticed between the state and most other human organisations. Membership of a state is not voluntary and the state is the only organisation which is empowered lawfully to use force which may find its expression in various of its agencies – police, armed forces, prisons, for example.

2. AUSTRIANS ON THE STATE

Austrian economists, to a much greater extent than the neoclassical school, have given prominence to their view of the nature of the state and its relationship with the individual. This has been largely a side-effect of their preference for free markets as allocative systems, but also it has a connection with their basic belief in the superior morality of individualism over collectivism. Also, although Austrians would wish to keep state power and activity closely limited, they differ as to precisely where these limits should be.

The Austrian view of the state has much in common with that of classical nineteenth-century liberalism, although in this, as in other areas, there are disagreements on the extent to which the state should use its powers of coercion. Mises and Hayek tend to be of the same mind, though the latter has supported, more than Mises, the idea of state action to redistribute income. Some critics see Hayek's position in this regard as rather ambiguous. The Rothbard wing of neo-Austrianism is more anarchistically libertarian than the Mises–Hayek position.

Mises' position is mainly the traditional liberal view of the state as a machine preferably regulated by democratic majority rule. The state has a monopoly of 'violent action' and is essentially for the purpose of preserving 'peaceful inter-human relations' (1949, p. 149). Democracy is seen by Mises as 'the very means of preventing revolutions and civil wars' (ibid., p. 150). Although he sees as desirable the Platonic ideal that the 'best fitted' should rule,[6] Mises accepts the possibility that the majority may prefer 'unworthy office-seekers'; this must be accepted as part of the price of liberty and he would not seek to change the choice of the democratic electorate other than by persuasion. In this connection Mises sees collectivists and universalists in all their varieties as being forced to rely upon 'theological' appeals rather than on peaceful rational persuasion. Any dictatorial minority must base its claim to power on some form of superhuman authority rather than upon the will of the majority. This external authority appears in various forms: divine right of kings, the historical destiny of the proletariat, the *Geist*[7] (Hegel) or *humanité* (Auguste Comte) (ibid., p. 151). Mises' objection to anarchy is that it overlooks the obvious fact that some people are 'either too narrow-minded or too weak' to grasp the benefits of free market 'social co-operation'. Even if there were no such individuals among the adult population there still remains the problem of the young, the old and the sick.[8] In general, Mises rejects anarchism on the grounds that the majority must be allowed to prevent, by the use of force if necessary, minorities from destroying the social order and accepts that this power is to be 'vested in the state or government' (ibid., p. 149). Thus, it is clear that Mises is fully in the tradition of liberal democracy and accepts the need for a powerful state, even though the extent of its powers should be severely limited. Mises points out the usefulness of the distinction in the English language expressed by the words 'government' and 'state'. The use of 'state' has been used in a mystical sense to legitimate dictatorial governments, although Mises accused Marxists of avoiding the term 'state' since it has an unpleasant sound to lovers of freedom and democracy, and substituting for it the word 'society' (1936, p. 129). For Mises the greatest danger to freedom comes from Utopians who wish to 'establish the perfect state of mankind' (1962, p. 95).[9]

Hayek's concept of the state is inseparable from his defence of individual liberty as a supreme good and his view of the rule of law. Throughout Hayek's work the predominant value is his concern for individual freedom against the encroachments of the collectivist state. This began in 1945 with the publication of *The Road to Serfdom*. This was the starting-point for more than thirty years' work in the field of law and social philosophy. Hayek's concept of freedom was developed in *The Constitution of Liberty* (1960) and followed by *Law, Legislation and Liberty* (3 vols 1973, 1976 and 1982). For the present we are only concerned to identify Hayek's view of the nature of the state; the discussion of further aspects of liberty is continued in Chapter 15. However, it must be noted here that for Hayek the supreme purpose of the state is the preservation of liberty, since liberty is the source of all other values.

Law in Hayek's view, is seen as older than law-making. Long

before the idea that law could be altered or invented there must have existed enforced rules of conduct which made possible peaceful existence in society. In early civilisation there was great respect accorded to 'law-givers' whose function was not to make new law but 'merely to state what law was and had always been' (1982, I, p. 81). This kind of law had developed quite spontaneously. 'It is no accident that we still use the same word "law" for the invariable rules which govern nature and for the rules which govern men's conduct' (ibid. p. 73). Thus Hayek sees the origin of law as organic and 'natural' but this does not lead him to view the state itself as organic – far from it. The modern idea that all law is the invention of a legislator is seen as 'an erroneous product of constructivist rationalism' (ibid). There is no distinguishable time in history when this idea of legal positivism first appeared, but there always existed the seeds from which it could grow. Rulers assumed the function of enforcing given laws and of organising defence against external enemies, and they found it advantageous to claim for these kind of administrative rules the same status as was accorded to those rules of conduct which had grown up spontaneously.

But as the concept came to be accepted in modern times that legislation is the sole source of law, two harmful side-effects followed. First, the belief that the power of the legislator should be unlimited, and secondly, that anything laid down by the legislator is law and only such action is law. This is, according to Hayek, not only logically fallacious but is the source of the chief threat to individual liberty by the state. For Hayek, the rule of law is a spontaneous creation which has evolved as an unintended consequence of human action. The idea which has developed in the twentieth century of the government's actions being judged according to some concept of benefits, such as Benthamite utilitarianism, is entirely different from Hayek's view, which is that such principles have been the chief determinant of the growth of collectivism, and the dangerous principle that it is a task of the state to organise 'social justice'. The best safeguard against the abuse of power by government is seen by Hayek as lying in some form of constitutionalism like the American system, in which the power of the legislature is circumscribed by overriding principles. A seemingly awkward fact for Hayek is that the US constitution was the product of deliberate design, a consciously-created, rational construction. He tries to escape from this dilemma (not entirely convincingly) by pointing out how much of the subsequent developments in the structure of American government were largely unforeseen – the results of historical accident (1960, p. 184).

Finally, in assessing Hayek's view of the rule of law, the position of the Anglo-American tradition of common law must be mentioned. As the 'rules of just conduct' (to use Hayek's phrase) developed spontaneously it became the task of the judges to 'find' the law. It is often said that such case law is 'judge-made'. This gives rather a superficial impression of the process. Hayek maintains that although the role of the common law judge is to decide between conflicting expectations in situations where there will be no known rules to guide him, he is still not free to decide in any way he likes; he must adjudicate between different views, one of which or even both may conflict with the requirements of an existing order. He thus may modify the law. This raises the question of the unpredictability of judicial rulings in the absence of codified, statute law and therefore European jurists have tended to favour codification. Hayek himself, in spite of nearly a lifetime of experience of this European tradition, came eventually to the opposite view. He does not rule out entirely the idea that legislation may be used to increase the certainty of the common law on occasions, but fears that the consequence of this practice if it becomes general is to require that '*only* what has been expressed in statutes should have the force of law' (1982, I, p. 116). The difference between the rules of just conduct which emerge from the judicial process, (the *nomos*[10] or law of liberty) and the rules laid down by a government lies in the fact that the former grow out of an unintentioned spontaneous order whilst the latter serve the needs of an organisation designed for specific purposes (ibid., p. 123). The second of these two kinds of rules is exemplified by the great structure governing the aims of social justice which we shall consider in Chapter 16. The essence of Hayek's view of the state is that it should, as far as possible, confine itself to the maintenance of institutions (such as the judiciary) and the rules governing their administration so as to safeguard the 'general rules of right behaviour' (*nomos*). Once, however, government-made law becomes the dominant form, we are well on 'the road to serfdom'.

Hayek's view of the state is fairly representative of the neo-Austrian School as a whole, but Rothbard takes a more uncompromising line. His views are set out at length in *Power and Market* and in 'The Anatomy of the State' (1974). Rothbard rejects entirely Aristotelian and Platonic concepts of the state as the embodiment of man's highest moral endeavours. This argument rests on the proposition that man is a social being and that therefore the state is a 'natural' institution through which man is able to fulfil his true nature. As Rothbard rightly points out this is no defence of the state since it first must be established that the state and 'society' are coextensive; the contention of libertarians is that the state is in fact an anti-social instrument (1970, p. 237). On the question of law, Rothbard, like Hayek, points to the existence of law, in the shape of common law, merchant law, etc. which preceded state legislation, and which grew out of voluntarily adopted rules of conduct.

The limitations of space forbid any extended exposition of Rothbard's views, therefore we shall concentrate on a brief summary of those aspects of his position which seem most interesting. A common rebuttal of the libertarian objection to coercion by the state is that 'we' *are* the government through the use of our democratic electoral system. But the state is not, like a club or a trade union, a voluntary association. It is that organisation which 'attempts to maintain a monopoly of the use of force . . . in a given territorial area' (1974, p. 70). The notion that in some mystical way the state is the 'human family' getting together to solve mutual problems is a fallacy. The state is seen as a legalised channel for the theft of private property which has first been created by the free market, thus the 'free market is anterior to the State' (ibid., p. 71). Once a state has become established, the problem of the ruling group is how to remain in power. One way, suggests Rothbard, is by using the intellectuals, who will mould the mass of opinion towards the idea that the state is good and wise. The intellectuals are 'bribed' by the state apparatus with a good income and prestige. One example of this was the alliance between the state and the intellectuals in nineteenth-century Berlin. Although many exceptions to this idea could probably be unearthed (Marx: Rothbard himself?), it does have the ring of truth about it and might well (partly at least) explain a number of modern phenomena, for example, the observable hostility of some teachers to commerce and their corresponding attraction to public service as vocations for their pupils. In the past, the union of Church (intellectuals) and state is an outstanding example of co-operation.

The hypothesis that the state is more interested in its own preservation than in the protection of its subjects may, says Rothbard, be tested by looking at its attitude to crimes against itself and comparing it with its attitude to crimes against the private citizen. For such crimes as counterfeiting money and tax evasion much greater energy is devoted to punishing the offender than is the case with, say, burglary or 'mugging' (ibid., p. 83).

Finally, Rothbard sees the recent development of public policy economics by enconomists such as Buchanan, Tullock and Downs as having 'taken a wrong turn'. The public policy economists have sought to get away from the idea of the state as it has hitherto been depicted in economic theory, as able to intervene wisely and with superior motives. They have wanted to analyse the state's role as simply an instrument of social action, like the market. Rothbard, however, regards government action and voluntary market action as diametric opposites (1970, p. vi–vii). Collectivists, of course, would agree with Rothbard but the difference is that, whereas the former tend to see the state as different from the market but beneficent, Rothbard sees it as different and almost wholly anti-social.

Free market critics of the state, it has often been suggested, apply double standards. They equate 'the state' with politicians and bureaucrats in order to divest the term of any suggestions of mystery and omniscience. It would be consistent therefore to equate the market with entrepreneurs and lawyers, 'the agents that liberal political economy regards as essential for upholding the market order'.[11] There is, indeed, a superficial correspondence between politicians and entrepreneurs on the one hand and bureaucrats and lawyers on the other hand, but the differences are greater than the similarities. The most important difference is that there exists no 'entity' operated by full-time agents called the 'market order' which has powers of coercion within a given territory. This is a holistic misconception. Also much of the work of lawyers arises from the needs of the state, not the market.

The Austrian view of the nature and functions of the state would confine it to the prime purpose of upholding the rule of law, ('the *general* rules of right behaviour'), what has been called the 'referee state', its use of coercion to be confined to the provision of true public goods including externalities. It should not be assumed that when the state acts, it reaches ideal solutions (e.g. as in the correction of externalities). Also there remains an important difference of principle between, for example, the collective voluntary cooperation of a private club or labour union, and collective action imposed by the state. This difference is, that a subject of a sovereign state cannot, so long as he chooses to live within its boundaries, decide not to join the 'club'. Ultimately, the state's power can be backed up by coercion and indeed must be. It is for this reason that the more libertarian 'wing' of the Austrian School, typically represented by Rothbard, regard recent studies designated 'the economics of politics', as obscuring this point. It cannot be denied that the power of lawful coercion resides in the state and that this distinguishes it from other collective organisations. Since this power is inevitable if there is to be any state at all, then the kind of analysis done by Buchanan and Tullock (see

Note 1) should be read by anyone who believes that the state is in some way free from the base motives often ascribed to capitalist entrepreneurs.

NOTES

1. Recently, economists such as Buchanan and Tullock, have used economic theory to analyse the actions of government. See, for example, James M. Buchanan *et al.*, *The Economics of Politics* (1978), London: IEA; and Gordon Tullock (1976), *The Vote Motive*, London: IEA.
2. See T.D. Weldon, *States and Morals* (1947), New York: McGraw-Hill, for a fuller exposition of the subject-matter in the text which follows.
3. Quotations from Hegel's *Philosophy of Law*, quoted in Popper (1945, p. 31).
4. The need to summarise Hegel's theory of the state in the present context omits a great deal. For a full introduction to Hegel, see George H. Sabine, *A History of Political Theory*, 3rd edn, 1951, London: Harrap, chapter XXX. For a withering critique of Hegel see Popper (1945, vol. 2). But see also a sympathetic study: Raymond Plant, *Hegel*, 2nd edn, 1983, Oxford: Basil Blackwell.
5. See Nozick (1974) for a profound analysis of political philosophy and one which includes a theory of how the state might have arisen in a 'state of nature'.
6. The dangers inherent in the Platonic ideal of the philosopher-king are, of course, recognised by Mises (1962, p. 95).
7. *Geist* is literally 'spirit'. Hegel conceived the state as the *spiritual* embodiment of a nation's will and destiny.
8. Actually Mises uses the term 'mentally sick' and expresses the surprising opinion that 'he who acts anti-socially should be considered mentally sick and in need of care' (op. cit., p. 149).
9. By far the most powerful critique of Utopianism is that of Karl Popper (1945). Curiously enough, Mises makes little reference to Popper in this context.
10. *Nomos* means 'usage' and is in contrast to *thesis* which may mean the adoption of given or made law. Hayek uses *nomos* to describe a 'universal rule of just conduct applying to an unknown number of future instances and equally to all persons'. In contrast, he uses

thesis to mean 'any rule which is applicable only to particular people or in the service of the ends of rulers' (*The Confusion of Language in Political Thought* (1968), London: IEA, p. 15). See also Hayek (1982), vol. I, pp. 94–145.

11. See Andrew Gamble, 'The free economy and the strong state', in *The Socialist Register* (1979), p. 24, n. 16.

14 Planning

In the desire to plan the economy we see an interesting fusion of holism, objectivism and historicism. The very word 'planning' suggests ordered procedures, predictability and rationality and it is a remarkable tribute to the unshakeable faith of its advocates that they continue to be apparently impervious to the lessons of experience.

Engels regarded the market as alien to man, 'imposed by nature and history' with man as the victim of *unplanned* forces. Only under socialism will 'the objective alien powers . . . *come under control*'.[1] It is to such visions that not only full-blooded socialism on the Soviet model owes its origins, but also the more diluted forms of collectivism which appear and vanish from the scene in the mixed economies of the West. The British experience since 1945 is instructive, with its successive blueprints meant to guide the various manifestations of the desire to plan. These have appeared under various names. (It is apparently thought prudent, by their advocates, to change the name each time, lest old memories be stirred of the disappointments consequent upon the failure of previous schemes.) In the aftermath of war the Labour government's planning was well-meaning, detailed and on the whole obstructive of a return to civilised existence. It was almost as if the general policy aim was to seek out the tender shoots of market forces springing from the dislocation of wartime controls and kill them off. The extent and idiocy of regulations was almost beyond belief.[2] Amazingly, it seems likely that there may be people who even now look back at the 1940s as a sort of golden age of planning.[3] Hayek's *The Road to Serfdom*, when it appeared in 1944, seemed a call to 'reaction' and away from the current starry-eyed faith in planning, and caused fury in 'certain circles'. Hayek, in his Preface to the 1976 edition of the book speaks of 'one well-known philosopher who shall be nameless [who] wrote to another to reproach him for having lauded this scandalous book.'

But it was not only convinced socialists who were anxious to plan. Sir Oliver Franks, for example, compared what had to be done in peacetime to what had been done by Churchill in 1940, and even to Stalin's Five Year Plans (Hutchison, 1968, p. 59). The West German policy of dismantling most of the controls was regarded as heretical by many economists. Such anti-Keynesian free market 'obsolete' philosophies would, it was predicted, have terrible consequences.

By the late 1950s and early 1960s, in spite of the fact that the West German economy had gone from strength to strength, the planners were still the loudest voices in Britain. Centralised controls on investment on the Soviet pattern were advocated, and Dr Kaldor thought that 'our economic strength [could be raised considerably] by a vigorous policy of economic planning'.[4] A recurrent theme in the planners' ambitions was the idea of reaching agreements on sharing out the 'national cake' and deciding targets for the growth of incomes and profits, etc. Thus we witnessed a series of 'national' plans, 'indicative' plans and whole new bureaucratic creations with grandiose titles such as the National Economic Development Council. Some of this ceaseless activity was partly on a microeconomic level, as exemplified by such bodies as the National Incomes Commission 1962, and the National Board for Prices and Incomes 1965. The finest flowering, in Britain, of the urge to plan was probably the setting up of the Ministry of Economic Affairs. Soon afterwards there emerged a National Plan[5] based on economic growth of 25 per cent between 1964 and 1970 and 'agreed' by both the TUC and the then Federation of British Industry. A common assumption of all these schemes was that there was a measurable entity called 'the economy' and a staggeringly armour-plated complacency concerning the ability of trade union leaders and the representatives of business to get their heads together and decide upon aggregate targets.

Even more numerous in these years than ambitious national plans was a bewildering variety of incomes policies, which (as was noted above) it was found necessary to call by different names, in order to allay scepticism. Some examples are the Macmillan Wage and Price Plateau, 1956; the Selwyn Lloyd Pay Pause, 1961–2; the Guiding Lights, 1963–6; the Wage Freeze, 1966–7; the Stages I, II and III 'Freezes', 1972–4; and the Social Contract, 1974–6. In spite of all these endeavours, or perhaps indirectly because of them, prices in the long run continued to rise, and average money wages continued to rise faster than prices. The chief effects of these policies, apart from a strong tendency to distort relative wages the longer they continued, was to slow down the growth of money wages when they were in force, only to be followed by an upsurge shortly after they ceased. One suggestion has been that the answer is to have a permanent incomes policy.[6]

Alongside these macroeconomics interventions, the relatively poor performance of British industry was the pretext for ambitious activity by the government on the microeconomic level. The Industrial Reorganisation Corporation (IRC) was set up in 1966 in the belief that market forces could not be relied upon to produce the desired structural changes in industry which 'could yield benefits to the whole economy' (sic). Why it was assumed that the IRC could know better than the market was not made clear. The National Enterprise Board (NEB) appeared in 1975 and had the avowed purpose, among other things, of engaging in 'direct, public initiatives',[7] that is, of supplying capital and assisting companies in financial difficulties. It also, like its predecessor the IRC, went in for promoting mergers. One problem with this aspect of its policy was that it came into conflict with another government creation, the Monopolies Commission, one of whose tasks was to spot mergers which were likely to result in monopolies 'against the public interest'.

2. THE FAILURES OF PLANNING

By the end of the 1970s most of the attempts at planning in the sense we have described had been unsuccessful and were being abandoned. The claim of government in all these ventures was that in some way (usually unspecified) it had access to knowledge which was unavailable to the thousands of individuals and firms within the country. It is the contention of Austrians that this is not the case and that the government is not only faced with the impossibility of gathering to one centre all the knowledge it *would* need, but that the necessary knowledge in all its thousands of varieties will quite simply not be generated otherwise than by freely-working markets.[8] A 'weaker' version of the case for government intervention is to argue that, although entrepreneurial expectations may well be subjective, the government can, through the use of fiscal policy, cause all firms to expand together; this would not imply that the government 'knows best'.[9] If fiscal policy includes items such as spending deficits by supporting particular industries and firms or transferring income from one group to another, Austrians would want to ask about the criteria being used. There is, of course, no intention to deny that planning is both sensible and necessary at many levels: firms, institutions, government departments, nationalised industries, families and individuals. But it is, allegedly, woolly thinking from an Austrian viewpoint to equate such units with the economy as a whole. Only some sort of slave economy could be planned in any meaningful sense.

3. THE AUSTRIAN CRITICS OF PLANNING

Mises saw the present age (writing in the third revised edition of *Human Action*, 1966) as one in which there is a 'passionate longing for government omnipotence' (p. 730). The interventionist, as Mises describes those attracted to planning, sees a sharp contrast between 'automatic forces' and 'conscious planning'. It seems obvious to such a mind that an attempt to plan consciously is much superior to its absence. This, says Mises, is a confusion; the issue is not 'automatism versus conscious action; it is autonomous action of each individual versus the exclusive action of the government' (1949, p. 731). An apparent virtue of planning, Mises points out, is that it appears more scientific than 'leaving things to the market; it appeals to our desire for handling problems rationally.' That this view is fallacious has been forcefully argued by Hayek in many of his writings.[10] Anyone who is not utterly fatalistic must plan his affairs and it is all the individual plans which may be good or bad, wise or foolish, which constitute the complexity of the open society. What central planners demand, however, is conscious direction, serving particular ends, of the whole society. The argument is not, therefore (as it is sometimes presented) between those who believe in planning and those who do not; no one in their right senses disputes the need for the best exercise of foresight. But the question is how will this best be done. Socialists have appropriated the word 'planning' to stand for central direction and organisation, with the unspoken implication that free markets are unplanned.

Throughout his work, Hayek has constantly stressed the fundamental difference between two kinds of law. While every law places restrictions on individual freedom to some extent, there is a distinction between the rule of law and arbitrary government. Under the rule of law, then, in the economic sphere, the government lays down rules in advance which decide the conditions under which resources may be used. Such formal rules guide people in general terms, without reference to particular circumstances. An example of this type of formal rule is the law which says that people should drive on one particular side of the road; it does not tell them where to go. Economic planning of the collectivist kind, however, involves something quite different – it must constantly decide questions which cannot be answered by formal principles alone, and which involve, for example, distinguishing quite arbitrarily between the needs of different groups of people. This is compared to ordering people which road to take rather than simply providing signposts for their general guidance. An apparent paradox is discernible in this. Under Hayek's rule of law principle the government confines itself to laying down general rules the effects of which it cannot foresee. To some this may appear less 'scientific' than the alternative (i.e. for government to be constantly alert to changing circumstances and laying down detailed regulations, the outcome of which it tries to predict). The paradox is resolved by going back once again to Hayek's concept of how knowledge of the economy is obtained. Only individuals faced with particular circumstances can possess such knowledge, and when these individuals use their knowledge they must be able to predict those actions of the state which may affect these plans (1944, p. 56). As planning becomes more extensive it becomes ever more necessary to leave the decision on particular cases to judges or, what is much more dangerous to freedom, to government officials. When Hayek was writing *The Road to Serfdom* in 1943 the greatest use of delegated legislation[11] had yet to be seen in the shape of the huge torrent produced by the Labour government elected in 1945. As such rules multiply, respect for the law becomes increasingly undermined. Undoubtedly one of the reasons for the fury with which 'certain circles' greeted *The Road to Serfdom* was that Hayek saw a connection between the decline of the rule of law in Germany and the rise of Hitler: 'a policy well advanced towards totalitarian planning had already done a great deal of the work which Hitler completed' (p. 58). It seemed inconceivable and monstrous to suggest to the builders of democratic socialism after the war that their wholly well-meant attempts at planning only good things could have anything to do with totalitarianism. Yet the multiplicity of wartime controls which became, if anything, more extensive with the peace, should surely have raised more doubts than they did among the faithful. Examples were everywhere to be seen of the effects which Hayek predicted, such as the flourishing 'black markets'.

The Road to Serfdom was largely concerned with the moral and political consequences of planning. By the time it was written the Austrians were satisfied that the argument over the economic efficiency of collectivist systems had been decided in their favour in the famous 'socialist calculation' debate[12] of the 1920s and 1930s. Thirty years later, Hayek, with evident exasperation, felt it necessary to lay the ghost of socialist calculation which had begun to appear in new forms. By the 1970s he was maintaining that apart from 'occasional flare-ups of old misunderstandings in lay circles, the efficiency argument for central economic planning has almost universally been abandoned' (1978c, p. 237). But although the 'new' advocates of planning accepted the argument against central direction on the grounds of efficiency, they still, as both British and American experience showed, continued to unveil a variety of schemes for national planning. The general obscurity of the aims of such proposals, Hayek maintained, was in itself 'the sure way to hell' (ibid., p. 238).

Some of the British examples of national planning have been referred to above. In the resumption of his critique of planning in 'The new confusion about "planning" ', 1976, Hayek used American examples, whose basic philosophy, in so far as one could be identified, was similar to those of Britain. Vagueness with regard to both the functions, and the likely benefits of their operations seemed to Hayek characteristic of all the proposals for Economic Planning Boards. Among the arguments for the proposed Balanced Growth and Economic Planning Act, 1975, popularly known as the Humphrey–Javits Bill, two varieties of planning could be distinguished. One was for the Planning Board to produce a kind of skeleton outline deciding the future distribution of resources as between industries. The hope was that individual firms would thereby be enabled to make better forecasts of those detailed pieces of knowledge which concerned them. Hayek saw this as a halfway house between a completely planned system and a free market ('the worst of all possible worlds') and a good example of how arbitrary decision-making by the government would introduce for the individual firm that very uncertainty which the 'Plan' was aiming to reduce. A second variety of planning which was advocated in the late 1960s both in America and Britain was 'indicative planning' following the French experiments of the early 1960s. The idea here was that the government would forecast targets at which industry should aim. Austrians saw quite clearly that this concept is utterly confused. There is no reason why the announcement of a target will cause the totals of output stated to be realised. And again, it contains the fallacious assumption that somehow the government possesses knowledge not available to individuals. This may, of course, be true in one sense. The government can collect data from individuals and publish aggregates, but it cannot have any sources of information other than what it receives from individuals, firms and other organisations within the economy, apart from those generated within the government machine itself.

A somewhat more favourable view of non-coercive planning is taken by Lachmann,[13] who compares it to gardening rather than to engineering, that is, cultivating the conditions which may assist economic growth rather than engineering growth by decree. Since the Austrian concept of market process stresses the role of knowledge dissemination it is difficult to see the objection to governments publishing data which increase knowledge, thereby informing individuals of one another's intentions. However there can be no certainty as to the effect of particular changes in the information available, at least not in the market as Austrians envisage it. There is no reason for assuming, for example, that all profit opportunities can be assessed objectively and the only judges of the 'efficiency' of particular courses of action are the individuals taking them; profit opportunities may be ignored for reasons known only to the individual.

4. THE TENDENCY FOR GOVERNMENT INTERVENTION TO ACCELERATE

The 'ratchet effect' whereby government intervention is difficult to reverse has received ample confirmation in recent times. In Britain, for example, in spite of the election of a radical Conservative government in 1979, up until 1983 the areas of government dominance in the economy have not been reduced to any marked extent.[14] Another tendency has been for private sector 'failures' to be the pretext for a further extension of collectivism. These market 'failures' have often largely been due to government interference or the threat of interference[15] in the first place, but the remedy has often been to prescribe more of the same medicine – further state control. Schumpeter spoke of price controls as facilitating the 'march into socialism'. 'The resultant frictions and deadlocks' would be blamed on private enterprise 'and used as arguments for further restrictions and regulations'.[16] Another influence tending to accelerate the growth of government control has been what has been called the nirvana[17] approach to questions of economic efficiency. Those who adopt this approach seek to discover discrepancies between a real market situation and some ideal which they have in their mind. When they find that the real is different from the ideal they conclude, first, that the former is inefficient, and secondly that some other arrangement such as one run by the government will inevitably perform better. The fallacies which underlie such arguments have been analysed by Harold Demsetz.[18] In the present context the most important fallacy is the assumption that the government will be able to improve on the market. The relevant choice should be based on a comparative institution approach in which the choice is not between the real and the ideal, but between which of alternative institutional arrangements is likely to be more satisfactory. It is the failure to adopt this approach which has led to the prevalence of blindness to the 'bad side' of intervention and the accompanying demands 'for ever more political controls such as employment laws, rent controls, incomes policies, and subsidies in all their infinite variety'. Austrians urge that as much attention be given to analysing the results of current and past interventions as is devoted to the analysis of 'market failure'.[19]

5. THE SOCIALIST CALCULATION DEBATE[20]

'Where there is no market there is no price system, and where there is no price system there can be no economic calculation' (Mises, 1936, p. 131). This statement contains the essence of the famous contention that socialism is 'impossible', which on the face of it sounds vague and unbelievable. Mises did not mean to deny the possibility of political institutions being created which would describe themselves as socialist. His point was in reference to the possibility of organising production and distribution in a centrally planned system *without private property*. 'Exchange relations in productive goods can only be established on the basis of private property in the means of production' (ibid., p. 132). Mises' critique first appeared in 1920 and years later caused Oskar Lange to admit that it had the effect of forcing socialists to recognise that there was a very real problem: how to carry out economic accounting in a socialist system. There then followed the famous 'debate'. Enrico Barone, in 1935, purported to show that the calculation problem could be solved. Assuming the necessary information was available, all appropriate equations existed for a solution. These were to be based on the possibility of a perfectly competitive Pareto welfare optimum. But both Barone and Pareto were very sceptical about the practicability of such a scheme. In 1938 Oskar Lange proposed a 'market socialism' model in which consumers would be free to choose and thus provide the 'guidance' to the central planning board as to what should be produced. As workers they would be free to choose between occupations. The pricing of final goods and factors of production was to be on the basis of equi-marginal rules which would ensure greater efficiency than under capitalism. The central planners would adjust prices by trial and error in response to observed shortages and surpluses. Abba Lerner contributed to the debate by showing how Lange's static model could incorporate a more dynamic element. All that remained was the problem of acquiring the necessary information and solving the equations. By the 1960s the increasing power of the computer coupled with linear programming techniques, could, it was suggested, provide all that might be required by a central planning board, not only to run a market socialist economy successfully, but to achieve greater efficiency than under capitalism. All these added up in the eyes of at least one economist to 'a final rebuttal of Mises';[21] this included Lange himself. All the modern Austrian arguments against the practicability of socialist central planning which will now be enumerated ultimately rest, it should be noticed, on their belief in subjectivism.

The setting of prices according to marginal principles would, claim the proponents of market socialism, achieve a Pareto optimum – a state not achievable under capitalism. The ideal condition of economic efficiency, neoclassical equilibrium with perfect competition in all sectors of the economy, would now be feasible. Hayek has shown clearly how great is the contrast between this view of competition and the Austrian view.[22] Competition is a dynamic process which is assumed away in the neoclassical perfectly competitive states. In such a state there would be no economic problem; there is nothing for human agents to do; all the problems of the real world are swept away: the world of constantly changing knowledge, expectations and opportunities, in short, *disequilibrium*. The advocates of market socialism argued that disequilibrium effects would be countered by trial-and-error price adjustments (iterative methods). Mises' objection to this method is that trial and error is inappropriate since there is no means of knowing in a socialist system, when a correct solution has been found. In a capitalist economy entrepreneurs learn after the event whether or not they guessed correctly by the computation of their profit or loss. In the absence of market prices such a calculation is not feasible. Trial and error is only suitable for the solution of problems for which the correct solution is recognisable by clear marks not dependent on the method itself (Mises, 1949, pp. 704–5).[23] In real-world competitive markets entrepreneurs try to anticipate future conditions, whereas in a centrally-managed system the authorities react passively to past situations.

In production under socialism the aim is to equate price with marginal cost. But costs as well as prices are, according to the Austrian view, ultimately subjective and can only be known to involved individuals and are not accessible to outside observers. Cost can exist only in the mind of the chooser.

According to Buchanan, the whole debate was never 'properly grounded'. 'The central issue is the critical interdependence between market choice itself and the informational content of this process, which can only be revealed as the process is allowed to occur' (Buchanan, 1979, p. 86). Furthermore, the actual process of buying and selling reveals information probably more cheaply (i.e. efficiently) than if it were the subject of central computation.[24]

One of the most persuasive arguments for socialist calculation is that it can, unlike capitalism, ensure full employment and render the business cycle obsolete. This is surely not such an impressive claim as it appears at first sight. As in an army camp, it really is not a terribly clever thing to find everyone something to do at all times. People can, in the absence of free markets, be set to work on *anything*, however remotely or vaguely the ultimate product may be related to the ways in which consumers' preferences are ranked.

Rothbard turns the question round and asks the socialists why, if central planning is more efficient than the free market, has it not come about through the creation of 'one big firm' by the voluntary market process? The fact that it needs the 'coercive might' of the state to establish such central planning 'demonstrates that the latter could not be the most efficient way of organising the economy' (Moss, 1976, p. 76). Whether or not this is accepted as conclusive it serves to draw attention to the essence of the debate. The reason why a socialist system cannot 'calculate' does not arise from the fact that it is socialist. It is because if one agent, be it the state or a hypothetical giant private monopoly, owns all economic resources, there is no possibility of calculation since production processes would be decided by what would amount to production engineering as in one large factory. There would be no external market data to guide decision-making.

Although, in this chapter, the term 'planning' has been used to embrace more than one meaning, what they have in common is that they rest on the proposition that governments are not only able to perceive desirable goals not apparent to individuals, but are better equipped to achieve such ends, whether this is at the 'macro' level of promoting economic growth or at the 'micro' level of 'picking winners' among industries or firms. The Austrian view is that governments cannot 'know' better than the market and that the evidence in support of this view is abundant in modern economic history. It is very difficult in practice, however, in many cases, to obtain firm *conclusive* evidence either way. Although, as measured by growth rates, the market-dominated economies, and especially the newly industrialised ones of East Asia, have been very successful, it should be noticed that the extent to which particular governments might justifiably claim responsibility for that success varies greatly between them. For example, the expansion of the South Korean economy may owe a good deal to successful state manipulation of investment, but in other cases, such as Hong Kong, most of the credit must go to market forces. On the available evidence, therefore, there is certainly no reason to assume, as a general principle, that the state is likely to 'plan' better than market forces either in promoting economic growth or identifying new and promising investment opportunities. Indeed if we include the dismal record of the Soviet bloc, any faith in the state's economic expertise must surely be drastically shaken.

NOTES

1. See Robert L. Cunningham (1979), p. 300.
2. For example, boxes containing pieces of wedding cake sent to friends abroad were emptied and sent on empty because the export of confectionery was prohibited; newspapers were fined for exceeding more than 55 per cent of advertising matter; the owners of private gardens were prohibited, except under licence, to bottle fruit and sell it to the public. For these and many more, see T. W. Hutchison (1968), pp. 56–8, who draws on J. Jewkes, *Ordeal by Planning* (1948).
3. Mr Michael Foot, leader of the Labour Party in the 1983 General Election campaign, spoke of doing again 'what we did after 1945 – getting the economy right'.

4. *Encounter*, March, 1963, p. 73. See Hutchison (1968), p. 217.
5. The National Plan was presented to the nation by Mr George Brown, who held up a document which he claimed embodied union, industry and government agreement. This event was sadly reminiscent of the famous occasion in 1938 when Neville Chamberlain returned from Germany with an agreement signed by Hitler.
6. See, for example, J.E. Meade, *Wage-Fixing* (1982), London: Allen & Unwin.
7. Notice the careful use of words in this phrase, suggestive at once of vigour, decisiveness and 'goodness' (through e.g. the use of 'public' – in practice, as Rothbard has pointed out, it is usually anything but 'public' if this means 'of the people').
8. See Littlechild (1978), pp. 67–72.
9. See Axel Leijonhuvhud, *Information and Co-ordination: Essays in Macroeconomic Theory* (1981), London: Oxford University Press.
10. Hayek's first attack on planning was in *The Road to Serfdom* (1944).
11. An instructive example of how a piece of planning legislation may result in the delegation to officials of vast and unpredictable powers is the British Town and Country Planning Act 1947. See Hayek (1967), chapter XXV.
12. See reference pp. 193–6.
13. Lachmann (1977), pp. 323–7.
14. Ironically, it was the private sector which bore the brunt of unemployment. Much of the fury against the Thatcher government's 'cuts' was probably due to fear of what the government *might* be planning, rather than what it actually did, plus resentment that the public sector did not continue to expand at the same rate as hitherto.
15. Private investment in a particular sector may be inhibited for years beforehand by the prospect that an incoming government intends to introduce controls or nationalisation. Fears for the future are already threatening the prosperity of Hong Kong, as the date when Britain's lease runs out gets nearer. The uncertainty among the owners of residential property concerning the intentions of future government policy on rent controls has probably played a significant part in aggravating British housing problems.
16. From J.A. Schumpeter, *Capitalism, Socialism and Democracy*, 3rd edn, 1950, New York: Harper & Row, p. 424.

17. The Buddhist state of sinlessness – a state of bliss.
18. Harold Demsetz, 'Information and efficiency: another view-point', *Journal of Law and Economics*, April 1969, 1–22.
19. One possible explanation for this double standard of judgement as between the market and the state may rest on an implicit assumption that restrictions on the freedom of the individual serve as corrections to what are seen as relative disparities in the economic power of the participants in a market order. This is regarded by Buchanan as an erroneous assumption. (See 'Public goods and natural liberty', in Wilson and Skinner (1976), chapter 9.)
20. See Mises, *Die Gemeinwirtschaft* (1922), reprinted as *Socialism* (1936); Hayek, 'The nature and history of the problem', in Hayek (ed.), *Collectivist Economic Planning* (1935), London: Routledge; Rothbard, 'Ludwig von Mises and economic calculation under socialism', in Moss (1976); also Steele (1981) and Bradley (1981). The latter is an excellent survey of the whole subject which brings out the central importance of subjectivism in any explanation of the modern Austrian attitude to socialism.
21. David Collard, *Prices, Markets and Welfare* (1972), London: Faber & Faber. This was his assessment of L.V. Kantorovich's *Best Use of Economics Resources* (1964). In 1977 Kantorovich in the Soviet Union and Koopmans in the United States won Nobel prizes for their construction of mathematical techniques based on linear programming.
22. 'Competition as a discovery procedure' (Hayek, 1978c, pp. 179–90). Hayek had argued along similar lines before this in 'The meaning of competition' (1948).
23. Mises illustrates the difference as follows: 'If a man mislays his wallet, he may hunt for it in various places. If he finds it he recognises it as his property; there is no doubt about the success of the method of trial and error applied; he has solved his problem' (1949, p. 704).
24. See Charles E. Lindblom, *Politics and Markets* (1977), New York: Basic Books, p. 101, who thinks that most economists would reject the feasibility of 'socialist calculation'.

15   Liberty and the Market

1. INTRODUCTION

The most persuasive and influential of all the arguments in favour of
government intervention in the free market are those based
essentially upon a redefinition of 'freedom', so as necessarily to entail
such state intervention. A free market may be cruel in its effects:
should people who are unemployed through no fault of their own bear
the full burden of the consequent misery? should the sick and the old
be dependent on the support of their families or friends? In the
market economy the standard of living of each individual is
constrained by his ownership of something marketable, but not
everyone owns something marketable. Those who, through good
fortune, earn large incomes, have the opportunity to accumulate
surpluses (wealth), and left to itself this process perpetuates, through
inheritance, undeserved inequalities in the command over wealth.
Even when a competitive market economy works 'ideally', the largest
share of total output goes to those with the most money. 'A rich
man's dog may receive the milk that a poor child needs to avoid
rickets.'[1] Such concerns, which are expressed in the saying that free
markets leave people 'free to starve', form the basis for discussions
around the question of whether income and wealth distribution
should be left to the play of competitive markets. Ultimately, this is
an ethical question and is now regarded by many economists as lying
beyond the boundaries of positive economics, following the work of
Arrow in his analysis of the impossibility of deriving a method of
comparing various possible states of social welfare. Arrow showed
that there are insuperable conceptual difficulties in justifying a choice
between individuals' different preference orderings.[2]
  However, there is, of course, absolutely no reason why a value
judgement is impossible concerning the morality of particular social

systems. A long-standing and widespread argument for socialism, or at least some degree of state intervention, runs roughly as follows: the unfettered market throws up inequalities of income and wealth; inequality is inherently morally reprehensible; therefore, the state should be used to achieve social justice (distributive justice). Only in this way is real freedom attainable for the many instead of the few. The loss of liberty consequent upon the inevitable coercion by the state needed for the achievement of equality is a price that should be paid in order to gain real freedom for the many people whom the impersonal forces of the market treat unfairly. Thus, it is clear that questions of liberty, equality and social justice are necessarily interconnected. The first aspect of this to be considered is the question of what we mean by freedom or liberty.[3]

2. WHAT IS FREEDOM?

Disagreements about the nature of liberty have been dominated by the competing ideas of negative and positive freedom. This debate is sufficiently wide-ranging and varied to fill a respectable-sized book in its own right. Reasons of space alone dictate that we shall be forced to select from among the many facets of the subject those which appear to be most relevant to the general aims of this volume.

In the nineteenth century there was a fundamental revision in English liberal thought which marked the origin of the expressions 'negative' and 'positive' liberty. The former had originated in the seventeenth and eighteenth centuries when liberty was regarded by many as a natural right given by God or Nature; it is associated in this form with, for example, John Locke and Adam Smith. In the nineteenth century the same idea appears in the thought of the classical economists, such as Ricardo and McCulloch, and the Utilitarians (e.g. Bentham); this has become known as the classical position on liberty. Its effect can be seen in regard to the question of freedom of contract: which gives rise to the general presumption that contracts agreed between sane adults should be free from coercion by a third party (e.g. the state), but that the state should uphold contracts freely arrived at. This rests in the belief that adults know their own best interests and should have complete freedom to promote them.[4] By the same argument, the state has no right to regulate conditions or hours of work if an employee has 'freely' entered into an agreement with an employer to work under certain conditions.

The revision of liberal theory which emerged in the 1880s is associated chiefly with the Oxford political philosopher, T.H. Green, who pointed out that the classical position tacitly assumes that law is the only restriction on liberty, and that this is not true unless freedom is arbitrarily defined as the absence of legal restraint. Green called this 'negative freedom', and proposed an alternative, 'positive freedom'. This defined freedom as the power of an individual to develop his own particular capacities. Freedom of contract by itself was not, according to Green, an end but a means to enable people to achieve the positive power to enjoy something. The coercion which an employer or landlord could exert on a worker or tenant was, he argued, much more dangerous to real freedom than the coercion which the state might employ to overrule a contract in the interests of the weaker party. This revised version of freedom is similar to Marx's distinction between 'formal' and 'material' freedom.

3. ARGUMENTS FOR POSITIVE FREEDOM

Professor Bernard Williams, in his essay 'The idea of equality',[5] states the case for income redistribution in which, by implication, he advocates the case for positive freedom by the use, as an example, of the provision of medical care. He contends that the only condition for the distribution of medical care should be ill-health: 'This is a necessary truth.' It is simply irrational, he argues, for the possession of wealth to be necessary in order to assure medical treatment.[6] Charles Taylor, in 'What's wrong with negative liberty?' (Ryan, 1979), regards the position taken by many proponents of negative liberty as too extreme and indefensible when analysed. One aspect of positive liberty involves what he refers to as an 'exercise concept', by which he means that freedom consists in 'exercising control over one's own life'. Negative freedom positions, on the other hand, rely on an 'opportunity concept', meaning that freedom involves only that there be no obstacle in the way of what we can do. Taylor argues that taking a stand on this line is inspired by a 'Maginot line' mentality – 'a desire to fight the Totalitarian Menace from a last ditch position.'[7] He then seeks to undermine the basic presumption of classical liberalism (that an individual is the best judge of his own interests) by arguing that there may well be internal obstacles to freedom, such as being influenced by fear, or 'inauthentically internalised standards or false consciousness to thwart your self-realisation'. This is what he means by an exercise concept of freedom.

If an individual does not, in this sense, know his 'true self' does not this open the way to the prospect of others (e.g. the state) putting him on the right track, perhaps by the use of force? Taylor's answer is quite clear He rejects entirely the idea that, in a liberal society, some authority may impose its will on people for their own good. However, the pure negative concept of freedom he sees as failing to distinguish between different degrees of infringements of freedom. For example, a new traffic light on a road junction is a sensible and quite trivial restriction, whereas a ban on religious observance is serious. The pure negative freedom concept would 'seem to make it possible to defend the idea that Albania is in some sense a freer country than Britain simply because there are less traffic lights in the former than the latter' (ibid., p. 182).[8]

Taylor's main opposition to the 'crude' version of negative freedom is based on the contention that there are many ways in which an individual may behave irrationally. For example, he may very much desire to learn to swim, but fear may prevent him from entering the water. Thus, even though there may be no external obstruction (i.e. coercion) preventing him from learning to swim he is just as effectively rendered unfree by his own fear. Whether we now go on from this to argue that true freedom is only realisable in a certain kind of society in which coercion is used for the sake of the individual's true interests is a question, says Taylor, which cannot be evaded simply by adopting the 'crude' negative position. It is not very clear what should count as an individual's 'true interest'. One could take the view, in the case of the frightened would-be swimmer, that he is behaving rationally in the sense that he, and only he, 'knows' that the 'pain' he would suffer from taking the plunge would not be sufficiently compensated by the pleasure he might get from learning to swim. Of course he might, if someone pushed him in the water, discover that his fears were groundless, but whether this gives anyone some sort of right or duty to push him seems doubtful.

In general, the concept of positive freedom is based on the idea that there is really no point in talking about freedom unless what that freedom enables an individual to do is specified – freedom means freedom to achieve or enjoy something. In its most radical form, that of the Marxist approach, we can see most clearly what might be implied by this way of defining freedom. The Marxist view is that the state should not only protect the individual from infringements of his freedom such as, physical assaults by the strong on the weak, but also the state should protect the worker from exploitation by the owner of capital. The notion that all the state has to do is to protect the free actions of individuals which do no harm to others is seen as ignoring the 'fact' that the state itself originated as the protector of class interests. The principle of negative liberty as enunciated by J.S. Mill is that the state should not interfere with the freedom of individuals to conduct their affairs and dispose of their property, except in so far as it was necessary to stop one person causing harm to another. Marxists object to this on the grounds that it implies that state intervention, by reducing negative freedom, is in itself harmful. Liberals assume that the freedom to buy and sell 'labour power' and appropriate its product is not harmful. Marxists maintain that real freedom, as distinct from merely legal or formal freedom, can only be realised through the replacement of a state which protects private property by a state which protects the individual worker from capitalist exploitation. For a trenchant (some might say dogmatic) statement of the Marxist case against negative freedom here are two brief quotations from a book by Maurice Cornforth, the title of which shows obviously that its chief target is Popper's anti-Marxism.[9]

By instituting social ownership of means of production we can institute social planning of production to employ available resources and labour to meet needs. (p. 303) [Who is the 'we' referred to?]

Happiness and personal relations – . . . their sources are poisoned by the free-for-all competition and the monopolising of resources, the 'I'm all right Jack' and 'dog eats dog' ethic of capitalist society. (ibid.) [Obviously no believer in the idea that exchange is not a zero-sum game].

Cornforth concludes that Marxists have always recognised that certain freedoms must be restricted in order to secure real freedom and equality, 'demonstrating therein a perfectly sound grasp of the so-called paradox of freedom'.

4. ARGUMENTS FOR NEGATIVE FREEDOM

One of the best-known statements of the case for negative freedom is that by Sir Isaiah Berlin.[10] Here is a summary of the case he presents: 'Mere incapacity to attain a goal is not lack of political freedom.' When a person is prevented by poverty from getting enough to eat, to call this by a term such as 'economic slavery', as Marxists do, implies a particular view of society concerning the cause of poverty. To regard such an individual as not free because of his poverty, Berlin regards as a confusion of terms. Supposing, for instance, one individual is willing to sacrifice some of his freedom for the sake of the greater equality of others, then it is a mistake to conclude that freedom has increased – if something is given up there must be less of it: 'liberty is liberty, not equality or fairness or justice or culture or human happiness or a quiet conscience. . . . Everything is what it is.' To say that in giving up individual freedom some other kind of freedom ('social' or 'economic') is increased is a 'confusion of values'. No matter where the line is drawn between individual liberty on the one hand and equality on the other, liberty in this sense remains liberty *from*, not liberty to do or enjoy something or to have a right to something. With regard to the argument that an individual may not be the best judge of his own interests and that therefore it is justifiable to coerce him in pursuit of some goal, which his 'higher' self wants, but which he is blind to because of ignorance, Berlin rightly points out the obvious danger that this opens the door to all manner of oppressive bullying. Even more seriously, this argument implies that since an individual may not know his own 'true self', coercion is in a sense 'willed' by a higher self than the one which foolishly rejects what has been decided for use for his own good. Thus freedom can depend on how we choose to define a 'self' or person. 'Enough manipulation with the definition of man, and freedom can be made to mean whatever the manipulator wishes.' Recent history shows what this can lead to.

Sir Karl Popper's position on the question is set out in *The Open Society and its Enemies*, the book which Cornforth criticised (see above). Popper is entirely in favour of the state protecting the weak against the strong, in the economic as well as the physical sense: 'a minority which is economically strong may in this exploit the majority of those who are economically weak' (p. 123); in this respect Popper agrees with Marx. But he differs sharply from Marx in that he argues strongly that the proper remedy for the *economically* weak is through *political* action. 'The State must see to it that nobody need enter into an inequitable arrangement out of fear of starvation or economic ruin.' This, of course, is a very interventionist position and Popper lists many of those services which have become known as the welfare state which together remove the citizen from economic intimidation. Marx, on the other hand, held that we cannot alter underlying economic reality by legal reforms alone, since economic power is more fundamental than political power. In Popper's view, Marx underestimated the dangers to liberty from political power, and completely failed to grasp the fact that *all* power, political or economic, is dangerous. Popper's surprising conclusion is that Marx was, ultimately, an individualist since his belief in the comparative unimportance of political power is analogous to the liberal belief that all that is necessary is equality of opportunity. Although Popper is by no means an extreme libertarian and accepts to some extent the arguments for positive freedom, he warns that state intervention should be no more than is necessary to protect freedom – freedom from both physical and economic oppression. He recognises that even this degree of state intervention carries with it great risks for freedom and is, of course, famous for his rejection of 'Utopian or holistic methods of social engineering'. In the end 'only freedom can make security secure'.

The two sides to the debate have now been outlined by reference to some of the main arguments of the protagonists and this will suffice as a background to a consideration of questions of equality and social justice from the Austrian point of view. But it needs finally to be mentioned that there is a good deal more which might have been said on the negative–positive freedom conflict. Political philosophers have introduced somewhat more sophisticated arguments than any of those referred to above.[11] For instance, some contend that some of the age-old discussion is quite simply confused and that when subjected to close analysis some of the problems melt away. As an example, T.D. Weldon regards the demand for any objective standards in politics as 'looking for something which it is nonsense to ask for at all'.[12]

5. The Austrian concept of liberty

In this, even more so than in any other topic we have discussed, Hayek is the predominating and authoritative influence. Simply to recall the titles of his major works emphasises the importance he attaches to the concept of liberty. The latter belong unmistakably in the 'negative' tradition. He defines freedom as 'that condition of men in which coercion of some by others is reduced as much as is possible in society' (1960, p. 11).[13] The aim of a policy of freedom should be to minimise coercion, even if it cannot eliminate it entirely. Throughout his work Hayek holds fast to the principle that freedom should be freedom under the law, and he quotes with approval John Locke. 'The end of law is, not to abolish or restrain, but to preserve and enlarge freedom . . . where there is no law there is no freedom' (ibid., p. 162). But he constantly distinguishes between different kinds of law. One is the rule of law, general principles laid down beforehand which allow individuals to foresee how the coercion of the state will be used; and the other kind which gives those in authority the power to do what they think fit as, for example, where the state acts, not according to rules previously laid down, but by judging each case 'on its merits' (1944, p. 62, n. 1). By giving the striving for equality and social justice, for example, priority over freedom as an ideal, the door is opened to all manner of coercion in the sense in which Hayek uses the term.[14]

There are obvious difficulties here in deciding which laws are necessary to the maintenance of a free society and which are not, especially in the area of economic policy, and many questions arise. In general, the important point is that all coercive actions of governments must be unambiguously determined by a permanent legal framework.[15] Some Austrians are more purely libertarian than Hayek. Rothbard, for instance, regards freedom as definable only as the absence of interpersonal restrictions, and contends that the 'freedom to starve' argument rests on a basic confusion between freedom and 'abundance of exchangeable goods'; these are two quite distinct concepts. That an individual is 'free to starve' is therefore not a condemnation of the free market, but a simple fact of nature. The best way to reduce poverty is through capitalist free markets – 'production must come first'. 'Force and violence may "distribute", but it cannot produce' (1970, p. 222).

Finally, it should be noticed that certain of the conflicts between the desire for personal freedom and the desire for things like order and equality may be amenable to analysis by using something like the indifference curve technique.[16] For example, more or less of individual freedom may be envisaged as being compensated for by more or less of some other end, such as protection against violence. From the Austrian point of view, the same criticisms would apply to this as apply to indifference analysis as a method of discovering any other preferences.

The Austrian definitions of freedom and coercion imply a complementary belief in individual responsibility.

Liberty not only means that the individual has both the opportunity and the burden of choice; it also means that he must bear the consequences of his actions and will receive praise or blame for them. Liberty and responsibility are inseparable.

These are the opening lines of Chapter Five of Hayek's *The Constitution of Liberty*. The attack on this belief in the inseparability of freedom and responsibility has been based largely on two views of the true nature of the human condition. One is that responsibility presupposes the ability to make rational conscious choices but that this is not always feasible, since psychology has shown that man is often driven by unconscious forces which overpower his capacity for rational action. The other is that economic forces over which he has no control can bear on the individual so powerfully as to significantly reduce the capacity for rational action (see Bosanquet, 1983, for a well presented argument based on such views).[17] If this picture of the individual is correct, then the case for some institutional arrangements to protect the individual both from himself and from economic 'forces' becomes convincing. However, there would seem to be nothing in the Hayek definition of freedom which excludes the creation of such institutions so long as they arise through *voluntary* action and are not imposed, for example, by the state. What Hayek does strongly maintain, however, is that freedom must be treated as a 'supreme principle' and never overruled on any pragmatic basis. For example, some specific intervention in the market order may be attractive and be judged as offering some obvious and immediate gain; but one often unappreciated value of freedom is that it provides opportunities which cannot be known in advance and that therefore we can never know what has been lost through the restriction of freedom in particular cases. If it becomes a habit to treat freedom as something to be traded off against *known* objectives, then Hayek's prediction is that freedom will inevitably be destroyed, and at an accelerating pace, by the unintentional effect which political actions themselves have in promoting the acceptance of principles which make further political actions necessary.

Although Hayek (and, of course many others) have argued persuasively in favour of negative liberty it may of course be the case that modern man is still not convinced and indeed will choose security rather than freedom. As Dostoyevsky's Grand Inquisitor puts it: 'I tell Thee that man is tormented by no greater anxiety than to find someone quickly to whom he can hand over that gift of freedom with which the ill-fated creature is born. . . .' (*The Brothers Karamazov*). This poses something of a dilemma for libertarians: suppose that all or a majority of the individuals in a society choose security, is not this in itself an exercise of individual free choice, the consequences of which must logically be accepted? Of course, individuals do not in practice deliberately choose slavery; they see themselves as accepting some degree of limitation on their freedom in exchange for some degree of protection and what could possibly be wrong with that? Hayek clearly fears that the desire for security over and above a specified minimum will eventually lead to increasing loss of freedom – there is really no half-way house – and that the individuals who made the original choice will live to regret it. There can of course be no settled conclusion on such a matter, but in the next chapter the Austrian view on two aspects of the demand for security is discussed.

NOTES

1. See Samuelson (1964), p. 42.
2. See Chapter 7.
3. In the present context 'freedom' and 'liberty' will be regarded as interchangeable.
4. See W.L. Weinstein, 'The concept of liberty in nineteenth-century English political thought', *Political Studies*, vol. XIII, no. 2, 1965.
5. Bernard Williams, 'The idea of equality', in P. Laslett and W.G. Runciman (eds), *Philosophy, Politics and Society*, 2nd series (1962), Oxford: Basil Blackwell, pp. 110–31; reprinted in Joel Feinberg (ed.), *Moral Concepts* (1969), New York: Oxford University Press.
6. For a criticism of this argument, see Nozick (1974), pp. 233–5, e.g. 'Williams says (it is a necessary truth that) the only proper criterion for the distribution of medical care is medical need. Presumably, then, the only proper criterion for the distribution of barbering services is barbering need.'
7. Taylor seems to be hinting that he regards the 'Totalitarian Menace' idea as having little substance: Hayek disagrees.
8. Cf. Hayek's distinction between road signs for guidance and an order telling people where to drive.
9. Maurice Cornforth, *The Open Philosophy and the Open Society* (1968), London: Lawrence & Wishart.
10. Sir Isaiah Berlin, *Four Essays on Liberty* (1969), London: Oxford University Press.
11. See, for example, G. MacCallum, Jr, 'Negative and positive freedom', *The Philosophical Review*, July 1967, 312–14; Lansing Pollock, 'The freedom principle', *Ethics*, vol. 86, no. 4, July 1976; H. Steiner, 'Liberty and equality', *Political Studies*, vol. xxix, no. 4. December 1981, 555–69; W.E. Draughon, 'Liberty: a proposed analysis', *Social Theory and Practice*, Fall 1978, 7–11;

R.B. Perry, 'What does it mean to be free?', *Pacific Spectator*, 7, 1953. For an outstandingly good and readable essay on the subject, which avoids the more esoteric knots of the philosophers, see Fritz Machlup, 'Liberalism and the choice of freedoms', in Streissler (1969), pp. 117–46. This essay also includes a convincing explanation of why 'liberal' in the United States has come to be associated with socialism, whereas in Europe it still mostly signifies 'pro-market'.

12. T.D. Weldon, *The Vocabulary of Politics* (1953), Harmondsworth: Penguin, esp. pp. 157ff and pp. 70–2.
13. Hayek's definition does not exclude coercion entirely as some people have thought. See his reply to a reviewer of *The Constitution of Liberty*, in 'Freedom and coercion', *Studies*, p. 348.
14. See Barry (1979), chapter 4, for an excellent analysis of Hayek's position on questions of liberty and coercion.
15. For Hayek's position on the permissible extent of coercion by the state, see *The Constitution of Liberty*, Chapter 15.
16. See Brian Barry, *Political Argument* (1965), London: Routledge & Kegan Paul. Attention was drawn to this by Samuel Brittan in *Left or Right: The Bogus Dilemma* (1968), London: Secker & Warburg, p. 148.
17. Nick Bosanquet, *After the New Right* (1983), London: Heinemann, pp. 92–102.

16 Equality and Social Justice

1. EQUALITY AS AN IDEAL

The ideals of equality and social (or distributive) justice have, alongside Keynesian economics, been the driving force behind much state intervention into the market order. It is the contention of the neo-Austrians that people who prefer freedom have been too complacent in the light of the dangers which these ideals pose for the whole basis of the liberal society.

We must first say something about equality[1] as an ideal, although there is only space to give a brief summary of some of the more relevant aspects of the subject. In the twentieth century, equality has become something of a sacred cow. The notion that anyone could seriously argue for inequality (especially gross inequality) is regarded in some circles as at best mad, and at worst, immoral. Faced with the fact that in a free society some individuals will, either through superior ability, hard work, cunning, inheritance or good luck, become richer than others there is a widespread belief that someone must be to blame and that the state (to which everything seems possible) should correct the situation in favour of the less fortunate, by redistributing income, either in cash or kind. It is remarkable that in a largely secular age the state is endowed with god-like powers of wisdom and benevolence. But faced with the ever-accumulating evidence of states that are neither omnipotent nor philanthropically disinterested, the advocates of equality now tend to say that 'society' should not tolerate inequality. The term 'society' is similar in its vagueness to its stablemate 'social' (of which more below).

Among the many arguments for equality one of the most compelling is what has been designated the argument from universal humanity – the idea that there exist between individuals many basic, essential and common needs (we are 'brothers'; if my brother is in need, I should help him). In a world in which millions are starving it is seen as morally wrong for others to enjoy useless and dispensable luxuries. This has been described as the 'Oxfam' argument.[2] The 'War on Want' argument, on the other hand, contends that redistribution of income is not the only, or even necessarily the best way of helping the poor. In the long run it may be better to help people to become independent of aid. People are not just passive, 'They need liberty and opportunity as well as food and medicines; stimulus as well as satisfaction' (Lucas, ibid, p. 262). Nothing in this view rules out the prospect of individuals or groups of individuals freely and *voluntarily* giving to others. Ironically, one of the arguments for state-managed redistribution is that it is morally better for the state to tax people in order to help the poor and needy rather than for them to be 'degraded' by receiving charity from voluntary associations. Whatever other arguments may be adduced for state-administered aid, it is difficult to see any grounds for it being morally superior to behave as a Robin Hood.[3] It is an essential ingredient of the Austrian ethical position – as it is of libertarians in general – that it is wrong to coerce people into charitable behaviour; furthermore, that such a policy tends to kill off private charity: 'Compulsory confiscation can only *deaden* charitable desires completely' (Rothbard, 1970, p.222).

It should be stressed that the differences between people's economic success may simply be due to a greater alertness to opportunities. What appears as luck (or other external forces) may, in part, be explained by the fact of one individual being better prepared than another to take advantage of opportunities which present themselves. If it is always assumed that people are equal, in the sense of being equally blessed with native ability and are equally enterprising, then differences in their economic welfare are only too easily explained by some hostile and powerful influence, such as the iniquitous capitalist system. Professor Bauer suggests that 'difference' is often a more appropriate term than 'inequality', which has come to be used as if it is synonymous with 'inequity'.[4] As well as there being many arguments *against* equality, there are also many *for* inequality, many of which are based on assumptions about liberty and justice, while others are of a more material nature. For example, Hayek contends that economic progress is very dependent on inequality: 'Progress cannot proceed on a uniform front but must take place in echelon fashion with some far ahead of the rest' (1960, p. 42). The motor car, for instance, would never have been produced on its present large scale had it not been for the fact that rich people could afford the first models in the early twentieth century. Another source of confusion is the habit of seeing any better-off or more able group as an élite and regarding this as inimical to egalitarianism. Élitism has evidently now become one of these words which is used to silence further discussion as soon as it is uttered.[5]

One final consideration is that it is desirable to have some people in a society who, by reason of their wealth, are independent of patronage or intimidation by state officials and can, if necessary, afford to fight against abuses of political power. This is often regarded too narrowly: that the rich cannot be pushed around so easily as the rest of the population and that this is unfair, is seen as justifying heavy taxation to bring them down to the level of the majority. However, the fact that there exist some rich people may well act as a brake on officials and make them more cautious in their dealing with the mass of people too.[6]

2. AUSTRIAN VIEW OF SOCIAL JUSTICE

Under the Tories West Indians and Asians are not getting their full *share* of the national product.

Of course we have got to have an agreement with the unions on how the increased wealth should be *allocated*.[7]

These two recent statements by leading politicians in the British General Election campaign, 1983 reveal clearly two presumptions about social policy: first, that there is a 'national cake' which it is someone's job to share out; and second, that these shares should be 'fair'. Austrians see such ideas as fallacious and harmful; a brief account of why they hold this view now follows.[8]

The two statements quoted above are good illustrations of how the appeal to 'social justice' has become the most widespread weapon in political discussion and the chief outlet for moral emotion replacing, even among churchmen, promises of justice in Heaven. In a free market order, the demand for 'social justice' raises two problems: first, whether the concept has any meaning, and second, whether it will be possible to preserve a market economy whilst continuing to extend the practice by which the needs and remuneration of different groups is decided, not by the market, but by the government. Hayek's answer to both these questions is a 'clear no' (1960, p. 68). The word 'social', by itself, might well be discussed at some length and has by now been used to mean so many different things as to be in danger of becoming entirely vacuous. A sure sign of the deterioration of a word in this way is when it starts to be heard in statements such as, 'Your views are anti-social'. Very frequently this only signifies, 'I do not agree with you'. Another use of 'social' is that it suggests that there are common aims governing the activity of the individuals in a society. A good test of the usefulness of a word is to try omitting it and then asking whether the phrase or sentence of which it formed part has altered in meaning. For example, take 'Social Democratic Party': how could there be a party which believed in democracy which was *not* social?[9] Hayek recalls how the first occasion of his disquiet concerning 'social' was when the Germans began to qualify the term 'free market economy' by calling it 'social market economy'.[10]

When someone complains that there is injustice in the existing distribution of goods in a free market economy he appears to be implying that some individual or group is to blame, and 'society' has become the focus of his indignation. But this would only make sense in the case of a command economy (e.g. an army), and in that case it would be entirely sensible to complain to the authorities that they should alter the criteria on which they are basing their distribution of total output. But in a system in which each individual is free to use his own knowledge for his own purposes nobody's *will* can determine relative incomes: 'differences in reward'[11] cannot meaningfully be described as 'just or unjust' (ibid., p. 70). Even in the interventionist mixed economies it is largely mistaken to believe that existing inequalities are the result of a conscious decision. The impersonal process of the market throws up results which depend on a mass of circumstances incapable of being grasped in their totality by any single person or group.

The Austrian defence of the free market does not depend on the proposition that it necessarily rewards merit.[12] As in a game, although the players must obey the rules there can be no assurance that the result will be just, and it is this apparently unfair (unjust) outcome of markets which may lie behind the demand for greater equality. 'In a free economy it is neither desirable nor practicable that material rewards should be made generally to correspond to what men recognise as merit' (Hayek, 1960, p. 94). If merit is to be rewarded then some way of measuring it must exist. We must be able, for instance, to assess how much use individuals have made of opportunities open to them; how much effort they have made. To judge merit presupposes that we are able to distinguish between that part of achievement which is due to luck, or inborn qualities for which they are not responsible, and that part which is due to hard work or self-denial. How much of any sportsman's success can be explained by his natural physical attributes, and how much by his devotion to training? It is quite impossible to assess. An accidental invention may turn out to have great value (i.e. as judged by others in the market), whilst another, which has taken years to perfect, may not sell. Although a society based on rewarding merit rather than value sounds attractive it would, in fact, be based on the entirely unwarranted presumption that an individual or group is capable of judging conclusively what a person is worth: it would be the opposite of a free society.[13]

Contemporary demand for social justice may be compared to the medieval search for the just price – and is equally futile. Wage disputes are often conducted in an atmosphere thick with moralising about justice, but this often only masks the underlying hard realities of relative bargaining power. The phrase 'value to society' is often heard, but this is just as meaningless as 'social justice'. The demand for equality or social justice would, if fully realised, mean the end of the free society, and paradoxically such a system would result in treating people unequally, since to ensure equality of material possessions for all, government would have to treat people differently in order to compensate for their excess or lack of ability, perseverance, and other qualities which it was not able directly to alter. Only a government with totalitarian powers could ensure full social justice.

It might well be concluded that the foregoing arguments, if accepted, would imply that all government action to provide social security is to be condemned. Mises is in favour of a combination of charity and private insurance against accidents, sickness, old age, the education of children and the support of widows and orphans (1949, pp. 837–8), and replies to two frequently heard criticisms of charity. First, that charities do not have enough funds to cope with the problems. This, says Mises, will become less of a problem as capitalism increases wealth. Government intervention only impedes this process. With the second – that charity is degrading, and corrupts both giver and recipient – Mises is in agreement: 'It makes the former, the giver, self-righteous, and the latter the receivers, submissive and cringing' (ibid., p. 838). However, it is only because people are used to the ethos of a capitalistic environment that people feel like this. Capitalism has substituted contracts for brotherly love. Ironically, those critics who condemn capitalism for its impersonality also condemn charity for its reliance upon feelings of kindliness. By substituting 'the discretion of bureaucrats' (as in government welfare agencies) 'for the discretion of people whom an inner voice drives to acts of charity' there is no certainty that the sick and old will be better-off (ibid., p. 540). Mises does not say how he thinks the needy are best to be helped *now*, but constantly emphasises the overriding aim of not adopting methods which are likely to 'curtail the productivity of human effort'. Neither the fit nor the unfit gain from a fall in the quantity of goods. This may well be true of the long run but in the short term such a policy risks appearing to use the same 'end justifying the means' argument as Stalinist Five Year Plans.

Rothbard's brand of libertarianism leads him to regard state 'poor relief' as a subsidisation of poverty, and state unemployment relief, similarly, as a subsidisation of unemployment. One generates recipients and thus increases the apparent extent of poverty; the other helps to keep wages above the level which would sufficiently increase the demand for labour to take up the unemployment.

Hayek's view on state aid is, surprisingly perhaps, not so firmly *laissez-faire*. He sees no reason why a government should not assure a minimum income to all: 'a floor below which nobody need to descend'. He gives two reasons: first, 'it may be felt to be a clear moral duty of all to assist, within the organised community, those who cannot help themselves.' Second, it 'may be in the interest of all' (1982, vol. II, p. 87). Hayek has been seen as somewhat inconsistent on this question since the implication of assisting 'within the organised community' is the existence of some coercion by the state. However, if we remember that all he aims for in his definition of liberty is that coercion be reduced to a minimum, the inconsistency disappears.

Many critics of the free market use the argument that an individual's liberty is almost wholly dependent on his ownership of something marketable, either property or labour services, and that in particular the existing distribution of property is not necessarily just. Even if it can be shown that the market is in some way 'just' in its distribution of income, that distribution is very much dependent on the ownership of property which may have been acquired unjustly. To explore fully the important questions raised by this proposition would demand more space than is now available.[14] In his Preface (1982), Hayek states that his own conclusions have been reached without taking full account of the work of Nozick and Oakeshott,[15] though he had found himself in substantial agreement with Rawls,[16] and in general the Austrian position is close to that of these political philosophers, especially of Robert Nozick, who believes that markets are a reasonable way of achieving a fair allocation of resources. He has been criticised, however, on the grounds that he gives no convincing account of how 'initial endowments' are to be determined,[17] that is, the 'rectification' of injustice in the initial distribution of wealth. Nozick's position is that an individual is entitled to his particular 'holding' (of resources), so long as it was acquired 'justly' or, alternatively, transferred to him justly from someone entitled to the holding.[18] Nozick claims that his theory is more acceptable than those theories which take insufficient account – when discussing the distribution of wealth – of the processes which have brought about current patterns of distribution. They are concerned only with 'a current time-slice of distribution'.

In Nozick's chapter 'Equality, envy, exploration, etc.' he discusses the objections of egalitarians to the free market on the grounds that as well as having unequal initial holdings (of wealth), some people are handicapped by unequal natural endowment, and that therefore the aim should be 'equality of opportunity'. This is one of those phrases, usually linked to 'rights' (e.g. 'everyone has a right to equality of opportunity'), which appear so superficially unobjectionable and which are guaranteed to produce nodding of heads in agreement from all parts of the political spectrum, but which hide real problems. For example, if it is argued that someone has 'rights' it usually involves rights to some material resources over which other people also have rights (e.g. their justly acquired holdings). Furthermore, the view of economic activity as a means to the end of equality is seen by Nozick as mistaken. Economic activity is not analogous to a race in which some people are handicapped by factors over which they have no control, such as being made to carry heavy weights or being forced to start behind the start line. In real life there is no centrally-administered 'race' with known prizes: 'No centralised process judges people's use of the opportunities they had; that is not what the processes of social co-operation and exchange are *for*.'[19] This is remarkably similar to Hayek's views on merit versus value, discussed above.

To many people, the way in which 'rewards' are distributed in free markets appears immoral; there is a constant yearning for 'distributive justice'. Austrians do not defend free markets on the basis that the most admirable (from the point of view of character, honesty or hard work) necessarily receive the highest incomes. What they ask is that critics of the market who would like to see it replaced by some other standard by which rewards are decided face up to the fact that any conceivable alternatives raise serious problems. Austrians believe economic freedom to be the basis of morality, an indispensable condition of all other freedom. If freedom is to work, it requires moral standards of a particular kind: the belief in individual responsibility and the general acceptance of a system which gives material rewards corresponding to the value which an individual's services provide for others. In the absence of such moral standards and their replacement by some sort of assessment of individuals' moral merit (by whom and using what criteria?) the way is opened for moral standards to become general which would destroy freedom and hence the basis of all moral values.[20]

Finally, there is one possibility to which there seems no simple answer: suppose, in spite of efforts to persuade them of their 'folly', the majority of people prefer a large degree of social justice administered by the government, and in its absence would create civil disorder and cause a breakdown of the rule of law. Should a government, whose aim is to protect freedom as the pre-eminent ideal, give way to the demands of the majority?

NOTES

1. Statistics have often been presented which exaggerate the extent of inequality. See Bauer (1981), p. 21.
2. See J.R. Lucas, 'Against equality again', *Philosophy*, 52, 1977, 255–80. This essay presents many of the arguments against equality for which there is insufficient space in the text. It also analyses what possible meanings might be understood by the term 'equality'.
3. Politicians often claim 'generosity' for their practice of distributing other people's money or accuse their opponents of 'meanness' for not doing so.
4. See Bauer, op. cit., p. 10.
5. It is fashionable nowadays to oppose an argument by calling it an '—ism', of some sort, as if this in itself constitutes a valid objection; it would be, however, if the élite in question were self-chosen.
6. The Crichel Down case of the 1950s is often cited as a clear example of the abuse of official power being successfully opposed only because the offence was against a rich man. See Lucas, op. cit., p. 274.
7. Although these two statements were made by leading Labour politicians it should not be assumed that Conservatives question the desirability of social justice. So deep-rooted and widespread

is the belief that social justice is a desirable ideal that few politicians dare oppose it.

8. The source for much of this section is Hayek (1982) vol. II, *The Mirage of Social Justice*, esp. chapter 9. See also Mises (1949), chapter XXXV.

9. Could it be that it would be more appropriately called 'Democratic Socialist'. Is 'social' inserted simply to avoid 'socialist'? What kind of party could properly be called '*Un*democratic Socialist'?

10. See 'What is "social"'? – what does it mean?', in Hayek (1967), chapter 17. Also *Encounter*, May 1983, p. 55.

11. Strictly speaking, it is misleading to speak of 'rewards' to factors of production. Factor incomes are more like signals guiding factors to their most profitable employment in the future, rather than rewards for past service.

12. This view is markedly different from some interpretations which seek to justify free markets on the grounds that merit necessarily is rewarded.

13. See Hayek (1960), pp. 93–9, for full discussion of the conflict between merit and value.

14. See Nozick (1974), esp. chapter 7; Rawls (1971); and Oakeshott (1975).

15. Hayek advises 'younger readers' that they cannot 'fully comprehend the present state of thought on these issues' unless they make the effort to digest Nozick and Oakeshott.

16. Hayek disagrees with Rawls, however, over his use of the term 'social justice' (1982, vol. II, p. 100).

17. See, e.g., H.R. Varian, 'Justice, welfare and fairness', in Hahn and Hollis (1979), chapter IX.

18. Cf. Hayek, who accepts that it may be just to 'correct positions which have been determined by earlier unjust acts . . . But unless such injustice is clear and recent, it will generally be impracticable to correct it' (1982, vol. II, p. 131). The problem is that rights which were acquired justly in the past may, in the context of a current set of values, now be judged unjust. See Lawrence C. Becker, *Property Rights* (1977), London: Routledge & Kegan Paul, p. 113.

19. This unavoidably sketchy account of Nozick's position tends to make it appear rather dogmatic; it can only be properly understood by a reading of the arguments which lead up to it.

20. See 'The moral element in free enterprise', in Hayek (1967), pp. 229–36; also 'Why the worst get on top' (1944), chapter X.

The horrifying possibilities for the growth of corruption in a collectivist 'merit-based system' are relentlessly brought out in Alexander Zinoviev's viciously satirical allegory, *The Yawning Heights* (1969).

17 Conclusion

The most important influence of the neo-Austrian school is due to their quite distinctive (subjectivist) explanation of how free market capitalism actually works, as opposed to some caricatures purporting to explain it. If, as Austrians (and others, of course) maintain, the free market based upon the private ownership of property is a necessary condition for the continuance of a society in which genuine personal freedom under the rule of law may be taken for granted, then it is obviously desirable that people should be offered a convincing explanation of why this is so. Ignorance of the capitalist market ethos (what can be expected of it, and what are its limitations) is, unfortunately, nearly as common among its supporters as among its opponents.

Today, all free societies face the problem that the causal relationship between capitalism and freedom is not properly understood by many people who enjoy the benefits of freedom. When the historical record of obvious incompetence and even of mass murder as practised by governments is compared to the comparative guiltlessness of capitalists it is a matter for wonder that government action is so often sought for the solution of a multitude of different problems by so many apparently optimistic individuals and groups. Is it 'multi-nationals' (one of the mysterious bogys of left-wing demonology) or 'big business' that has been responsible for the horrendous slaughter, in the twentieth century, through war and genocide? Of course, this point might be met by the (untestable) assertion that governments in capitalism are mere tools of the property-owning classes (like the Jews in Nazi Germany?). Why capitalism has had such a bad press is, of course, a subject which has received a good deal of attention. The attitude of intellectuals (opinion-formers?) has been suggested as a consistently anti-capitalist influence (e.g. Hayek, 1954; Stigler, 1963). A variety of explanations have been offered: a fairly plausible one is that an intellectual resents the material success and even sometimes higher social standing achieved by some businessmen who supply what the customers want. This gives rise to suggestions by them that the customers do not 'really' want the goods. This is especially the case if the goods in question are of a kind which they find aesthetically or morally repellent. It may also lead intellectuals to suggest various forms of state coercion to stop what they disapprove of. Curiously enough, some critics of capitalism see the intellectuals quite differently. The New Left see the universities, for example, as being quite important instruments for the 'legitimation' of the bourgeois capitalist state, in spite of the popular myth that they are centres of dissent (See e.g. Milliband (1969), *The State in Capitalist Society*, London: Weidenfeld & Nicolson).

The case for capitalism being a necessary condition for liberty, prosperity and even of true social justice is more subtle and difficult to understand than is the case for socialism. The argument that the blindness of market forces to questions of justice is a sufficient justification for state intervention or the replacement of capitalism, is easily understood.

The Austrian defence of free market capitalism, whilst it often takes the form of a direct attack on socialism, receives some indirect support from its critique of neoclassical economic theory; this has more than simply technical implications, and is seen in the Austrian theory of market process. Many students have probably been drawn to economics partly because they have conjectured that as it claims to be a social science, it would not only be useful as a guide to understanding inflation, the money supply, the banking system, the balance of payments, and such-like, but would also have something convincing or interesting to say about human behaviour in its economic aspect. But when presented with the seeming irrelevancies of equilibrium models and mathematical complexities which seem to have little realism it has not only been the stupid or lazy but also the thoughtful student who has turned away from the subject. The perfect competition model, for example, has led to the misunderstanding that it is a picture of how real markets function; it is little wonder that the reaction has sometimes been anti-capitalist, and that the Marxian version has been found more attractive. The Austrian picture of markets and entrepreneurial action would appear to offer a more acceptable alternative to either the neoclassical or Marxist approaches.

There are now, fortunately, some signs that mainstream economic theory is paying increasing attention to subjects such as public policy economics, the role of the entrepreneur, uncertainty and expectations; subjectivism too is now being taken more seriously. But the process of change may take a long time; and well-known weaknesses and difficulties in orthodoxy may not find their way into the textbooks and unusual perspectives may remain ignored (See Barnes, *T.S. Kuhn and Social Science* (1982), London: Macmillan). It is hoped that the present volume may contribute in some small way to the process of modification of orthodox teaching texts.

The Austrian view is that opponents of capitalism have a holistic fallacy at the heart of their case. 'Capitalism' is not a system which was imposed on humanity; it evolved spontaneously and is a web of interlocking relationships rather like a natural ecological system: *no individual or group masterminds it*; it is what emerges when individuals are free to engage in mutually beneficial exchange. This view would, of course, be regarded by Marxists as extremely simplistic in its apparent disregard for the processes of history. The possibilities of debate about this are, of course, only too well known and the question is likely to remain unsettled. There are some areas, however, in which the Austrian school, especially its libertarian wing, pose some awkward questions for the anti-capitalist. Supposing capitalism does depend upon self-interest; what can or should be done about it? First, it should be recalled that the Austrian view of capitalist free markets is not that they necessarily depend upon self-seeking behaviour but only that they allow the individual to choose some particular line of action. This could, at one extreme, be purely altruistic or, as Dostoyevsky puts it, the freedom to do exactly as one chooses even if it means acting against one's own self-interest. Supposing, however, that the individuals in a society do act selfishly (say towards the sick and old), how far should the state go to compel people to behave morally better? Is coercion itself a moral act? and if it is not, should it still be used to compel people to behave 'better'? Is the concept of making people behave decently by force even feasible?

Sometimes it is argued that free market capitalism is an outworn concept in a 'shrinking' world of increasingly complex technology. Western liberal, capitalist-type democracies have never been very common among the nations and perhaps there are historical forces already at work hastening their disappearance. Such systems may come to be seen in the not so distant future as historical curiosities. People may also prefer security to freedom. But one aspect of the capitalist free market which would probably disappear, apart from individual freedom, would be the immense variety of human activity which is so characteristic of free markets. The collectivist societies to date do seem to be marked by a painfully dull uniformity. Nor is this disadvantage offset by any increase in what Orwell described as 'common decency', unless we believe with Solzhenitsyn that prisons foster a higher morality.

In the meantime, one of the services rendered by Austrians – and especially by Hayek – has been to expose some of the confusions and prejudices which they see as dangerous to our present civilisation, and to reshape and restate the arguments of classical liberalism. Of these misconceptions, perhaps the most dangerous is the scientistic belief that the free market could be replaced or irreversibly modified by more 'rational' arrangements without the possibility of some quite unpleasant unintended consequences.

Finally, it is to be hoped that the neo-Austrian school will themselves keep in mind the need to try to avoid those 'pretences of knowledge' which, quite understandably and indeed logically, are the stock-in-trade of constructivists and Utopians.

Biographical Notes on the Leading Representatives of the Austrian School

Carl Menger, 1840–1921

Founder of the Austrian school. Professor of Political Economy, University of Vienna, 1873–1903. Best-known work, *Principles of Economics* (1871), in which he used subjectivism to undermine the classical ideas of objective value theory. His ideas were not well received at the time, especially in Germany, then dominated by the 'Historical' school. Sought to vindicate his position in *Problems of Economics and Sociology* (1883). Schumpeter ranked him with Adam Smith and Karl Marx.

Friedrich von Wieser, 1851–1926

Together with his brother-in-law and fellow student Böhm-Bawerk, spread Menger's ideas to a wider audience. Two chief theoretical contributions: the interpretation of costs as sacrificed utility and a theory of factor shares (the concept of 'imputation'). In his *Origin of Economic Value* (1884), developed Menger's theory of value and coined the term *Grenznutzen* (marginality). Taught that the social sciences should use the *Verstehen* method, which became a characteristic of Austrian methodology.

Eugen von Böhm-Bawerk, 1851–1914

Three times Austrian Minister of Finance. Chief work *Capital and Interest*, vol. 1 (1884), vol. 2 (1889). Later editions combined in a three-volume work (1909–14). Developed a theory of interest in terms of marginal utility in order to refute Ricardian and Marxian distribution theory. Adopted the definition of capital as 'roundabout production'. His other famous work is *Karl Marx and the Close of His System* (1896), a classic critique in which he contended that Marx's 'error' lay in his use of the labour theory of value instead of the more 'scientific' subjectivist theory. Described by Schumpeter as 'one of the five or six great economists of all time'. Frank Knight, however, criticised *Capital and Interest* as being too wordy.

Ludwig von Mises, 1881–1973

Attended Böhm-Bawerk's seminars; taught at the University of Vienna; became professor in Switzerland, 1934. In 1940 emigrated to the United States: became Professor of Economics at New York University until his death, and influenced a new generation of students who became the founders of the neo-Austrian school (e.g. Kirzner, Rothbard, Machlup). His *magnum opus* is *Human Action*, first published when he was in Switzerland (first English edition, 1949). Did important work on monetary economics (*Money and Credit*, 1912; Eng. trans., 1934). Leading figure in the 'socialist calculation' debate, in *Die Gemeinwirtschaft* (1922), (first Eng. edn, 1938). Adopted the ideas of Menger and Max Weber, arguing the case for 'methodological individualism'. Methodology rigorously apriorist. Outstanding gifts as a teacher and defender of classical liberalism. Mises' ideas reached the Anglo-American world by various routes, but the most noteworthy is that which went via the lectures given by his former student at the London School of Economics in the 1930s, Hayek.

Friedrich August von Hayek, 1899–

By far the most influential of the modern Austrians. His work has encompassed political philosophy, social theory and psychology as well as technical economics. It is quite impossible to condense into a paragraph an appraisal of the breadth and power of his ideas. The reader is recommended to consult Machlup (1977) for essays on Hayek by a group of eminent writers who have studied his work. Hayek's academic work has taken him to Vienna, London, Chicago, Freiburg and Salzburg. First appointment in the English-speaking world at London School of Economics, 1931–50. Published his *Pure Theory of Capital* (1941), in which he developed the ideas of Böhm-Bawerk. In 1944 there appeared *The Road to Serfdom*, his best-known work. *The Counter-Revolution of Science* (1952), attacked 'scientism'. His increasing concern for the individual against the encroachments of the state is shown in such persuasive and profoundly thoughtful writings as *The Constitution of Liberty* (1960), and *Law, Legislation and Liberty* (3-vol. edn, 1982). A constant critic of Keynesian economic policies, seeing in them the seeds of trouble in the shape of inflation and unemployment. His work is agreed, even by most of his critics, to be marked by tireless dedication, scholarship and an absence of virulence towards his opponents. As well as having written many books, he is also the author of some 200 articles, essays and pamphlets, many in German.

Ludwig M. Lachmann, 1906–
Studied under Hayek at the LSE. In the 1970s with Kirzner set up the Austrian Graduate Program at New York University. He sees the proper task of the Austrian school today as that of applying subjectivist and *Verstehende* methodology to a critique of mainstream mathematical economic models. An excellent introduction to his ideas is to be found in *Capital, Expectations and Market Process* (1977).

Israel Kirzner, 1930–
A student of Mises at New York, where he is now Professor of Economics. Has applied Austrian methodology to the study of market processes and especially to the entrepreneurial function. Best-known works are *The Economic Point of View* (1960), *Competition and Entrepreneurship* (1973), and *Perception, Opportunity and Profit* (1980). Has done much to provide a welcome and alternative way of looking at entrepreneurial action.

Murray N. Rothbard, 1926–
Has followed the strictly a priori method of Mises, and has drawn from it the most radically libertarian conclusions and policy prescriptions of any of the neo-Austrians. His most important works are *Man, Economy and State* (1962), *Power and Market* (1970), and *Ethics of Liberty* (1982). He is Professor of Economics at the Polytechnic Institute of New York. In his writing he follows the logical implications of his initial axioms with vigour, clarity and persuasiveness. He is prominent in the American Libertarian movement and author of *For a New Liberty* (1973). He regards most state intervention as disastrous, and resting ultimately on the use of force.

Other Neo-Austrians
New York became the chief centre of neo-Austrian studies in the United States, but there is evidence of Austrian influence today in several other university economics departments. A good deal of work is supported and funded by institutes such as The Liberty Fund, The Center for Libertarian Studies and The Cato Institute. Among scholars who have produced work in Austrian or related fields, are

James M. Buchanan, E.G. Dolan, Tibor Machan, Laurence S. Moss, Gerald O'Driscoll, L.M. Spadaro, Leland Yeager, and many others.

In Britain, where the Austrian school had its first base in the Anglo-American world at the LSE in the 1930s, there is today a noticeable revival of interest as represented by scholars such as N.P. Barry, S.C. Littlechild, B. Loasby and D.W. Reekie.

Selected Bibliography

Alchian, Armen A. (1977), *Economic Forces At Work*, Indianapolis: Liberty Press.

Arrow, Kenneth J. (1974), 'Limited knowledge & economic analysis', *American Economic Review*, vol. LXIV, 1974, 1–10.

Balogh, Thomas (1982), *The Irrelevance of Conventional Economics*, London: Weidenfeld & Nicolson.

Barry, Norman P. (1979), *Hayek's Social & Economic Philosophy*, 1982 edn, London: Macmillan.

Bauer, P.T. (1981), *Equality, The Third World and Economic Delusion*, London: Weidenfeld & Nicolson.

Becker, Lawrence C. (1977), *Property Rights*, London: Routledge & Kegan Paul.

Bell, D. and Kristol, I. (1981), *The Crisis in Economic Theory*, New York: Basic Books.

Binks, M. and Coyne, J. (1983), *The Birth of Enterprise*, Hobart Paper 98, London: IEA.

Blaug, Mark (1968), *Economic Theory in Retrospect*, 2nd edn, London: Heinemann.

——(1980), *The Methodology of Economics*, Cambridge: Cambridge University Press.

Böhm-Bawerk, Eugen von (1949), *Karl Marx and the Close of His System*, Clifton, NJ: Augustus M. Kelley.

——(1959), *Capital and Interest*, South Holland, Ill.: Libertarian Press.

Bradley, Robert Jr (1981), 'Market socialism: a subjectivist evaluation', *Journal of Libertarian Studies*, vol. V, no. 1, 23–39.

Brittan, Samuel (1979), *Participation Without Politics*, 2nd edn, Hobart Paper Special 62, London: IEA.

Brodbeck, M. (ed.) (1968), *Readings in the Philosophy of the Social Sciences*, New York: Macmillan.

Buchanan, James M. (1959), 'Positive economics, welfare economics, and political economy', *Journal of Law and Economics*, vol. 2.

——(1969a), *Cost and Choice*, Chicago: Markham.

——(1969b), 'Is economics the science of choice?', in Streissler (1969).

——(1979), *What Should Economists Do?*, Indianapolis: Liberty Press.

——and Thirlby, G.F. (1973), *L.S.E. Essays on Cost*, London School of Economics: Weidenfeld & Nicolson.

——, Burton, J. and Wagner R.E. (1978), *The Consequences of Mr. Keynes*, Hobart paper 78, London: IEA.

Carter, C.F. and Ford, J.L. (1972), *Uncertainty and Expectations in Economics: Essays in Honour of G.L.S. Shackle*, New Jersey: Augustus M. Kelley.

Casson, Mark (1980), *Entrepreneurship: An Economic Theory*, Oxford: Basil Blackwell.

Cordato, R.E. (1980), 'The Austrian theory of efficiency and the role of government'. *Journal of Libertarian Studies*, vol. IV, no. 4.

Cunningham, Robert L. (ed.) (1979), *Liberty & The Rule of Law*, College Station and London: Texas A. & M. University Press.

Dolan, Edwin G. (1976), *The Foundations of Modern Austrian Economics*, Kansas City: Sheed & Ward.

Ebeling, Richard M. (1983), 'Austrian economics – An Annotated Bibliography', *Humane Studies Review*, vol. 2, no. 1.

Friedman, David (1978), *The Machinery of Freedom*, New York: Arlington House.

Friedman, Milton (1962), *Capitalism & Freedom*, Chicago: Chicago University Press.

Garrison, Roger W. (1978), *Austrian Macroeconomics: A Diagrammatical Exposition*, Menlo Park, Cal.: Institute for Humane Studies.

Gilbert, J.C. (1982), *Keynes's Impact on Monetary Economics*, London: Butterworth.

Gravelle, H. and Rees, R. (1981), *Microeconomics*, London and New York: Longman.

Green, H.A. John (1971), *Consumer Theory*, Harmondsworth: Penguin.

Hahn, F. and Hollis, M. (1979), *Philosophy & Economic Theory*, Oxford: Oxford University Press.

Hayek, F.A. (1931a), 'Reflections on the pure theory of money of Mr. Keynes', *Economica*, August 1931.

——(1931b), *Prices and Production*, 1967 edn, New York: Kelley.

——(1933), *Monetary Theory & The Trade Cycle*, 2nd edn, 1966, New York: Kelley.

Hayek, F.A. (1935), *Prices and Production*, 2nd revised edn, 1967, New York: Kelley.

——(1937), 'Economics and knowledge', *Economica*, 4, 33–54; reprinted in Hayek (1948).

——(1941), *The Pure Theory of Capital*, 1976 edn, London: Routledge & Kegan Paul.

——(1944), *The Road to Serfdom*, rep. edn, 1979, London: Routledge & Kegan Paul.

——(1945), 'The use of knowledge in society', *American Economic Review*, XXXV, no. 4, September, 1945, 519–30. Reprinted in Hayek (1948).

——(1948), *Individualism & Economic Order*, Chicago: Chicago University Press.

——(1952), *The Counter-Revolution of Science*, 2nd edn, 1979, Indianapolis: Liberty Press.

——(ed.) (1954), *Capitalism & The Historians*, London: Routledge & Kegan Paul.

——(1960), *The Constitution of Liberty*, rep. edn, 1976, London: Routledge & Kegan Paul.

——(1967), *Studies in Philosophy, Politics and Economics*, rep. edn, Chicago: Chicago University Press.

——(1968), *The Confusion of Language in Political Thought*, Occasional paper 20, London: IEA.

——(1975), *Full Employment at Any Price*. Occasional paper 45, London: IEA.

——(1976), *The Sensory Order*, first published 1952, London: Routledge & Kegan Paul.

——(1978a), *A Tiger by the Tail*, 2nd edn, Hobart paperback 4, London: IEA.

——(1978b), *The Denationalisation of Money*, 2nd edn, Hobart paper 70, London: IEA.

——(1978c), *New Studies in Philosophy, Politics and the History of Ideas*, London: Routledge & Kegan Paul.

——(1982), *Law, Legislation & Liberty*, 3 vol. edn, London: Routledge & Kegan Paul.

Hazlitt, Henry (ed.) (1960), *The Critics of Keynesian Economics*, Princeton, NJ: Van Nostrand.

Hey, John D. (1979), *Uncertainty in Microeconomics*, Oxford: Martin Robertson.

Hicks, J.R. (1967), 'The Hayek story', in *Critical Essays in Monetary Theory*, Oxford: Oxford University Press.

——(1973), *Capital and Time: A Neo-Austrian Theory*, Oxford: Clarendon Press.

——(1974), *The Crisis in Keynesian Economics*, Oxford: Basil Blackwell.

Hirsch, Fred (1977), *Social Limits to Growth*, London: Routledge & Kegan Paul.

Hunt, E.K. and Schwartz (eds) (1972), *A Critique of Economic Theory* Harmondsworth: Penguin.

Hutchison, T.W. (1968), *Economics & Economic Policy in Britain 1946–1966*, London: Allen & Unwin.

——(1977), *Knowledge & Ignorance in Economics*, Oxford: Basil Blackwell.

——(1981), *The Politics and Philosophy of Economics*, Oxford: Basil Blackwell.

Institute of Economic Affairs (1980), *Prime Mover of Progress*, London: IEA.

——(1983), *Agenda for Social Democracy*, London: IEA.

Jevons, W. Stanley (1871), *The Theory of Political Economy*, London and New York: Macmillan.

Katouzian, Homa (1980), *Ideology and Method in Economics*, London: Macmillan.

Kauder, Emil (1965), *A History of Marginal Utility Theory*, Princeton, NJ: Princeton University Press.

Keynes, J.M. (1972), *Collected Writings*, Vol. X, *Essays in Biography*, London: Macmillan.

——(1973), *Collected Writings*, Vol. VII, *The General Theory*, London: Macmillan.

Kirzner, I.M. (1963), *Market Theory and the Price System*, New York: Van Nostrand.

——(1973), *Competition & Entrepreneurship*, Chicago: Chicago University Press.

——(1979), *Perception, Opportunity & Profit*, Chicago and London: Chicago University Press.

Kornai, Janos (1971), *Anti-Equilibrium*, New York: American Elsevier.

Koutsoyannis A. (1979), *Modern Microeconomics*, 2nd edn, London: Macmillan.

Lachmann, Ludwig M. (1969), 'Methodological individualism and the market economy', in Streissler (1969).

——(1973), *Macroeconomic Thinking and the Market Economy*, Hobart paper 56, London: IEA.

——(1976), 'Toward a critique of macroeconomics', in Dolan (1976).

——(1977), *Capital, Expectations, and Market Process*, Kansas City: Sheed, Andrews & McMeel.

Laidler, David E.W. (1982), *Monetarist Perspectives*, Oxford: Philip Allan.

Lancaster, Kelvin (1969), *Introduction to Modern Microeconomics*, Chicago: Rand McNally.

Layard, P.R.G. and Walters, A.A. (1978), *Microeconomic Theory*, New York: McGraw-Hill.

Lekachman, Robert (1959), *A History of Economic Ideas*, New York: Harper & Row.

Lepage, Henri (1978), *Tomorrow, Capitalism*, Eng. trans., 1982, La Salle, Ill.: Open Court.

Lipsey, R.G. (1975), *Positive Economics*, 5th edn, London: Weidenfeld & Nicolson.

Littlechild, S.C. (1978), *The Fallacy of the Mixed Economy*, Hobart paper 80, London: IEA.

Loasby, B.J. (1976), *Choice, Complexity & Ignorance*, Cambridge: Cambridge University Press.

Lucas, J.R. (1979), 'Liberty, morality & justice', in Cunningham (1979).

Lukes, Steven (1973), *Individualism*, Oxford: Basil Blackwell.

Machan, Tibor R. (1974), *The Libertarian Alternative*, Chicago: Nelson-Hall.

Machlup, Fritz (ed.) (1977), *Essays on Hayek*, London: Routledge & Kegan Paul.

Marshall, Alfred (1890), *Principles of Economics*, 7th edn, 1916, London: Macmillan.

Menger, Carl (1950), *Principles of Economics*, trans. J. Dingwall and B. Hoselitz from first edn, 1871, Glencoe, Ill.: Free Press.

——(1963), *Problems of Economics and Sociology*, ed. L. Schneider, trans. F.J. Nock from the German edn, 1883, Urbana: University of Illinois.

Mises, Ludwig von (1934), *The Theory of Money & Credit*, London: Jonathan Cape.

——(1936), *Socialism: An Economic & Sociological Analysis*, trans. J. Kahane, reprint, 1974, London: Jonathan Cape.

——(1949), *Human Action*, 3rd edn, 1966, Chicago: Contemporary Books.

——(1962), *The Ultimate Foundation of Economic Science*, 1978 edn, Kansas City: Sheed, Andrews & McMeel.

Mishan, E.J. (1961), 'Theories of consumer behaviour: a cynical view', *Economica*, February 1961.

Morris, Derek (ed.) (1979), *The Economic System in the U.K.*, 2nd edn, Oxford: Oxford University Press.

Moss, Laurence S. (ed.) (1976), *The Economics of Ludwig von Mises*, Kansas City: Sheed & Ward.

Nagel, Ernest (1961), *The Structure of Science*, London: Routledge & Kegan Paul.

Nell, Edward J. (1981), 'Value and capital in Marxian economics', in Bell and Kristol (1981).

Nozick, Robert (1974), *Anarchy, State & Utopia*, Oxford: Basil Blackwell.

——(1977), 'On Austrian methodology', *Synthese*, 353–92.

Oakeshott, Michael (1975), *On Human Conduct*, Oxford: Oxford University Press.

O'Brien, D.P. (1975), *The Classical Economists*, reprint edn, 1978, Oxford: Clarendon Press.

O'Driscoll, Gerald P. (1978), *Economics as a Coordination Problem*, Mission: Sheed, Andrews & McMeel.

——(1979), 'Rational expectations, politics & stagflation', in Rizzo (1979).

Pasour, E.C., Jr (1981), 'The free-rider as a basis for government intervention'. *Journal of Libertarian Studies*, vol. V, no. 4, pp. 453–64.

Perrin, Robert G. (1981), 'The dynamics & dialectics of capitalism', *Journal of Libertarian Studies*, vol. V, no. 2.

Popper, Karl R. (1945), *The Open Society and Its Enemies*, 2 vols, 5th edn, 1966, London: Routledge & Kegan Paul.

——(1957), *The Poverty of Historicism*, 2nd edn, 1979, London: Routledge & Kegan Paul.

——(1979), *Objective Knowledge*, revised edn, Oxford: Clarendon Press.

Ramsey, James B. (1977), *Economic Forecasting – Models or Markets?*, Hobart paper 74; London: IEA.

Rawls, J. (1971), *A Theory of Justice*, Cambridge, Mass.: Harvard University Press.

Reekie, W. Duncan (1979), *Industry, Prices & Markets*, Oxford: Philip Allan.

Rizzo, Mario J. (1979), *Time, Uncertainty and Disequilibrium*, Lexington, Mass.: D.C. Heath.

Rothbard, M.N. (1956), 'Toward a reconstruction of utility and welfare economics', in Sennholz (1956).

——(1962), *Man, Economy & State*, 2 vol. edn, 1970, Los Angeles, Cal.: Nash.

——(1970), *Power & Market*, 2nd edn, 1977, Kansas City: Sheed, Andrews & McMeel.

——(1974), 'The anatomy of the state', in Machan (1974).

——(1976), 'The Austrian theory of money', in Dolan (1976).

——(1982), *Ethics of Liberty*, Menlo Park, Cal.: Institute for Humane Studies.

Routh, Guy (1975), *The Origin of Economic Ideas*, London: Macmillan.

Rowley, C.K. and Peacock, A.T. (1975), *Welfare Economics: A Liberal Restatement*, London: Martin Robertson.

Ryan, Alan (ed.) (1979), *The Idea of Freedom: Essays in Honour of Isaiah Berlin*, Oxford: Oxford University Press.

Samuelson, Paul A. (1964), *Economics*, 6th edn, New York: McGraw-Hill.

Schumpeter, J.A. (1950), *Capitalism, Socialism & Democracy*, 3rd edn, London: Allen & Unwin.

——(1954), *History of Economic Analysis*, 4th reprint, 1961, London: Oxford University Press.

Seldon, Arthur (1980), *Corrigible Capitalism, Incorrigible Socialism*, Occasional paper, 57, London: IEA.

Sennholz, Mary (ed.) (1956), *On Freedom & Enterprise: Essays in Honor of Ludwig von Mises*, Princeton, NJ: Van Nostrand.

Shackle, G.S. (1949), *Expectation in Economics*, Cambridge: Cambridge University Press.

——(1961), *Decision, Order & Time in Human Affairs*, 1969 edn, Cambridge: Cambridge University Press.

——(1967), *The Years of High Theory*, Cambridge: Cambridge University Press.

——(1970), *Expectations, Enterprise & Profit*, London: Allen & Unwin.

——(1972), *Epistemics & Economics*, Cambridge: Cambridge University Press.

——(1973), *An Economic Querist*, Cambridge: Cambridge University Press.

——(1979), *Imagination & The Nature of Choice*, Edinburgh: Edinburgh University Press.

Sowell, Thomas (1977), *Markets & Minorities*, Oxford: Basil Blackwell.

Spadaro, L.M. (ed.) (1978), *New Directions in Austrian Economics*, Kansas City: Sheed, Andrews & McMeel.

Steele, David Ramsay (1981), 'Posing the problem: the impossibility of economic calculation under socialism', *Journal of Libertarian Studies*, vol. V, no. 1.

Stewart, I.M.T. (1979), *Reasoning and Method in Economics*, London: McGraw-Hill.

Stigler, George J. (1960), 'The influence of events and politics in economic theory', *American Economic Review*, May, 1960, 36–45.

——(1963), *The Intellectual and the Market Place and Other Essays*, New York: Collier-Macmillan.

Streissler, Erich (1969), *Roads to Freedom*, London: Routledge & Kegan Paul.

Sweezy, A.R. (1934), 'The interpretation of subjective value theory', *Review of Economic Studies*, June 1934.

Trevithick, J.A. (1977), *Inflation*, Harmondsworth: Penguin.

Weintraub, E. Roy (1979), *Microfoundations*, reprinted 1980, Cambridge: Cambridge University Press.

White, Lawrence H. (1977), *Methodology of the Austrian School*, New York: Center for Libertarian Studies.

——(1978), 'Comment on Shackle's notion of opportunity costs', *Austrian Economics Newsletter*, vol. 1, no. 2 Spring 1978, p. 10.

Wilson, T. and Skinner, A.S. (1976), *The Market & The State*, reprint edn, 1978, Oxford: Oxford University Press.

Index

Alchian, A.A., 92
Alienation, 62n26
Altruism, 73, 115, 122
Apriorism, 2–3, 49
Aristotle, 23, 119
Arkwright, R., 79
Armentano, D.T., 134n9
Arrow, K.J., 34, 36, 42n11, 67, 71, 109, 199

Balogh, Lord, xiii
Barnes, T.S., 222
Barone, E., 193
Barry, N.P., 27
Bauer, P.T., 211
Baumol, W.J., 91
Becker, L.C., 106
Bentham, J. 93, 108, 180, 200
Berlin, I., 203
Bernoulli, J., 16
Berry, M., 14
Blaug, M., 36
Böhm-Bawerk, 23, 45, 46, 47, 57
Boland, L.A., 12n2
Bosanquet, N., 207
Boulding, K. 42n15
Bourgeois counter-attack, 47
Bourgeoisie, 47, 178
Brittan, S., 135n23
Brodbeck, M., 13n10
Brownstein, B.P., 102, 111n11
Buchanan, J.M., 45, 54, 100, 182, 195, 198n19
Bukharin, N., 47
Burke, E., 9
Burman, P., 13n15

Burton, J., 172n9
Business cycle, 147–57
    forced savings in, 150
    Hayek on, 150–4
    historical background, 147–8
    Mises on, 149–50
    obsolescence of, 195
    Rothbard on, 155

Cairnes, J.E., 17, 19
Calculus, 16, 17, 22, 29n1
Calvinism, 44
Cambridge School, 142
Cantillon, R., 77, 171n7
Capitalism, 48, 74n2, 195, 220–2
Capitalist, 63, 78, 86–7
Cassell, G., 34
Casson, M., 90
Catallaxy, 71–3, 75n17
Chesterton, G.K., 14n25
Closed shop, 132–4
Clower, R.W., 155
Coase, R.H. 54
Coercion, 66, 182, 183, 195, 200, 205
Collard, D., 198n21
Collective goods, 98–103
Competition, 94
Comte, A., 7
Concertina effect, 151
Congdon, T., 172n19
Constructivism, 9, 12, 180
Consumer preferences, 106–7
    manipulation, 116–19
    theory, 46–53
Cordato, R.E., 113n29
Cornforth, M., 203

Cornuelle, R., 101
Cost-benefit analysis, 104
Costs, 44, 53–7, 195
Cournot, A., 16, 41n4
Critical rationalism, 10
Cunningham, R.L., 76n21

Debreu, G., 34
Demand, 49–52
   for money, 160–1
Democratic Socialism, 190
Demonstrated preference, 50, 52
Demsetz, H., 193
Disequilibrium, 194
Dostoyevsky, 207, 222
Dray, W.H., 13n19
Dupuit, A.J., 16

Econometrics, 16, 20, 25, 27, 28
Economic efficiency, 110, 115, 192–4
Economy
   and catallaxy, 71–2
   as an entity, 187
   as a holistic term, 13n11, 75n16
Edgeworth, F., 18, 49
Edwards, P., 13n19
Engels, F., 186
Entrepreneurs, 77–97
   in Austrian theory, 82–6
   as capitalists, 86–90
   as innovators, 80
   morality of, 121
   supply of, 92–4
Equality, 200
   as an ideal, 210–12
Equilibrium, general, 32–42
   Austrian view of, 37–40
   definition, 34–5
   and expectations, 40
   in Jevons, 33
   Kaleidic, 40
   and knowledge, 38
   of market, 70
   in Marshall, 33
   neoclassical critics of, 35
   Walrasian, 34
Evenly rotating economy, 37
Externalities, 98 ff

Falsification, 27
Fisher, I., 18, 49

Flew, A., 120
Freedom, (see Liberty)
Friedman, D., 73
Friedman, M., xiv, 65, 66, 111n7, 170, 175
Frisch, R., 20

Galbraith, J.K., 105, 117–18
Gamble, A., 185n11
Games, theory of, 50–1, 129
Gödel's theorem, 8
Green, T.H., 201

Hahn, F., 35
Harrod, R., 107
Hayek, F.A., on,
   business cycle, 150–4
   collective goods, 100–1
   constructivism, 9
   democracy, 94, 97nn26, 27
   dependence effect, 117, 123n6
   equilibrium, 38
   knowledge, 8–9, 66–7, 74n9, 190
   law, 10, 180–1, 189–90, 205–6
   liberty, 205–8
   markets, 64, 66–7
   mathematics, 25–6
   money, 152
   monopoly, 125
   perfect competition, 69–71
   profit, 121
   self-interest, 124n15
   scientism, 6–7
   socialist calculation, 191
   social justice, 212ff
   the state, 179–80
   statistics, 27–8
   trade unions, 167
   value, 45, 54
   welfare economics, 112n28
Hegel, G., 177, 184n4
Historicism, 7, 186
Holism, 4–6, 183, 186
   Popper on, 4–5
Hey, J.D., 14n26, 37
Hicks, J. 139
Hilferding, R., 57
Hirsch, F., 106–7
Hume, D., 8
Hutchison, T.W., 27, 30n13 35

Immorality of profit, 119–22
Incomes policies, 165–6, 187–8
Indifference theory, 18, 49–51
Individualism, 4–6
Inflation, 13n17, 161–2
  Austrian policy for, 164–6
  and full employment, 168
Institute of Economic Affairs, 65
Intellectuals as anti-capitalists, 220–1

Jay, P., 168
Jevons, W.S., 16–22, 33, 43, 46, 54
Johnson, H.G., 20

Kaldor, Lord, xiii, 35, 187
Kantorovich, L.V., 198n21
Kauder, E., 30n19, 44
Keynes, J.M.,
  on Austrians, 148–54
  on equilibrium, 32
  General Theory, 34, 151
  and Hayek, 139–41
  on mathematics, 17
  on probability, 91
  on rentier class, 95n3
  on self-interest, 123n5
  as subjectivist, 143
Keynesianism, 136, 138, 145n4
  dissolution of, 154–5
Kirzner I.M., on
  cost theory, 56–7
  entrepreneur, 78–90,
  equilibrium, 71
  profit, 84–5
Knight, F.H., 80, 82
Knowledge, 7–9, 190
Koopmans, T., 21, 30n15
Kornai, J., 35
Kuhn, T.S., xiii
Kühne, K., 58, 157n13

Labour theory of value, 57–9
Lachmann, L.M., on
  aggregates, 142
  business cycle, 155
  entrepreneur, 87–8
  equilibrium, 37, 39
  indifference theory, 51
  planning, 192
  profit maximisation, 92
Laidler, D., 134n14

Lange, O., 193
Law, 10, 180–2
L'Ecole Polytechnique, 6
Leibniz, G., 16
Leontief, W., 20, 30n17
Lepage, H., 112n15
Liberty, 199–209
  Austrian concept of, 205–6
  basis for morality, 216
  Berlin I., on, 203
  and capitalism, 220
  formal, 201
  and markets, 65, 66
  Marxist view of, 202, 204
  nature of, 200–1
  negative, 203–5
  and *nomos*, 181
  Popper on, 204–5
  purpose of state, 179
  and responsibility, 206–7
  source of values, 179
  supreme principle, 206
Lindbeck, A., 65 73
Lindblom, C.E., 198n24
Littlechild, S.C., 85–6
Lloyd, H., 16, 46
Loasby, B.J., 39
Locke, J., 8, 44, 200
London School of Economics, 54–6
Longfield, S.M., 46
Lucas, J.R., 116, 211, 217n2
Lukes, S., 5

Machan, T., 14n29
Machlup, F., 152
Macroeconomics, 136–46
  Austrian critique, 137–44
  as holistic, 141
  microfoundations, 34
McKenzie, L.W., 34
Malthus, T.R., 147
Mandeville, B., 9
Marginalism, 17
Marginal revolution, 16, 44
Marginal utility, 22, 46–9, 50, 109
Market, 63–76
  Austrian view of, 66–71
  cruelty, 199
  as discovery process, 70, 78
  disequilibrium, 83–4
  efficiency, 91

and entrepreneur, 82–3
equilibrium, 33, 34–5, 38
failure, 98–124, 192
and merit, 213–14
nature of, 65–6
origin of, 64
process, 23–4, 37, 66
and self-interest, 116
terminology, 63–4
Marschak, J., 30n16
Marshall, A., 17, 19, 29n5, 33, 41n5, 43, 44, 53–4, 60n14, 114
Marshall's synthesis, 48
Marx, K., 43, 45, 47, 57–9, 78, 119, 177, 204
Marxist economics, 19, 142
Mathematical economics, 15–31, 33
Matthews, R.C.O., 148, 156n3
Menger, C., 8, 22, 33, 43 ff, 57, 69, 159
Meredith, H.O., 157n15
Methodological individualism, 4–6
Methodology, 1–14, 44
Mill, J.S., 17, 78, 203
Milliband, R., 221
Mises, L.von, on
business cycle, 149–50
coercion, 121
costs, 54
demand for money, 160–1
econometrics, 25
entrepreneur, 82–3
equilibrium, 37–8
Keynes, 141, 146n13
market economy, 66
mathematics, 23–4, 28
planning, 189
praxeology, 2
profit, 84–5
profit maximising, 91
socialist calculation, 193–5
social justice, 214
state, 178–9
Mishan, E.J., 53, 103, 111n13
Monetarism, 162, 166
Money, 158–73
Austrian theory of, 39, 162–4
definition, 159
demand for, 160–1
denationalisation of, 168–9
and GE theory, 39

origins of, 159–60
supply of, 166, 170
Monopolies Commission, 188
Monopolistic competition, 129
Monopoly, 125–35
Austrian view, 126–8
origins, 127–8
orthodox view, 125–6
state and, 130–1
Moss, L.S., 156n6

Nagel, E., 5, 11
National income, 144
Nell, E.J., 52
Neoclassical economics, 2, 14n26, 34, 43–4, 48, 68–70, 175
New Left, 66, 106, 116
Newton, I., 16
Nirvana approach, 193, 198n17
Nomos, 181, 184n10
Nozick, R., 50, 51, 128, 184n5, 208n6, 215–16

Objectivism, 60n10, 43, 46, 186
O'Driscoll, G.P., 157n19
Oligopoly, 128–9
Opportunity cost, 56, 61n18
Orwell, G., 74n3, 119
Overspill effects, 103–6

Pareto optimum, 69, 75n20, 109, 115, 194
Pareto, V., 34
Perfect competition, 68–70, 221
Pasour, E.C., 103
Patinkin, D., 161
Peacock, A.T., 168
Peston, M., 172n15
Petty, Sir W., 15
Phelps-Brown, H., 20
Phillips curve, 30n24, 155
Pigou, A.C., 100
Planning, 186–97
Plant, R., 184n4
Plato, 176
Political economy, 175
Popper, Sir K., 4, 10, 25, 176, 184n4, 204–5
Positivism, 52
Praxeology, 2–3
Prest, A., 29n6

Prices,
  as signals, 67–8
  equilibrium, 35
  index of, 170
  just, 43, 60n2, 119
  oil, 74n10
  stability of, 170
Prisoner's dilemma, 107–8
Probability theory, 21
Profit, 77–97
  arbitrage theory, 84
  Austrian theory, 82–6
  entrepreneurial, 88
  excess, 130
  maximisation, 86, 91–2
  monopoly, 80
  morality of, 119–21
  sharing, 167
Protestantism, 93, 121
Public goods, 99
Public ownership, 99
Pure interest rate, 96n14

Rational expectations, 36, 157n18, 163
Rawls, J., 215
Reekie, W.D., 86
Rentier class, 48, 95n3
Revealed preference, 49
Ricardo, D., 17, 43–7, 57, 78, 200
Ricardo effect, 151
Rizzo, M.J., 172n20
Robbins, Lord 74n8, 82, 138
Robinson E.A.G., 145nn4, 10
Robinson, J., 142
Rothbard, M.N., on,
  altruism, 115
  business cycle, 155
  capitalists, 87
  collective goods, 101–3, 105
  consumer preference, 49, 52
  econometrics, 27
  freedom, 206
  Galbraith, 118
  mathematics, 27, 31n29
  money, 159–60
  monopolistic competition, 129
  oligopoly, 128–9
  socialism, 195
  social justice, 215
  state, 181–2
Rousseau, J.J., 176–7

Rowley, C.K., 168
Rule of Law, 189–90, 205–6
Russell, B., 114

Samuelson, P.A., 49, 50, 99, 101
Savings, forced, 150
Say, J.B., 77
Scholastics, 44
Schumpeter, J.A., 15, 30n18, 46, 57, 78, 85, 192
Scientism, 6–7
Self-interest, 72–3, 75–6n20, 114–16
Sen, A., 12, 112n25, 123n3
Shackle, G.L.S., on
  cost theory, 54–5
  entrepreneur, 82, 84
  equilibrium, 40
  games theory, 50–1, 129
  Keynes, 155
  profit, 81
  subjectivism, 3
Shaw, G.B., 119
Smith, A., 9, 12, 15, 33, 44, 72, 100, 200
Shenoy, S.R., 172n12
Social, meaning of, 212–13, 218n10
Social costs, 98
Socialism, 186, 192, 194, 200, 208n11, 218n9
Socialist calculation, 191, 193–5, 198n20
Social justice, 122, 181, 200, 212–17,
Social welfare functions, 109
Sociologism, 60n8
Sowell, T., 135n20
Spontaneous order, 64, 133, 180
Sraffa, P., 35, 139
State, 174–85
  belief in, 210
  and monopoly, 130–1
Statistics, 15, 21, 27–8
Steedman, I., 58
Stigler, G.J., 29n7, 97n25
Streissler, E., 14n22, 157n17
Subjectivism, 3–4, 23, 25, and,
  capitalism, 220
  costs, 53–7, 102
  demand, 49
  entrepreneur, 84
  religion, 44
  value, 43, 44–6, 50–1
Supply and Demand, 23, 35, 44, 53

Tawney, R.H., 93
Taylor, C., 201–2
Thirlby, G.F., 54, 61n16
Thünen, J.H. von, 16
Tintner, G., 92
Totalitarianism, 190
Trade Disputes Act, 132
Trade Unions, 128, 131–3, 167
Trevithick, J.A., 167
Tullock, G., 182

Uncertainty, 7–10, 80, 81
Unemployment, 152–3, 170
Unintended consequences, 8, 10, 130

Value, 43–62
    and costs, 53–7
    and marginalism 48–9
    labour theory, 57–9
    paradox of, 46

Varian, H.R., 218n17
Verstehen, 4, 49

Wagner, R.E., 169
Walras, L., 17, 18, 34, 43, 46
Watkins, J.W.N., 13n19
Weber, M., 4
Weintraub, E.R., 34
Weldon, T.D., 184n2, 205
Welfare economics, 108–9
Wells, H.G., 119
Whitehead, A.N., 142
Wicksell, K., 149, 156n11
Wicksteed, P., 136
Wiener, N., 21, 30n14
Wieser, F. von, 23
Williams, B., 201
Williams, R., 28
Worswick, G.D.N., 20, 30n12

Zinoviev, A., 218n20